"No Real Madrid book, or sports book for that matter, has ever been written like it. Mandis's unique background in business and academics and outsider's perspective produce an essential book for any Madridista's library collection."

—GABE LEZRA, founder and editor-in-chief emeritus of ManagingMadrid.com

"The Real Madrid Way delivers ground-breaking insights about the success formula for a legendary sports franchise. An in-depth exploration of organization culture provides a great balance to the role of sports analytics and makes this a must-read leadership book for anyone interested in sports management."

—VINCE GENNARO, director of the Masters of Science
in Sports Management program at Columbia University,
author of *Diamond Dollars: The Economics of Winning in Baseball,*
and president of the Society for American Baseball Research (SABR)

"Mandis explains the incredible power of community brands—where a global community feels so deeply passionate about the brand that the brand is synonymous with one's identity, values, and much more."

—ANDREW MESSICK, CEO of IRONMAN

"The Real Madrid Way explains how Real Madrid has created and maintained a culture that drives both financial and on-the-field success. An educational and inspiring example for sports fans and executives alike."

—Lindsay McGregor and Neel Doshi, cofounders of Vega Factor and
New York Times bestselling coauthors of *Primed to Perform: How to Build the
Highest Performing Cultures Through the Science of Total Motivation*

"Mandis has created a gripping narrative exploring how Real Madrid has done the seemingly impossible: used a strong culture and shared values to overcome the problem of the too-much-talent effect. The book is a must for anyone interested in culture, leadership, and high performance."

—ADAM GALINSKY, chair and Vikram S. Pandit Professor of Business
at Columbia Business School and coauthor of *Friend & Foe*

THE
REAL MADRID
WAY

HOW VALUES CREATED
THE MOST SUCCESSFUL SPORTS TEAM
ON THE PLANET

STEVEN G. MANDIS

BENBELLA BOOKS, INC.
DALLAS, TEXAS

Photos used courtesy of Real Madrid Club de Fútbol.

BenBella Books, Inc.
10440 N. Central Expressway, Suite 800
Dallas, TX 75231
www.benbellabooks.com
Send feedback to feedback@benbellabooks.com

Printed in the United States of America
10 9 8 7 6 5 4 3 2 1

Copyediting by Scott Calamar
Proofreading by Brittney Martinez and Sarah Vostok
Indexing by Amy Murphy Indexing & Editorial
Text design and composition by John Reinhardt Book Design
Front cover by Bradford Foltz
Full cover by Sarah Dombrowsky
Author photo by Alexandra Mandis
Logo courtesy of Real Madrid
Printed by Lake Book Manufacturing

Distributed by Perseus Distribution
www.perseusdistribution.com

To place orders through Perseus Distribution:
Tel: (800) 343-4499
Fax: (800) 351-5073
E-mail: orderentry@perseusbooks.com

Special discounts for bulk sales (minimum of 25 copies) are available.
Please contact Aida Herrera at aida@benbellabooks.com.

This book is dedicated to the people of Spain.

*My family and I admire your beautiful
and fascinating culture, history, and language.*

Most of all, we appreciate your warmth and kindness.

"Real Madrid's secret to success on the field and off the field, more than money, talent, and data analytics, is the values and passion in its fans' hearts and souls. It starts and ends there."

—A Real Madrid Executive

CONTENTS

Appendices

PREFACE

Essential Message of the Book

The sports industry is a $620 billion global business,[1] as competitive and dynamic as any industry on the planet. To rise to the very pinnacle of this arena, as Real Madrid has done, is an extraordinary accomplishment. Generally unnoticed, in the space of fifteen years Real Madrid has gone from near bankruptcy to becoming the most valuable sports team on the planet. Their secret to success, revealed here, is a fascinating story, with implications for industries and organizations worldwide.

How the Book Came to Be

On a weekday morning in 2014, I passed through security at what is considered one of soccer's cathedrals: Santiago Bernabéu Stadium in Madrid, Spain. It is the home of the celebrated Real Madrid soccer team, but I was not going to a game. Rather, I was headed to a meeting in the executive offices located inside the stadium.

When I arrived, Carlos Martínez de Albornoz, Real Madrid's director and a key member of the executive team responsible for turning Real Madrid into an international powerhouse, warmly greeted me.[2] He looked distinguished, dressed in a conservative suit and tie, his silver hair parted to the side. When he shook my hand, he drew me closer, as

---

[1] A.T. Kearney White Paper, *The Sports Market*.

[2] Fabio López, a successful asset manager from Madrid that married a close family friend and then became a close friend himself, had set up the 2014 meeting with Carlos. Fabio knows Carlos because Fabio's father, Pedro López Jímenez, is on the board of directors of Real Madrid. I am an adjunct professor at Columbia Business School, after having worked in finance for more than twenty years. Fabio and Pedro thought Carlos and I would enjoy speaking together and that Carlos would be a great guest speaker for a popular Columbia University Business School class that I teach in Madrid for one week each January.

if we were old friends. He walked me to his office, and as we talked he came across as levelheaded, thoughtful, and analytical, but he had the Latin warmth of a Spaniard and father of four.

I asked Carlos, "Did you grow up as a Real Madrid fan?"

He chuckled and replied, "Before this job, I didn't even like soccer. My background is in engineering and managing engineering-related companies. The president of the club plus my wife and kids had to talk me into taking this job."

What?!

One of the most important executives running one of the most important soccer teams in the world didn't even like soccer and didn't want the job! As I sat down, I thought to myself, *This should be interesting.*

After a few hours, we adjourned to my favorite restaurant in Madrid, El Landó, and continued the meeting over a traditional Spanish lunch. I was fascinated by what Carlos had to say about Real Madrid's history, ownership structure, financial turnaround, investment in facilities and people, global fan base, style of play, and ability to attract the best players and get them to work together. Since he was a former engineer and now responsible for reporting Real Madrid's financial performance, I expected that he would have talked about income statements or balance sheets or data analysis and performance metrics. However, what really stood out to me were the numerous times Carlos used the words *community, passion, values, expectations, transparency,* and *culture.*

Carlos explained that he had previously worked with Florentino Pérez in various executive and board positions at engineering-related companies. Florentino, a Spanish businessman, civil engineer, and former politician, is chief executive officer of Grupo ACS, the largest engineering and construction company in the world with €35 billion ($38.5 billion) in sales and 210,000 employees. In July 2000, he was also elected president of Real Madrid.

Florentino's election was a surprise because the incumbent had won the UEFA[3] Champions League titles in May 1998 and May 2000. At

---

[3] The Union of European Football Associations (UEFA) is the administrative body for association football (soccer) in Europe and organizes the competition. It is one of six continental confederations of the world soccer's governing body, Féderation Internationale de Football Association (FIFA).

the time Florentino was elected, however, Real Madrid was close to bankruptcy. In the media, Florentino is most associated with lifting the debt-laden club to their current position as the most valuable sports team in the world and ushering in the period during which Real Madrid signed the best of the best players from around the globe. The term *galácticos* ("a galaxy of stars") has been used in the media to describe Florentino's signing of star players and also as a nickname for the team.[4]

After the club members elected Florentino to be president of Real Madrid in 2000, he asked Carlos to take the executive role of Director General and focus on selected day-to-day activities—in particular administration, finance, and legal. The fact that Carlos was neither a soccer aficionado nor a Real Madrid fan was precisely why Florentino wanted Carlos to join the executive team. Florentino wanted someone who wouldn't be swayed by biases or swept up in the glamour or intimidated by the star power of the players. He wanted someone he knew and could trust to apply and execute their knowledge of what was needed to successfully run a global corporation.

Carlos has a son, Lorenzo, who, like me, had worked at Goldman Sachs. By coincidence, not knowing that his father and I would one day meet, Lorenzo had given Carlos a copy of my book, *What Happened to Goldman Sachs? An Insider's Story of Organizational Drift and Its Unintended Consequences* (Brighton: Harvard Business Review Press, 2013), which was my dissertation for my PhD in sociology from Columbia University. Its focus is on organizational culture. During our meeting, when Carlos said he had enjoyed reading my book, I thought he was merely being polite. Then he walked across his office and pulled it off his bookshelf. When he opened the book, I could see pages he had marked and sentences he had underlined. I was stunned. Not only had he read my book, I now had a sense of how meticulous and curious he was.

As I got to know Carlos better, my inquisitiveness and fascination remained unabated. The more I learned, the more I wanted to know.

---

[4] I remember first hearing the word or idea of "galácticos" a few days after my seventh birthday in May 1977 when my soccer-loving father, who had immigrated to the United States from Greece, took my older brother Dean and me to Chicago's Soldier Field to watch a North American Soccer League game between the Chicago Sting and the New York Cosmos with its star "galácticos" players: Brazilians Pelé, Carlos Alberto, and German Franz Beckenbauer.

During another visit to Madrid and lunch at El Landó, I told Carlos that I wanted to do a rigorous study of Real Madrid,[5] taking an analytical and dispassionate approach similar to the one I used in researching and analyzing Goldman Sachs. Unlike any other book written about a sports team, I wanted to investigate both the on-field and business aspects of the club and see if, and how, the two were linked.

One of the things in the back of my mind was Michael Lewis's bestselling 2003 book, *Moneyball: The Art of Winning an Unfair Game* (New York: W. W. Norton & Company, 2004), about the Oakland Athletics baseball team and its general manager, Billy Beane.[6] The book describes how Beane, a former professional baseball player, uses an unconventional, analytical, evidence-based, sabermetric approach to assemble a competitive baseball team, despite the Athletics's disadvantaged revenue situation compared to large-market teams like the New York Yankees. Lewis's book, which is one of my favorites, captures the moment when baseball changed its player selection strategy from a reliance on instinct to data analysis of past performance, a shift that revolutionized baseball and sports management.

The enormous popularity of the book and then the 2011 film *Moneyball* (starring Brad Pitt and Jonah Hill) solidified the power of data-driven decision-making in the minds of the general public and corporate management teams around the world. While the power of data analysis is undeniable, I was interested in what and how large of a role it played in the overall success of Real Madrid.

Carlos described to me an equally dramatic shift in Real Madrid's business model, but one that was utterly *unlike* Beane's. Instead of being driven by data analytics, the Real Madrid revolution stemmed from an organizational culture centered on the shared values and expectations of the club's fans. Also, while Beane was a baseball insider, Real Madrid's revolution was being led largely by a bunch of outsiders! One of the things they had

---

[5] My family and I had moved from New York to Madrid for approximately six months in 2013 to immerse ourselves in Spanish culture and improve our Spanish. While living in Madrid, we attended one Real Madrid regular season game together. I am a very enthusiastic fan of the city of Madrid, its people, and its culture, but no one would call me a hard-core Real Madrid fan. I don't own any Real Madrid merchandise. I am equally delighted to see Real Madrid, Atlético Madrid, Getafe, or Rayo Vallecano win because my friends in Madrid typically root for one of the local teams.

[6] Billy Beane is an advisor to Dutch professional soccer team AZ Alkmaar. He also is a part owner in MLS's San Jose Earthquakes but does not advise the team.

in common, however, was that both innovations were driven out of financial necessity and constraint. I was fascinated by the potential the Real Madrid way has beyond the sporting world—potential that I felt the need to explore and identify. Big money and glamorous stars tended to camouflage what the executives were really doing, and what they were doing can be appreciated far beyond the realm of soccer or Real Madrid.

Real Madrid provided me with unprecedented access, both to people and to data. Over two years, I conducted more than 100 hours of semi-structured interviews with more than twenty people associated with Real Madrid, from the president of the club to current and former players and coaches, to people who work in the stadium, academy, and practice facilities. My research included an entire week in Madrid during which I was given complete access to the club, including being allowed to meet with whomever or see whatever I wanted. Real Madrid staff also thoroughly and promptly responded to at least fifty or so very long information request lists from me. I was provided financial information and statistical data, some of which Real Madrid makes publicly available in its commitment to be transparent. (Real Madrid regularly issues annual reports of approximately 300 pages.)

In addition, I sought my own data and independently interviewed community members; soccer and sports experts; current and former executives and players at competing teams; academics who have studied Real Madrid, soccer, sports, or organizations; sports agents and legal advisors; data analysts; and members of the media. I agreed that I would keep all interviewees' participation confidential and not quote them, unless the quote was already in the press. I also researched business school cases, news reports, and books about Real Madrid and other relevant teams. The purpose of going beyond what Real Madrid provided was to gain a broader picture and challenge, support, and illuminate my data, analysis, and conclusions.

It is not my intent to glorify or vilify any individual, group, or era, although I suspect parts will be interpreted or used to do so. I've tried not to be influenced by nostalgia, and I have tried to recognize that people I interviewed were looking back in hindsight and may have had agendas or other issues, something I tried to overcome by speaking to many different sources and balancing the interview data with other information and analysis. I've tried not to be affected by people's passion for Real Madrid, their own favorite and rival soccer teams, the sport of soccer and sports generally, or recent events having too much weight simply because they are fresher in our minds. I have relied on publicly available data to confirm and disprove various claims and theories advanced by those I interviewed.

My primary reasons for writing this book were intellectual curiosity and academic contribution. *Any money that I have received, or will receive, for writing the book from the publisher has been, and will be, donated to charity.* I did not receive any compensation whatsoever from Real Madrid. For example, I did not ask for or receive one ticket to a game, nor did I ask for or receive a single player's photograph or autograph. Before publication, as a matter of professional courtesy, I did show drafts of parts of the book to Real Madrid, as well as a few other teams and leagues mentioned, to see if any material facts were incorrect or misrepresented. However, Real Madrid was not involved in the editorial or analytical process and did not approve or authorize this book. Any mistakes and all of the judgments, conclusions, and analyses are my own.

The book is written in American-sports English primarily to make it easier to understand for most American readers. Therefore, I use American terms, such as soccer for football, team for club (except when referencing Real Madrid, the club, or other teams that are actually member-owned clubs), field for pitch, game for match, locker room for dressing room, jersey for shirt, cleats for boots, uniform for kit, speed for pace, etc. I sincerely apologize in advance if this causes any annoyance or confusion for non-American readers. In addition, I try to convert amounts of money discussed in the book to US dollars using the average exchange rate for the year.

There are sidebars at the end and throughout most of the sections. The sidebars are related topics that don't fit the narrative on Real Madrid but shed light on the topic discussed in the chapter. Often the sidebars relate to American sports examples or an analysis of data or academic theories in order to illuminate an idea or help readers better understand the discussion.

Writing a book is a lengthy process—as well as is editing it, translating it, designing it, producing it, and marketing it. In order to have the book published in English and Spanish at the same time, which I felt was important, and to come out by a certain date, I had to submit my final draft to the publisher before the conclusion of the 2015–16 Real Madrid season. Therefore, the book does not reflect the entire season, but the data does include that Real Madrid won their eleventh Champions League trophy, La Undécima, in Milan, Italy, on May 28, 2016.

Lastly, I anticipate that I will take criticism from many sides. Many people have very passionate opinions regarding Real Madrid, their own favorite and rival soccer teams, the sport of soccer, and sports generally. The passion is so great that even respected scholars sometimes seem to put aside objective or critical thinking when it comes to the topic. When I interviewed people, I discovered many of their opinions are based on experience or gut feelings or simply what they have read or heard in the media, rather than facts or data. I am not sure they realize it, but some of their opinions have both strong and subtle biases, sympathies, and prejudices, and sometimes motivations. I know I have some, too, but I take the steps of challenging them as best I can, as described in my methodology. I do think approaching this study essentially as an outsider without

La Undécima. A photo of the players and coach lifting the 2016 UEFA Champions League trophy in Milan on June 28, 2016, after defeating Atlético Madrid. It is Real Madrid's eleventh European Cup. After extra time, the final finished with the score still tied 1-1, and Real Madrid won 5-3 in a penalty shootout. Lucas Vázquez, Marcelo, Bale, and Ramos scored their penalty kicks. Cristiano Ronaldo scored the decisive penalty kick after an Atlético Madrid player missed his. Sergio Ramos, the team's captain who also scored Real Madrid's goal, is seen lifting the trophy. The coach, Zinedine Zidane, is dressed in a suit and tie.

preconceived history, loyalty, or family ties to an European soccer team, not having really lived in Spain or Europe for a long time (but having spent enough time in Spain and Europe to understand some important nuances), and having limited experience-bias does help produce fresh and original ideas and research.[7]

As you read the book, keep in mind that I am using my best efforts to draw on my academic training and to shed light on a fascinating topic via a scholarly framework. Readers may agree or disagree or even feel like other aspects should be mentioned or examined further. I genuinely welcome constructive feedback. As an academic and curious person, I am always learning and trying to get to the most reasonable conclusion.

If you have any thoughts or comments about the book, please feel free to email me at my Columbia Business School email: sgm2130@columbia.edu. I can't promise that I will respond to every message, but I can promise you that I will read each one.

---

[7] In a 2014 interview with Sean Ingle of the *Guardian*, Billy Beane said, "I've got brilliant staff...One of my right-hand guys...has a PhD in behavioral economics from the University of California, Berkeley. He never played much baseball. Isn't that a disadvantage? It would be hard to imagine many English clubs doing the same...but he has no experience-bias when he comes to my office, so he is able to question the obvious...A guy like myself, who has been in the game his entire life, may not be able to spot when the emperor is not wearing any clothes."

INTRODUCTION:
LA DÉCIMA

ON THE COOL EVENING of Saturday, May 24, 2014, Real Madrid's soccer players walk onto the field for the 2014 UEFA Champions League final and look up at a screaming full-capacity crowd of 65,000 in Lisbon, Portugal's Estádio da Luz ("Stadium of Light"). The world's most watched annual sporting event is about to air in more than 200 countries, drawing an estimated global audience of 400 million viewers. (To put this into perspective, only an estimated 160 million people worldwide watched the 2014 Super Bowl, 114 million of them in the United States.) The Real Madrid players are dressed in their traditional gleaming white jerseys, the front of which are adorned with "Fly Emirates," a Real Madrid sponsor's logo. On the upper-left front of their jerseys, over their hearts, is the club's famous emblem with a royal crown on top. On the upper-right front is the logo of Adidas, another Real Madrid sponsor. The crest on the left sleeve shows the number of European Cups won by Real Madrid. With the temperature hovering around fifty-nine degrees Fahrenheit, some of the players have chosen to wear long-sleeved jerseys.

The tournament is referred to as the UEFA Champions League (previously known as the European Cup until it was renamed in 1992) because it is a tournament of the soccer teams that finish in the top few teams of their country's respective soccer leagues. Real Madrid had last won the competition—their ninth title—in 2002. After over a decade of chasing La Décima ("the tenth"), Real Madrid is ninety minutes away from realizing that goal. Their opponent in the final is cross-city rival Atlético Madrid, wearing their traditional red-and-white striped jerseys. There had been two teams from the same country in the Champions

League finals before, but there had never been a Champions League final between two teams from the same city. There was such high demand from Real Madrid's club members for the tickets the club was allocated by UEFA that the team had to award the tickets by means of a draw. In addition, Real Madrid sold out its 81,044-capacity home-city stadium, Bernabéu Stadium, to *Madridistas* (a nickname for people who support Real Madrid) to watch the game on big screens.

With a tenth European trophy for Real Madrid or a first for Atlético Madrid at stake, the Madrid versus Madrid battle for the title of best team in Europe—which generally translates as the best team in the world—is historically earth-shattering even before the prime-time kickoff.

Real Madrid's team of galácticos consists of amazing star players, including Portuguese forward Cristiano Ronaldo,[8] who is considered one of the two greatest soccer players in the world (along with Argentine forward Lionel Messi, who plays for rival club Barcelona). Ronaldo's jersey number is 7, and he is sometimes referred to as CR7. During the 2013–14 season, Ronaldo had truly established himself as one of Real Madrid's contemporary icons, along with previous galácticos like Zinedine Zidane, Raúl González, and Luís Figo. Ronaldo finished at the top of the Spanish La Liga season's goal-scorers list with fifty-one goals in forty-seven games—more than one goal per game average is an astonishing statistic. Though it is often overlooked, Ronaldo also contributed nine assists that season to add to his impressive stats. Beyond his good looks, his sculpted body reflects the incredible winning mentality and hard work that he puts into striving to be the best and to set an example for his teammates.

Ronaldo has a fearsome scoring partnership with Welsh winger Gareth Bale and French striker Karim Benzema. Benzema joined Real Madrid in July 2009, one month after Ronaldo, when Real Madrid paid

---

[8] There is debate in the media about whether Cristiano Ronaldo or Gareth Bale holds the world record for the highest transfer fee ever paid for a player, both by Real Madrid. Ronaldo joined the team in 2009 for what was reported at the time to be a €94 million ($131 million) transfer fee, while Bale's fee was originally reported to be €91.5 million in 2013. However, because Bale's fee was to be paid in installments, the total resulted in around €100 million. Spanish newspaper *Marca* reported that Ronaldo's contract also had installments and the total amount was actually €104.7 million, which would make Ronaldo the world's most expensive player.

The starting lineup of the Real Madrid team that won the 2014 Champions League final. Back row (left to right): Casillas, Ramos, Varane, Khedira, Benzema, Ronaldo. Front row: Di María, Bale, Coentrão, Carvajal, Modrić.

a €35 million ($49 million) transfer fee to French team Lyon, with the fee rising to as much as €41 million ($57 million) including incentives. Before the 2013–14 season started, Real Madrid had paid English team Tottenham €91 million ($120 million) for Bale. The three star players were nicknamed the "BBC" by the Spanish media—for Bale, Benzema, and Cristiano.

Despite the perception that Madrid simply buys its star players, the goalkeeper for this epic game is Spaniard Iker Casillas, who started his career at the age of eleven in Real Madrid's youth academy, which is sometimes referred to as La Fábrica ("The Factory"). In 1999, at age eighteen, he was promoted to the first team.[9] As the longest-serving member on the team, Casillas was automatically appointed captain during the 2010–11 season. As a product of the Real Madrid development

---

[9] The first team is the main, upper level team that plays in the first (top) division and major competitions.

academy, he knew and exemplified the ethos of Real Madrid. In fact seven out of the twenty-five players (28 percent) on the first team in the finals are graduates of the academy. Together they share the spirit, expectations, history, and essence of Real Madrid with the new players.

Real Madrid's coach that season, Carlo Ancelotti, is well suited to manage their superstars, not only because of his calm temperament on and off the field but also because of the respect he commands as a former star player and winning coach. Ancelotti likes to stretch the game and take advantage of open spaces, but Atlético's coach, Diego Simeone, has proven enough times that he is a tactical genius and will not be overwhelmed by the occasion.

The media has marketed the game as David vs. Goliath. Real Madrid generated €550 million ($726 million) in revenue during the year, compared to Atlético's €170 million ($224 million). Real Madrid paid their players an average of $7.6 million compared to Atlético's $2.6 million. Real Madrid has a powerhouse balance sheet, probably one of the strongest in all of sports, while Atlético had such serious debt problems three years prior that they fell behind in their tax payments. Although any link between winning in sports and profitability has been disproven in several studies (see sidebar below), the media has been speculating that an Atlético win would increase the value of their brand and profitability. The media seems to have forgotten that, after winning the Champions League in May 1998 and May 2000, Real Madrid was close to bankruptcy by 2000.

Most Soccer Teams Lose Money

Simon Kuper, writer for the *Financial Times*, and Stefan Szymanski, former professor of economics and current professor of sports management at the University of Michigan, made the argument in chapter three of their book *Soccernomics* (New York: Nation Books, 2009) that most soccer teams lose money. According to the authors, the buyers of soccer teams are wrong if they assume that if they can get their teams to win trophies, profits will inevitably follow. The authors analyzed the Premier League from 1992–93 to 2011–12 and discovered that even the best teams seldom generate profits. They also detailed how unprofitable the overall industry is. In addition, they showed that there was little correlation between success on the field and making money. Instead, Kuper and Szymanski found that most teams didn't care about profits. They were spending what they believed it took to win games. The majority of teams even paid players more money than they had or could produce, so the teams would borrow money, and most had a precarious amount of debt.

In a 2008 unpublished MBA thesis at Judge Business School in Cambridge, Francisco Cutiño showed that winning games doesn't necessarily help soccer teams make profits. Rather, the effect works the other way. If a team finds new revenues, those revenues can help them win games because they can help buy/ retain better players:

> But contrary to the common idea that good [on-field] performance will drive good financials, there is evidence that better revenue-generating structures can have a significant impact in the performance of the team... only with good financial results clubs can buy and retain good players and create good teams.

Therefore, a team should develop a sustainable economic-sport model to make profits to buy/retain better players, which leads to better results.

In *Winners and Losers: The Business Strategy of Football* (New York: Viking, 1999), Szymanski and researcher Tim Kuypers analyzed ten years of the English Premier League (1990–99) and discovered that the one variable with the highest correlation to winning is: the teams that pay the highest salaries for the best players win the most often. It probably doesn't take a lot of classes on data analytics to figure that out. I believe in a competitive industry with competitive owners who have lots of money to spend, a team needs a distinctive competitive advantage to maximize the performance of these best players as well as to help generate more money to pay the salaries.

The game ends Real Madrid 4–1 Atlético Madrid. It's Real Madrid's tenth Champions League trophy, their first since 2002, and they couldn't have won it in a more dramatic fashion, coming from behind to tie the score in the ninety-third minute and forcing the game into extra time (for more details, see "Play-by-Play of La Décima" sidebar on page xxvii).

To add to Real Madrid lore, the team won the game utilizing one of its core values: never giving up, which means competing until the final whistle. Real Madrid was 150 seconds away from defeat, yet they never gave up hope and played as hard as they could until the very end. Putting aside the rivalry or La Décima, what makes the evening so special to Real Madrid's management is that the players lived up to the community's expectations.

On Sunday morning, the team arrived at Madrid's Plaza de Cibeles with the trophy. There were still tens of thousands of Real Madrid fans in the square after celebrating throughout the night. "Thank you for waiting," Captain Casillas told the supporters and then added the obvious, "It's time to think about the Eleventh (La Undécima)."[10] Vice-Captain Sergio Ramos, with the second-most seniority on the team, spoke into the microphone: "This is dedicated to Pitina, who helps us from above.[11] Hala Madrid!" "Hala Madrid" is difficult to translate exactly. It means something like "Go, Madrid, Go!" or "Forward, Madrid!"

Real Madrid define themselves by results, and in particular by their performance in the Champions League. Anyone who plays for or manages Real Madrid is left in no doubt about the top priority every season.[12] The pride of the community at the team's record number of wins is matched only by their passion for doing it in their own unique way. In Lisbon, the team's players felt the full weight of the community's expectations, which went beyond simply winning. There is an intense sense of responsibility and pride that comes with representing what the community is and the values they stand for. Real Madrid's secret to dominance on and off the field is the passion and values of their community members.

---

[10] Rob Hughes, "The Never-Ending Job at Real Madrid." *New York Times*. http://www.nytimes.com/2014/05/28/sports/soccer/the-never-ending-job-at-real-madrid.html?_r=0.

[11] Ramos was referencing the beloved Pitina Sandoval, Florentino's wife of forty-one years and mother of their three children, who died in May 2012.

[12] Michael Owen, "Champions League final 2014: Real Madrid ruled by Europe so they dare not lose to Atletico Madrid." *Telegraph*. http://www.telegraph.co.uk/sport/columnists/michael-owen/10852545/Champions-League-final-2014-Real-Madrid-ruled-by-Europe-so-they-dare-not-lose-to-Atletico-Madrid.html.

Play-by-Play of La Décima

Exactly 19:45. It is time for business. The atmosphere is electric. Real Madrid gets the ball first and kicks it from left to right. Atlético is defending deep, as expected. In the ninth minute, Diego Costa, Atlético's leading goal scorer, jogs off the field, injured. Since he isn't carried off, the announcers speculate that he hadn't torn his hamstring again, like he did in the semifinals against Barcelona, but clearly he knows he can't carry on. The announcers speculate whether Costa will be sidelined by injury, and, if he is, the gamble that playing him could cost his team one of only three valuable substitutions allowed very early in the game.

Real Madrid continues to control the ball, but Atlético is so well organized on defense that Real Madrid can't develop any serious threats. As excellent as Atlético has been defensively, however, it has been ineffective going forward. At thirty-two minutes into the game, Real Madrid gets their best chance to score when Bale takes advantage of an Atlético midfielder's careless pass. Space opens up, and thirty yards out the Welshman uses his world-class speed to sprint toward the goal. Bale fights off a sliding tackle (had Bale gone down, he might have drawn a penalty) and perhaps is somehow distracted enough that he then pokes the ball just wide of the post from twelve yards. Bale throws both hands over his face. The magnitude of his regret over the missed opportunity highlights how rare scoring opportunities are in soccer and how precious the ability to finish and score is.

Only four minutes later, Atlético responds. An Atlético corner is headed away by Real Madrid, then an Atlético player heads the ball back into the penalty area. There seems to be little threat, but Real Madrid goalkeeper Casillas sprints off his goal line into no man's land. Atlético's center back rises above a Real Madrid defenseman near the penalty spot to head the ball over the out-of-position goalkeeper who is too far off his line. Casillas is already desperately retreating, realizing that he misjudged his ability to reach the ball. He manages to get a hand on the ball heading toward the empty net, trying to claw it back, but to no avail. The ball crosses the line. GOAL! The goal scorer is tackled by his teammates on his celebratory run and ends up under a mass of Atlético players. Even though Real Madrid had seemed to be in control for most of the first half, they are losing. To make things worse, all Atlético has to do now is sit back, clog things up, eliminate space between players, and defend—which is what they are most comfortable doing.

As halftime approaches, Real Madrid players seem increasingly frustrated by Atlético's defensive approach, which is tactically designed to break up Real Madrid's typical beautifully fluid attacking play. Real Madrid looks like they need a break to regroup.

Halftime: Real Madrid 0–1 Atlético Madrid. During the fifteen-minute break, an announcer on one broadcast makes the point that Ronaldo and Benzema barely touched the ball near the Atlético goal area during the first half. Bale only had one real opportunity, which he missed.

When the second half begins, there is a desperate air to Real Madrid's attacks. Atlético has moved more players to defense, which continues to frustrate Real Madrid, but Real Madrid is advancing the ball deeper and getting a few more opportunities to score. A Ronaldo free kick is deflected by the Atlético goalkeeper and off the bar at fifty-four minutes. A Ronaldo header glances wide at sixty-two minutes. And after an exhilarating sprint, Bale's shot tamely goes into the side netting at seventy-eight minutes.

After eighty minutes, Atlético players seem like they are on their last legs, tired of chasing after and closing down on Real Madrid's players and passes. Atlético uses their third, and last, substitution at eighty-three minutes. It seems Atlético can't clear the ball out of their own third, never mind their own half. The pressure seems to be escalating to an explosion.

At eighty-nine minutes into the game, the Atlético coach implores the fans to cheer his team to the finish. At the ninety-minute mark, the referee decides to add five minutes of stoppage time. Three minutes into stoppage time, a Real Madrid corner kick by Croatian midfielder Luka Modrić from the right swings toward the penalty spot. Sergio Ramos gets clear of everyone and powers a masterful header into the far corner of the net. GOAL! English TV commentator Ray Hudson, known for his descriptive color commentary, screams, "…magisteeerial…the corner kick sails in…and Ramos leaps…like a fresh salmon from a summer stream…it's an exquisite header…with power and accuracy measured down to a pixel!"

The moment the ball swishes the back of the net, a man in a conservative blue suit leaps in front of King Juan Carlos of Spain in the center of the stadium's VIP suite. The typically levelheaded and controlled Florentino Pérez, president of Real Madrid, raises his arms in celebration. Realizing that his passion is getting the best of him, he quickly pulls his arms down, wipes his glasses, straightens his suit jacket, and sits back down. He is trying to be sensitive and respectful to the president of Atlético Madrid, who is sitting near him.

A TV announcer screams, "We are heading for extra time!"

During the break before extra time, which is divided into two fifteen-minute halves, Atlético's exhausted and disheartened players stretch out on blue mats laid out on the field, while Real Madrid players gather in a huddle to motivate themselves.

The first fifteen minutes of extra time is sloppy. When the second half of extra time begins, it's still Real Madrid 1–1 Atlético Madrid. Atlético's players' minds now seem as tired as their bodies, and they start making mental errors.

GOAL! Gareth Bale had missed a few opportunities, but in the 111th minute he scores. Real Madrid's Ángel Di María uses fancy footwork to surge down the left side between two or three weary Atlético players and flicks the ball toward the goal with his outside foot. The Atlético goalkeeper makes an incredible save with his left foot, but the ball still deflects toward the far post. Bale reads the trajectory and spin of the ball and maneuvers his body to head the ball at an acute angle from very close range just inside the top right post.

Ray Hudson jumps off his chair, screaming, "...it's as electrifying as a hair dryer thrown into a bathtub...look at the balance...the timing...he's like a master thief stealing the silverware in the dark night...the galácticos are gladiators tonight...and Gareth Bale is Spartacus!"

Looking for an equalizer, Atlético starts to attack harder than they have throughout the game. Their aggressiveness leaves them vulnerable to counterattacks. GOAL! In the 118th minute, the big-haired Brazilian Marcelo takes advantage, driving a low shot right through the left arm of the plunging Atlético goalkeeper. Imagine Andrés Cantor, the Argentine-born Spanish-language sportscaster, yelling his familiar, "Gooooooooooal," with the "o" stretched out over fifteen seconds—and then repeating it.

To make matters worse for Atlético, two minutes later, a tired Atlético player accidentally trips Ronaldo in the penalty box, and Ronaldo is awarded a penalty kick. GOAL! With a right-footed shot, Ronaldo puts the penalty into the back of the right corner of the net with precision and power. Ray Hudson describes the moment: "...absolute precision from the Dark Invader...this one is a death-ray hit from Real Madrid's glamour boy..." It is Ronaldo's seventeenth goal of the tournament, a record at the time.

PART ONE

How Real Madrid Became the Most Successful Sports Team on the Planet

Chapter 1

REAL MADRID'S ON- AND OFF-FIELD DOMINANCE

A T THE CENTER of the Real Madrid way for success are the values of their community and resulting culture. Real Madrid management believes the culture has translated into continued success on the field thus creating a profitable and sustainable enterprise that people can identify with and turn to, embracing it as a meaningful and steadfast cornerstone of their own personal value and identity. Before examining the Real Madrid way, it is worth understanding its results, beyond its record 107 official competition trophies in its 114 year history.

When I ask US sports fans, "What is the most valuable sports team in the world?" the most common answers are "the New York Yankees" or "the Dallas Cowboys." When I tell them the answer is Real Madrid, most people are completely shocked. American-centric sports fans will be absolutely astonished by the data below.

Financials

Real Madrid is worth $3.44 billion according to *Forbes'* World's 50 Most Valuable Sports Teams in July 2015.[13] They rank it the most valuable sports team, which surprises many Americans, but if one thinks

---

[13] In September 2015, *Forbes* revalued NFL teams. The valuation for the Dallas Cowboys was higher than Real Madrid's valuation in July 2015. However, at the time, Forbes did not revalue any soccer or baseball teams.

about it, soccer is the most popular sport in the entire world. Soccer has 3.5 billion fans globally, while baseball, basketball, and American football's fans *combined* do not equal the number of soccer enthusiasts.[14] The 2012 Deloitte Football Money League reported that in 2010–11, European professional soccer teams generated a combined €17.5 billion ($23.7 billion) in revenues. In an article about ranking sports' popularity in September 2011, the *Economist* reported that "This compares with the NFL's $9 billion, MLB's $7.2 billion, and the NBA's $4.1 billion in 2011."[15]

Regardless of the rankings of *Forbes* and others, recent sports industry transactions may suggest that Real Madrid is actually the most valuable team. MLB's Los Angeles Dodgers was acquired for $2 billion, more than eight times its revenues in 2012. NBA's Los Angeles Clippers was acquired for $2 billion, fifteen times revenues in 2014 (*Forbes* valued the team at $430 million the previous year). Real Madrid has larger revenues and profits than either team, a more differentiated global brand, and a larger global fan base in the world's most popular sport. Real Madrid would also have a much wider potential buyer universe than an American sports team.[16] Just using the Dodgers' eight times revenues transaction multiple, Real Madrid would be worth over $5.7 billion. Of course, the value of the team in a sale transaction is very theoretical because Real Madrid is a not-for-profit organization with approximately 92,000 club members that "own" the club (this will be discussed in detail later).

---

[14] "Top 10 List of the Internet World's Most Popular Sports." *Topend Sports*. http://www.topendsports.com/world/lists/popular-sport/fans.htm.

[15] "Ranking Sports Popularity: And the silver goes to…". *Economist*. http://www.economist.com/blogs/gametheory/2011/09/ranking-sports'-popularity.

[16] I spoke to a leading sports industry mergers and acquisitions expert who has sold many leading sports franchises. He agreed that theoretically Real Madrid should be the most valuable sport team because of their sustainable economic-sport model, differentiated brand, and large global fan base in the world's most popular sport. The potential buyers could be larger and more global than those for North American sports teams. A possible list would not only include billionaires who could leverage the sports team and its stars playing friendly games abroad to help their image and companies but also sovereign wealth funds, such as Qatar Investment Authority buying Paris Saint-Germain to help promote a country. In addition, unlike North American sports leagues where other owners must approve a potential buyer (which could restrict interest or those eligible), there are no such restrictions in European soccer. However, he raised the issue that at some point the potential valuation amount is so large that the potential buyers for the entire amount become limited, which could restrict the valuation.

The chart below from *Forbes* values Real Madrid at five times revenues (the same multiple of revenues as the sale of NBA's Milwaukee Bucks in 2014, which really does not compare to Real Madrid).

Table 1.1: Ten Most Valuable Sports Teams 2015 by *Forbes*

Global Rank	Team	Value (2015) ($ billions)	Sport
1	Real Madrid	$3.44	Soccer
2	Dallas Cowboys	$3.20	Football
2	New York Yankees	$3.20	Baseball
4	Barcelona	$3.16	Soccer
5	Manchester United	$3.10	Soccer
6	Los Angeles Lakers	$2.60	Basketball
6	New England Patriots	$2.60	Football
8	New York Knicks	$2.50	Basketball
9	Los Angeles Dodgers	$2.40	Baseball
9	Washington Redskins	$2.40	Football

Real Madrid has the most revenues, $675 million in 2014, of any sports team in the world according to Forbes.[17] Great sports teams in major markets like the MLB's Dodgers and NFL's New York Giants don't even make the top ten. NBA's Los Angeles Lakers 2014 revenues were $293 million, less than half of Real Madrid's. Real Madrid has been at the top of the Deloitte Football Money League for eleven straight years, including the 2014–15 season.

---

[17] The revenues by given years can differ or be inconsistent because of different season ends, different fiscal years, and currency exchange moves. The revenues for Real Madrid's 2013–14 season were €550 million ($726 million).

Table 1.2: Ten Highest Sports Teams Revenues 2014 by *Forbes*

Global Rank	Team	Revenues (2014) ($ millions)	Sport
1	Real Madrid	$675	Soccer
2	Barcelona	$627	Soccer
3	Dallas Cowboys	$620	Football
4	Bayern Munich	$561	Soccer
5	Manchester United	$551	Soccer
6	Paris Saint-Germain	$518	Soccer
7	New York Yankees	$508	Baseball
8	New England Patriots	$494	Football
9	Washington Redskins	$439	Football
10	Manchester City	$411	Soccer

Community Support and Brand

The power of the Real Madrid brand goes well beyond soccer, Madrid, or Spain. Experts estimate that Real Madrid has approximately 450 million fans around the world—more than American football has in total. Perhaps the best evidence of the power of the brand and identity lies in the club's social media following. In 2015, Real Madrid had a total of 200 million followers across all global social media platforms, including those in China. A truly global presence, Real Madrid had approximately 100 million Facebook fans and Twitter followers on social media in 2015. To put this into context, the American sports team with the highest social media following was the Los Angeles Lakers at around 25 million, which also reflects the global appeal of basketball. In contrast, the New York Yankees had about 10 million fans on social media, which did not make the top fifteen of the chart below.

Table 1.3: Fifteen Most Popular Sports Teams on Social Media 2015

Global Rank	Team	Total followers (millions)	Facebook fans (millions)	Twitter followers (millions)
1	Real Madrid	100	83	17
1	Barcelona	100	85	15
3	Manchester United	71	65	6
4	Chelsea	49	43	6
5	Arsenal	40	33	6
6	Bayern Munich	33	31	2
7	Liverpool	30	26	4
8	AC Milan	27	24	3
9	Los Angeles Lakers	25	21	4
10	Paris Saint-Germain	22	20	2
11	Manchester City	22	19	3
12	Juventus	21	19	2
13	Chicago Bulls	20	18	2
14	Miami Heat	19	16	3
15	Galatasaray	18	12	6

According to BBDO Consulting, Real Madrid has the highest brand value among European soccer teams. As of 2007 this value of 1.063 billion ($1.45 billion) was based on current and future income and expert opinion. The ranking is based on research that determines brand value using current and future income flow and expert opinion. BBDO Consulting states that its approach went beyond depicting only financial performance—it also analyzed scientific behavioral values such as brand popularity, image, sympathy, and loyalty. Income was examined in great depth, right up to the levels of sponsor contracts, merchandising, and revenue from season tickets, etc. The behavioral scientific side of the valuation comes from a survey of around 400 international experts.

Table 1.4: Five Most Valuable Soccer Brands 2007 by BBDO Consulting

Global Rank	Team	Value (millions)
1	Real Madrid	€1,063 ($1,450)
2	Barcelona	€948 ($1,290)
3	Manchester United	€922 ($1,245)
4	Chelsea	€828 ($1,120)
5	AC Milan	€824 ($1,115)

According to PR Marketing, Real Madrid has the highest average jersey sales per year in soccer from 2009–10 to 2013–14. This demonstrates the passion, loyalty, and number of Real Madrid fans around the world. Adidas is the uniform manufacturer for Real Madrid. Sponsorship is provided by the Dubai-based Emirates Airlines. Many people believe that Real Madrid's jersey sales are driven by individual star players only. While it is undeniable that players' fans drive a lot of jersey sales, I will present some evidence later that the club's community values may have more to do with jersey sales than people expect.

Table 1.5: Soccer Jersey Sales 2009–10 to 2013–14 by PR Marketing

Rank	Team	Average Sales per Year
1	Real Madrid	1,580,000
2	Manchester United	1,490,000
3	Barcelona	1,180,000
4	Bayern Munich	945,000
5	Chelsea	875,000
6	Arsenal	825,000
7	Liverpool	805,000
8	Marseille	385,000
9	Juventus	375,000
10	Paris Saint-Germain	335,000
11	Fenerbahce	325,000
12	Inter Milan	300,000

Championships

On the field, Real Madrid has won eleven Champions League titles since the tournament of the best teams from each European league was established in 1955. The next closest competitor in terms of wins is AC Milan, which has won the Champions League seven times. Three teams (Barcelona, Bayern Munich, and Liverpool) are tied at five wins each.

Real Madrid has won a record thirty-two Spanish La Liga titles. Barcelona, in second place, has won twenty-four. Whenever Real Madrid plays their archrival Barcelona, it is commonly referred to as *El Clásico*. Real Madrid leads the head-to-head results in competitive games with ninety-two wins to Barcelona's ninety. Whenever Real Madrid plays their crosstown rival Atlético Madrid, it is commonly referred to as the *El Derbi Madrileño* ("The Madrid Derby").[18] Real Madrid leads the head-to-head results in competitive games with 107 wins to Atlético Madrid's 53.

Table 1.6: European Champions League Titles

Global Rank	Team	Number of European Titles	Number of Domestic Titles
1	Real Madrid	11	32
2	AC Milan	7	18
3	Barcelona	5	24
	Bayern Munich	5	26
	Liverpool	5	18

In 2015, UEFA released its ranking of the most successful teams in Champions League competition history. These rankings were based on three points for a win, one for a draw, and zero for a loss.

---

[18] Games between two rivals of close geographical proximity are usually called a "local derby," or simply "derby." In North America, the term "crosstown rivalry" is used.

Table 1.7: Top Teams in European Cup History (2015)

Rank	Team	Points
1	Real Madrid	729
2	Bayern Munich	565
3	Barcelona	508
4	Manchester United	455
5	AC Milan	404

Real Madrid was recognized as the FIFA Club of the 20th Century in 2010, winning the award with 42.4 percent of the votes. Manchester United was a distant second with 9.7 percent.

Table 1.8: FIFA Club of the 20th Century Voting (2010)

Rank	Team	Percent
1	Real Madrid	42.4%
2	Manchester United	9.7%
3	Bayern Munich	8.2%
4	Barcelona	5.6%
5	Ajax	5.1%

Differences between MLB, NBA, and European Professional Soccer

With *Moneyball* being such an imposing force on how we think about sports, it is important to remember that *Moneyball* is about an MLB team. There are several differences between the MLB, NBA, and European soccer leagues that are worth highlighting because they can have a meaningful impact on strategic decisions both on the field and off the field. The differences will highlight that Real Madrid needs to have a strategy in place regarding teamwork because of the interdependence of the sport (see "Interdependence" sidebar on page 39).

Drafts, Taxes, and Revenue Sharing

In European professional soccer, there are no drafts and no salary caps or luxury taxes. It is an open market. European professional soccer teams can either develop players through their own youth academies or buy the rights to players in the transfer market and pay them whatever they want. In 2011, UEFA enacted financial fair-play rules. Since then, teams that qualify for UEFA competitions essentially have to prove throughout the season that they have paid their bills. Since 2013, teams have also been assessed against break-even financial requirements, meaning that they have to balance their spending with their revenues, which restricts teams from accumulating too much debt. Without a salary cap or luxury tax on players' salaries, only a limit based on breaking even, teams are economically incentivized to expand their fan bases, cultivate sponsorships, and find other ways to increase revenues to afford better players.

The NBA and MLB, in contrast, have organized annual drafts to select players. Typically, the teams that finished with the worst record the previous season get to select first. This is to help with competitive parity. Therefore, a baseball or basketball team can draft a star player and not have to bid competitively for him. MLB has a "competitive balance tax" or "luxury tax" that is the punishment for large market teams that spend too much money. While MLB does not have a set salary cap, the luxury tax costs teams with high payrolls a considerable amount of money, giving them ample reason to want to keep their payrolls below the threshold level. The NBA utilizes a soft salary cap, meaning that while there is a salary cap, there are a variety of exceptions that allow teams to exceed it. In addition to the soft cap, the NBA utilizes a luxury tax system that is applied if a team's payroll exceeds a separate threshold that is higher than the salary cap. Historically, around half of the NBA's teams are over the cap. In both the NBA and MLB, big market teams like MLB's New York Yankees or the NBA's New York Knicks can generate revenues with their own sponsors and local television broadcasts and can afford to pay up to the cap or to pay the luxury tax if they go over the cap. Also, billionaire-owners such as the NBA's Brooklyn Nets owner Mikhail Prokhorov, who was charged a reported $80 million in luxury taxes in 2014, can simply pay the tax. Small-market and other teams like the MLB's Oakland Athletics in *Moneyball* may not have the financial resources, sponsorships, or local television broadcasts to pay up to the threshold, or may simply choose not to do so. However, the

Athletics receive money from those that pay the luxury tax. In addition, in order to combat the growing revenue disparity among major league teams, MLB first instituted a revenue-sharing program in 1996 that, among many things, requires that every team pay 31 percent of their net local revenue, and then that money is divided up and equally distributed to every team (the NBA and NFL also have revenue sharing). Therefore, the small-market MLB teams have less of an economic incentive than a European soccer team to grow revenues because the latter would have to share the upside. The business conditions for a small-market team in MLB are similar to a "socialist" economic system, while European soccer is much more of a "free-market" economic system. The "socialist" economic system prevalent in North America has the leagues, rather than the teams, playing the dominant role in many marketing functions, especially internationally. A team like the Athletics has some constrictions in revenue growth, such as limits to their market place, sharing a market with a much bigger and wealthier team, and being the only MLB team to share a stadium with an NFL team. The Athletics' innovation in data analytics was driven, in part, because they have limitations. On the other hand, Real Madrid owns their stadium and benefits more directly from their innovations in broadcasting, marketing, and commercial revenues.

"Tanking"

No matter how bad the performance of an MLB or NBA team becomes, the team's place in their respective "major league," and their share of the national television contract, is assured. Therefore, in MLB or the NBA, teams can be incentivized to "tank," or lose on purpose, in order to get a better pick for the draft. In addition, an MLB or NBA team can afford "rebuilding" years in which the team's performance is bad, because they have the upside of being able to get a high draft pick to start to put together a good team and, in contrast, can't get kicked out of the league.

European professional soccer teams have a much higher economic incentive to win because of "promotion" and "relegation." Promotion and relegation are processes where teams are transferred between two divisions (think Major Leagues and AAA or NBA and Development League)[19] based on

---

[19]   This example is illustrative, but can be a little misleading. It is important to note that teams in the lower divisions in European soccer are not farm teams and are independent. Affiliated teams cannot be in the same division or league.

their performance for the completed season. The best-ranked teams in the lower division are promoted to the higher division for the next season, and the worst-ranked team or teams in the higher division are relegated to the lower division for the next season. This would mean the Philadelphia 76ers, for example, would be moved down to the Development League if they finished in last place in the NBA, and the Santa Cruz Warriors or Rio Grande Valley Vipers would move up to the NBA if they finished at the top of the Development League.

In European soccer, being relegated means a team no longer participates in the revenue share of the first division, which can have a significant impact on a team's finances and value.[20] Therefore, even the teams at the bottom of the standings are fighting to win each and every game. The teams that can afford the highest payrolls and better talent might not be as concerned about relegation. However, it is possible for them to miss qualifying for the Champions League. In addition, in the English Premier League, national TV revenues are apportioned by standing, once again encouraging teams to fight for each win to finish in a position in the league standing that at least maintains their share of TV revenues from the previous year. Therefore, it puts pressure on the coaches of the top teams to play their best players more often, which increases tiredness and risk of injury. In contrast, there may be nights that a strong NBA team, for example, can rest their star players and still defeat a team that is "tanking." In soccer, a team resting their best players risks losing points and standing in the league, which can have a financial impact. This has implications not only on how coaches must use their players but also the risks the organizations are willing to take. For example, in a 2014 interview with Sean Ingle of the *Guardian*, Billy Beane said it is arguably riskier for a European professional soccer manager to place huge faith in statistical analysis because, unlike in American sports, there is relegation. Beane said, "You don't have a lot of time to be right in football. So ultimately, before you mark on anything quantitative, you have to make sure you have scrutinized the data and have certainty with what you are doing, because the risk is very high."

---

[20] In the English Premier League, for example, there is a "parachute system" of payments for a few years to smooth out the financial impact of relegation.

Chapter 2

THE REAL MADRID WAY

AT THE CENTER of the Real Madrid way for success on and off the field are the values of their community and the resulting culture. Simply put, the shared ethos, expectations, and values of the Real Madrid community dictate the operations, behavior, and mission of every aspect of the entire club. The values and expectations of the community drive the decision-making throughout the organization, from on the field (in player selection, player behavior expectations, style of play, and priorities) to off the field (in business and management characteristics, strategy, marketing, investments, financial reporting, human resources, and technology). The Real Madrid management team spends their time reinforcing and solidifying increased personal connections, relationships, and communication directly with their community members. Management also pushes the community's values throughout the organization and to their players. Management's goal is to help the community connect to their intense passion of *living* Real Madrid.

Real Madrid's management team believes that *the community does not exist to serve the business or management; rather, the club exists to serve the Real Madrid community.* While the community has a shared identity as Real Madrid fans, the club recognizes that members and fans are individuals with a wide variety of needs, interests, and responsibilities.

Professor Susan Fournier from Boston University and Lara Lee, former executive at Harley-Davidson, wrote an article titled "Getting Brand Communities Right" in the April 2009 issue of *Harvard Business Review*. According to them, "A community-based brand builds loyalty not by driving sales transactions but by helping people meet their needs."[21] Essentially, that is what Real Madrid is doing. The club is constantly trying to better understand their community members' values, give them what they want, and improve and inspire their lives. They learned that those needs are not just about gaining status or identity through brand affiliation. Fournier and Lee wrote, "People participate in communities for a wide variety of reasons—to find emotional support and encouragement, to explore ways to contribute to the greater good, and to cultivate interests and skills, to name a few. For members, brand communities are a means to an end, not an end in themselves." To this idea, Real Madrid would most likely add that their members participate in their community to be empowered, inspired, escape, enjoy, celebrate, connect, share, and socialize. Real Madrid seeks to help raise the self-esteem, self-confidence, joy, and happiness of hundreds of millions of people around the world. The community—the people—is the foundation. The reasons why Real Madrid's community members participate are different, but the jubilation—and sometimes tears—unites them all. For Real Madrid's fans and members, the community is a "means to an end, not the end itself."[22]

Therefore, the management team put at the center of their strategy the members' and fans' values and expectations. For example, if the community wants content to share, Real Madrid seeks to provide the best and most relevant exclusive content in the best and most convenient ways through Realmadrid.com and their social media accounts. Technology enables the content for experiences and engagement to be scalable around the world. The access fuels the connection and passion, while the club's traditions and rituals reinforce the identity association. Thus, Real Madrid's community's values, expectations, and desires became the touchstone for developing and aligning strategy, culture, and identity to win on the field and in business.[23]

---

[21] Susan Fournier and Lara Lee, "Getting Brand Communities Right." *Harvard Business Review*. https://hbr.org/2009/04/getting-brand-communities-right.

[22] Ibid.

[23] Albert M Muniz, Jr. and Thomas C. O'Guinn wrote a paper published by the *Journal of Consumer Research* in 2001 titled "Brand Community." They state that "a brand community is a specialized, non-geographically bound community, based on a structured set of social relations among admirers of a brand…brand communities exhibit three traditional markers of community: shared consciousness, rituals and traditions, and a sense of moral responsibility…Brand communities are participants in the brand's larger social construction and play a vital role in the brand's ultimate legacy."

With this approach, Real Madrid was able to bring together a passionate global community by creating a sense of belonging and shared values felt so deeply by fans around the world that they are synonymous with one's identity and much more. It is impossible to tell where the fan's identity and life as a Madridista and the club's identity and purpose start and stop. There is no question that the identity of a Madridista and the club is one and the same. The history, feelings, and emotions are intertwined. The closest corporate examples would be Harley-Davidson, Ferrari, and IRONMAN, where in each case the brand and the identity, life, and lifestyle are absolutely intertwined. Owning a Harley-Davidson motorcycle allows you to be a member of the "HOG" (Harley Owners Group); buying a Ferrari allows you to be called a "Ferrarista"; finishing a 140.6-mile IRONMAN race allows you to call yourself an "Ironman."[24] The commercial power of the identity, life, and lifestyle is demonstrated by the fact that all three brands have thriving global apparel sales, sold both online and in specialized stores, yet none of them are apparel companies. A HOG, Ferrarista, Ironman, or Madridista benefits from the community with new friendships, a sense of belonging, shared experiences, recognition, and increased self-esteem. In addition, the internet and digital technology have allowed sophisticated, active community engagement.

At the center of everything Real Madrid is and does is their relationship with the community. The Real Madrid management team cares as much about bringing joy to the community and spreading and sharing the community's positive values (far beyond the ninety minutes of a game) as they do about winning championships, in their unique way. In addition, they make efforts to reach well beyond their brick-and-mortar stadium venue via digital technology, social media, and a partnership with Microsoft; international and friendly exhibition games around the world; and Real Madrid supporters clubs to reinforce and intensify interaction and engagement.

---

[24] Alexander Chernev, Professor of Marketing at Northwestern University's Kellogg School of Management, classifies Real Madrid as a "personality brand," just like Harley-Davidson, Ferrari, and IRONMAN. According to Chernev, "Personality brands express consumers' individual values and preferences. Personality brands are less about asserting an individual's status, wealth, and power; instead, they reflect an individual's idiosyncratic beliefs, preferences, and values. Unlike status brands, which have a price point that makes them unattainable by the majority of the population, personality brands are not differentiated on price, which makes them accessible to a larger segment of the population."

The secret of the Real Madrid way is creating enterprise value from community values and expectations. Florentino and his Real Madrid leadership team figured out a *sustainable*, circular model to win both on and off the field (this is my interpretation and representation, not Real Madrid's). The word "sustainable" is important because Real Madrid is owned by approximately 92,000 club members, not a billionaire or corporation that can support losses. Many sports teams, including several Spanish soccer teams,[25] have strong sporting values or expectations on the field; the genius of the executives at Real Madrid is that they have harnessed the values for both on- and off-field success.

As demonstrated in the figure on page 20, Real Madrid gets the world's best players that match the community's values to play an attacking, beautiful style of soccer with class to win championships and capture the imagination and inspire a current and potential global audience and community. Take Cristiano Ronaldo as an example. He is the most followed person on social media in the world. In 2015, Ronaldo had 167.9 million followers on all social media.[26] According to jersey sales, he's also the most popular player—and for good reason. Ronaldo is a champion and has been voted, multiple times, the best soccer player in the world. He is talented, stylish, exciting, multilingual, and multicultural. The Real Madrid community expects the management team to sign players like Ronaldo to be inspirational to them.

Winning is not enough to the Real Madrid community. This is in direct contrast to the idea of "win at all costs" or "the end justifies the means," or selecting players based on data analytics first, or "taking a calculated risk" in signing a troubled talented player that can "help the team win now." The Real Madrid community has a different standard and demands more. They want the team on the field to reflect the values and expectations of the community, which is winning with a team philosophy, class, style, and elegance. The Real Madrid community wants the club to be

---

[25] For example, Athletic Bilbao has a policy of exclusively signing and fielding players meeting the criteria to be deemed as Basque.

[26] Ronaldo sells the most jerseys in the world and has the largest social media following. Therefore, the data indicates that Ronaldo is the world's most liked soccer player. Messi had 101.6 million total followers (66.3 million fewer than Ronaldo). The first non-soccer player on the list is basketball player LeBron James, who had 56 million total followers (111.9 million fewer than Ronaldo).

"champions and gentlemen." If the team loses, the community wants at least to see effort until the end, courage, and dignity. This is what makes them happy, and Real Madrid always tries to satisfy their needs.

Florentino believes that when Real Madrid represents the ideals of the community members, the community responds with more engagement, passion, and loyalty. Since Real Madrid's community values are inclusive and universal, the community itself grows globally, which leads to worldwide sponsors spending big money for association with and access to the Real Madrid community, as well as television broadcasters paying lots of money to distribute the game to the large, passionate global audience. The passion leads to an increase in stadium receipts, the value of broadcasting rights, and marketing and sponsorship opportunities, which contribute to higher revenues. Since Florentino and his executives implemented their sustainable economic-sport model, revenues have soared as fans more closely identified with the club and their players and became more passionate and loyal. Coming full circle, the high revenues allow the club to sign the world's best players who share their community values.[27] Real Madrid wants their community to see a player on the team and think, "I want to play like, and be like, that player; I want my son or daughter to play like, and be like, that player; I want to win playing that style and with those values."

The resulting increase in revenues from the community values-centric approach funds not only signing the world's best players but a bigger, more modern venue that makes the stadium experience itself a way to connect with the team. It also provides the best training facilities and a youth academy that develop talented homegrown players who learn, from the age of seven, the history, traditions, values, and expectations of Real Madrid to complement and indoctrinate the imported stars. To the community and to Florentino and his executives, Real Madrid is much more than any one current or past player, coach, or president.

---

[27] On the correlation of revenue and performance, Francisco wrote in his unpublished 2008 thesis: "The point we want to make with this argument is that other things being equal, making money and investing it on players is the best way clubs can make sure they enter in the virtuous circle of winning games, attracting more fans, having more TV audience, selling more merchandising, and making more revenue to reinvest in players."

Figure 2.1: The Real Madrid Way: Sustainable Economic-Sport Model

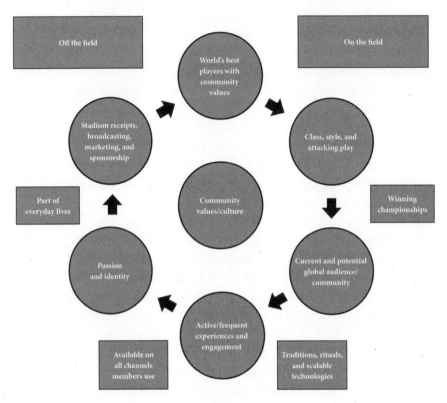

SOURCE: Steven G. Mandis

Real Madrid isn't just providing a soccer game; they are providing a larger experience or entertainment that draws in a community member to actively participate, for a memorable sensation. It is the experience from before and after the game as well as the satisfaction of the work of the club's charitable foundation. Off the field, the Real Madrid community wants the club to adhere to accountability, transparency, trust, and good corporate governance. Interestingly, if Real Madrid's community feels the club has not followed their values, the club's unique ownership structure enables those members to express their frustration by—along with not buying tickets or merchandise—voting a president out of office.

Although the team is often referred to as Real Madrid, or simply Real, its official name is Real Madrid Club de Fútbol. The reason Real

Madrid is referred to as a club is that it actually *is* a club.[28] Unlike most professional sports teams that are owned by billionaires or corporations, Real Madrid, since its founding in 1902, has been owned by club members called "socios." Today, Real Madrid has 91,846 members, of whom 66,671 are between fourteen and sixty-five years old, 19,797 are under fourteen years old, and 5,378 are over sixty-five years old or have been a member for more than fifty years. Real Madrid has 73,680 male and 18,166 female members. Adult members pay €123.30 per year as a membership fee. Any person who has been a member for over fifty years is exempt from paying membership fees. Any prospective new members must also be recommended by two existing socios to finalize their application for membership, although membership has been closed to new members since June 2009. A few people have been named "honorary members," including Placido Domingo (2011), Rafael Nadal (2012), Sergio Garcia (2012), and Julio Iglesias (2012).[29]

A new policy of only admitting descendants of present socios as new socios was established in June 2011 because the demand for season tickets is far greater than the seats in the stadium. Today, if someone is not a descendant of a present socio but wants to be an "official" part of the Real Madrid family, he or she can join the Official Madridistas Supporters and receive an official supporter card ("Carnet Madridista") and other benefits. The approximately 610,000 card-holding Official Madridistas Supporters are very much a part of the Real Madrid community but have no season ticket or voting privileges.[30] Non-socios can also join a local Official Real Madrid Fan Club and receive other benefits.

On the other hand, socio membership privileges include the right to vote for president and board of directors and to be a candidate for

---

[28] The club isn't simply a soccer team. The club also owns a basketball team. The basketball team was added in 1931 and has won a record twenty-five Spanish Cup championships and an unprecedented nine Euroleague championships (a tournament of the best professional basketball teams from each European country's premier league). The basketball team is discussed further in chapter seven in "Not All about the Numbers: Real Madrid Basketball."

[29] Julio Iglesias was a goalkeeper in the Real Madrid Academy until he was seriously injured in a car accident at age twenty. While recovering, he discovered his musical talent.

[30] For more details, see http://www.realmadrid.com/en/fans/madridistas/international. Even though Official Madridistas Supporters may not have "voting privileges," Real Madrid management views them, as well as Real Madrid Fan Club members, as critical active contributors to their global community and values.

A September 2015 General Assembly Meeting of club members representatives. They vote by a *mano alzada* (holding up their hands), a normal practice of Spanish-listed companies. An independent company counts the votes.

General Assembly (though the socio must have been a member for at least one year and has to be eighteen years or older in these cases). Socios also have easier access to tickets. As noted, Santiago Bernabéu Stadium has a capacity of 81,044. There are 61,287 socio season ticket holders for the 2014–15 season (76 percent of capacity).[31] The remaining seats are for the general public. Socios are subject to disciplinary action for failing to pay any due fees or failing to adhere to a proper code of conduct on Real Madrid property or away games.

As expected, any operating decisions that require the voting of approximately 92,000 people would be a cumbersome process. Thus, the socios hold an election to form the General Assembly ("Socios Compromisarios"), which comprises around 2,000 members elected by

---

[31] How does a socio becomes a season ticket holder? There are a limited number of season tickets, and during the last ten years there have been no vacancies. In 2013, the club offered a package of 5,000 season tickets for all socios, with a series of priorities such as seniority, number of years as e-ticket holder (being a socio), number of matches attended during the last seasons, etc. This package was sold out in a few weeks and has not been offered again.

the socios for four-year terms. The General Assembly's main responsibilities revolve around the financial aspects of the club, such as approving the club's budget for the season. The General Assembly also has certain other powers such as the ability to discipline the club president, as well as authorizing the club to borrow money.

Ownership Structure

Ownership structure of soccer clubs has evolved over time and across geographies, creating both advantages and disadvantages. Before 1990, Spanish soccer clubs were structured as mutual organizations owned by, and run for, the benefit of their members. By the 1980s, poor financial management, such as spending too much money on players and having too much debt, threatened the financial viability of almost every club. With uncertainty about who was accountable in the event of default of debt by a club (many members thought a local government entity would bail out their club), in 1990, the Spanish government intervened and created Sports Law 10/1990 to regulate the legal structures of the clubs. The regulation required all clubs that could not prove they were financially viable, with a positive balance in their accounts during the 1985–86 season, to convert into a what is called a Sociedad Anónima Deportiva (SAD), which is like a limited liability company (LLC), to increase financial accountability. The SAD structure still did not prevent the clubs from being financially irresponsible and borrowing too much money, but now most people recognize that it is the SAD entity that is accountable. Initially, the ownership of the SADs was very diverse, but over time ownership became concentrated, so that today most SADs are controlled by high-net-worth individuals. Of the forty-two professional clubs in Spain, only Real Madrid, Barcelona, Athletic Bilbao, and Osasuna were able to prove they were financially viable and stay member-owned clubs.[32, 33] Member-owned clubs are not-for-profit organizations and do not provide financial distributions to mem-

---

[32] According to the Sports Law 10/1990, the elected president and board of directors of a member-owned club have to personally pledge 15 percent of total expenses and assume 100 percent of losses. This legal provision was added in order to increase the financial accountability and responsibility of the member-owned clubs.

[33] In Germany, legislation mandates that members must own at least 51 percent of all clubs. Bayern Munich is 75.1 percent owned by club members. In 2014, Bayern Munich sold an 8.33 percent stake for €110 million ($150 million) to German insurance company Allianz as part of a deal to help the club pay down debts on its stadium and to sponsor a youth academy. Adidas and Audi already owned 8.33 percent stakes in Bayern Munich.

bers. The profits, if any, are reinvested for the benefit of the members and provide for internal financing to sustain and grow the organization.[34]

This divergence of structure among clubs has created financial advantage for some and challenges for others. For example, billionaires buying Chelsea and Manchester City made them contenders overnight and significantly increased the competition and cost for talent, which affects teams like Real Madrid. Recently, Wanda Group, a large conglomerate owned by Chinese billionaire Wang Jianlin, acquired a 20 percent stake in Atlético Madrid for €45 million, giving Wanda a seat on the board of directors. Now Atlético has access to more resources to buy talent.

Member-owned clubs such as Real Madrid and Barcelona do not have a billionaire owner or corporation or a wealthy investment owner to absorb losses or provide increases of capital, etc. Therefore, the clubs owned by members are at a competitive financial disadvantage, which forces them to seek a sustainable economic-sport model. In addition, with elections by club members for the president and board, it's more difficult for the club to seek long-term financing as the lenders don't know who will be running the club in the future and what their strategies may be. The election is also similar to a political election in that candidates may make promises that are good in the short term but disastrous in the long term. Or an incumbent may take actions to make the finances look better than they are, hiding problems, or sacrifice the financial future to win in the present.

On the other hand, having community membership invokes the opportunity for clubs to have a closer relationship with local residents and fans. It really is their team. They have a say and vote. The structure of Real Madrid ensures a high level of fan involvement and engagement. This could lead to an ability to generate greater passion and loyalty. It may be difficult for a billionaire owner to turn over how the team is run to their community. Another advantage worth noting is that member-owned clubs have consistency in ownership. Many sports teams are bought and sold over the years, and the owners can have different priorities and values. Real Madrid has had its socios ownership from the beginning, so it may be easier to draw values from them. When the elected presidents of Real Madrid have drifted from the values, the socios have taken action, including voting out an incumbent president.

---

[34] For more information about the taxation of Real Madrid as a member-owned club, see chapter eleven, "Comparison of Financial Performance."

Too much debt can also impact strategic decisions and ownership structure. Manchester United was purchased in a leveraged buyout. To help pay down debt, Manchester United went public on the New York Stock Exchange in 2012 by selling shares to investors. Now Manchester United also has to answer to financial investors who may have different values and priorities than the fan community. Before going public to raise equity to pay down debt, Manchester United sold Cristiano Ronaldo to Real Madrid in 2009 and gained financial flexibility. In contrast, since Real Madrid cannot sell shares and strives to be economically responsible, it has to find innovative ways to fund operations and develop a sustainable economic-sport model.

Billionaire owners and investment groups are starting to buy or invest in sports properties in other cities or sports to generate synergies. For example, Manchester City and the New York Yankees purchased a majority of a Major League Soccer franchise in New York for an estimated $100 million.[35] This may be more difficult for nonprofit, member-owned clubs to replicate and place them at a competitive disadvantage.

The NFL's Green Bay Packers is the only nonprofit, community-owned major league professional sports team based in the United States.[36] While the Packers are the smallest market team in the NFL, they—like Real Madrid—sell the most jerseys in their league. In addition, while differences exist between the Packers and Real Madrid,[37] their league-leading jersey sales may suggest that

---

[35] David Conn, "Manchester City and New York Yankees join forces to create new MLS team." *Guardian.* http://www.theguardian.com/football/2013/may/21/manchester-city-new-york-yankees-major-league-soccer.

[36] There is intransigent opposition of the major sports leagues to community ownership. The NFL passed a rule in 1960 that outlawed not-for-profit franchises, effectively eliminating not only any copycat Packers but even such notions as giving the public a share of ownership in exchange for taxpayer stadium subsidies. And baseball has been equally antagonistic toward public ownership. When Ray Kroc, the founder of McDonald's and owner of the San Diego Padres, died and his widow, Joan, tried to give the team to the city of San Diego as a public trust, MLB stepped in and stopped the deal. There have been a few US sports teams that have sold stock for brief periods—the Cleveland Indians and Boston Celtics—but these have always been minority shares with no actual voting control. Generally, team owners dislike the idea of their finances becoming publicly available (although the players' unions get some information; and if one knows how to access evidence in "discovery" in league and team litigation, some information is available). Besides, ruling out public ownership is a great way to stop fans and politicians from claiming that they should be allowed a stake in their local team. With community ownership it also would be impossible for a team to move cities, which could benefit not only the team owner but also the revenue-sharing league.

[37] Unlike Real Madrid members, Packers shareholders are not given special priority for season tickets. They do have a vote in electing members of the forty-five person board of directors, who in turn select a seven-person executive committee that is the brain trust that makes the actual franchise decisions with the president, who does not need to be from the pool of shareholders.

community-owned teams share characteristics that are more appealing even
beyond their local communities, which can lead to more commercial success.

Table 2.1: Ownership of Selected European Professional Soccer Teams

	TEAM	OWNER
Club Membership	Real Madrid	Club members (100%)
	Barcelona Bilbao, Osasuna	Club members (100%)
Joint Club Membership and Corporate Ownership	Bayern Munich	Club members (75.1%), Adidas (8.3%), Audi (8.3%), Allianz (8.3%)
Controlled by Billionaire	Chelsea	Roman Abramovich
	Arsenal	Stan Kroenke (67%) (also owns NBA's Denver Nuggets, NHL's Colorado Avalanche, and 40% of NFL's St. Louis Rams), Alisher Usmanov (29%)
	Manchester City	Sheikh Mansour (also controls MLS's NYC FC and Melbourne FC)
	Monaco	Dmitry Rybolovlev (67%), House of Grimaldi (33%)
	Valencia	Peter Lim (70.4%) (also controls Mint Media, which owns Cristiano Ronaldo's image rights)
	Milan	Silvio Berlusconi
Publicly Traded with a Billionaire Controlling Owner	Manchester United	Glazer (75%) (also own NFL's Tampa Bay Buccaneers)
	Juventus	Agnelli's Exor (64%), Libyan Investment Authority (7.5%)
Publicly Traded with an Ownership Group	Roma	A US-based investment group (DiBenedetto, Pallotta, Ruane, D'Amore, Starwood Capital)
Ownership Group	Liverpool	A US-based investment group (Fenway Sports Group [Henry, Gordon, DiBenedetto, Vinik, others], which also owns MLB's Boston Red Sox)
Sovereign Wealth Fund	Paris Saint-Germain	Qatar Investment Authority
Ownership Group with a Billionaire/Corporate Owner	Atlético Madrid	Two Spanish families (72%), Wang Jianlin's Wanda Group (20%)

After Florentino and his executives allowed community values to drive decisions, operating revenues have grown on average by 12 percent annually. Today, marketing, which includes sponsorship deals with twenty-five global firms such as Emirates Airlines, Adidas, Audi, and Microsoft, plus the sales of jerseys, is the largest contributor to revenues (in 2000, the largest contributors to revenues were from membership fees and stadium tickets).

Figure 2.2: Real Madrid's Operating Revenues 1999–2000 to 2014–15

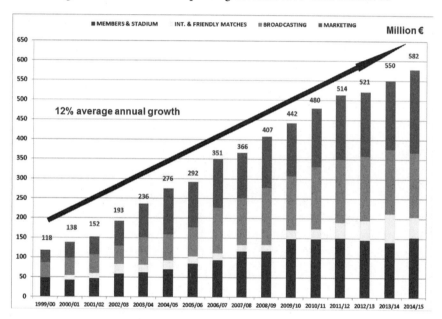

This growth highlights the effectiveness of the Real Madrid community's values-centric approach in generating extraordinary loyalty and passion—with community members buying merchandise and global sponsors paying to get access to and association with the community members. As an example of how much the passion, loyalty, and community has increased exponentially, in 1997 Real Madrid had a contract with Adidas for ten years, which paid out in total €100 million ($111 million), of which €95 million ($105 million) was paid out in the last three years. The average number of jerseys sold per year was around 150,000, most of which were sold in Spain. The current Adidas contract with Real Madrid, which lasts until 2020, was estimated to produce income of around €70 million ($92 million) per year, with 3.7 million garments sold per year (1.3 million in Spain and 2.4 million in the rest of the world), of which the number of jerseys sold between 2007–12 was estimated at 1.4 million per year, according to Sports Intelligence Report. By contrast, Real Madrid reported that in 2015 the number of Real Madrid Adidas garments sold increased to over 5.1 million, of which 2.6 million were jerseys.

The community values driving decisions at Real Madrid, as seen through growth in broadcasting revenue, are global. As the community expands, broadcasters are eager to deliver the games to this loyal, passionate, and very large community. International and friendly game revenues have grown as the community grows around the world and loyally supports the team when Real Madrid physically appears in their area. The awareness of brand and community values increases with the international exposure.

In 2000, membership dues and ticketing represented 32 percent and broadcasting represented 33 percent, and were the two largest components of revenues with combined 65 percent. In the 2000–01 season, income due to ticket sales to the general public was €14 million ($13 million), which represented 10 percent of the total income (€138 million, $126 million). Total income generated by the stadium (general public tickets, club members' season tickets, VIP seats and boxes, conferences, museum, and tours) was €42 million ($38 million, 30 percent of total income). By the 2013–14 season, income due to ticket sales to the general public represented only 5 percent of total income. As can be seen in the figure on the next page, in 2015, members and ticketing represented 26 percent of revenues. The largest revenue generator was marketing, which includes sponsorships, at 37 percent, which grew from 26 percent in 2000 as membership dues and ticketing combined with broadcasting now totaled 54 percent. In addition, international and friendly games now make up 9 percent of revenues.

Figure 2.3: Operating Revenue Percentage Breakdown 1999–2000 and 2014–15

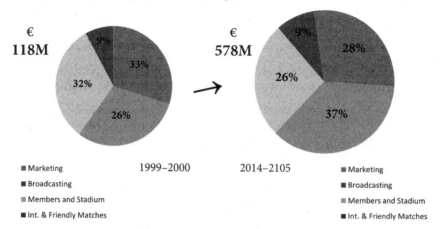

€ 118M   1999–2000   2014–2105   € 578M

- Marketing
- Broadcasting
- Members and Stadium
- Int. & Friendly Matches

The trend shows two very important and fast-growing segments: broadcasting and marketing rights. The growth of these areas illustrates that professional European soccer is a global entertainment business, in which Real Madrid has been a leader. Real Madrid executives—realizing that the club's games and best players captivated live, global audiences—sold broadcasts from which they generated marketing activities, sponsorships, and licenses.

Another key metric captures Real Madrid's success: wages-to-turnover ratio—the salaries and wages paid for all employees divided by total business revenues. The lower the ratio (the lower the percentage of revenues going to pay salaries), the more financial flexibility a team has to make other investments. The maximum threshold recommended by the UEFA's European Club Association is 70 percent.[38] After a transition period from 2000–01 to 2002–03, Real Madrid's wages-to-turnover ratio has been below 50 percent, one of, if not the, lowest in European professional soccer.[39]

---

[38] The European Club Association (ECA), the only association officially recognized by UEFA, promotes the health of European soccer teams through democratic representation.

[39] The wages-to-turnover ratio in the North American leagues is around 50 percent, but it varies by team. Collective bargaining agreements with player unions for the various leagues typically address this topic.

Figure 2.4: Real Madrid Wages-to-Turnover Ratio

WAGES TO TURNOVER RATIO

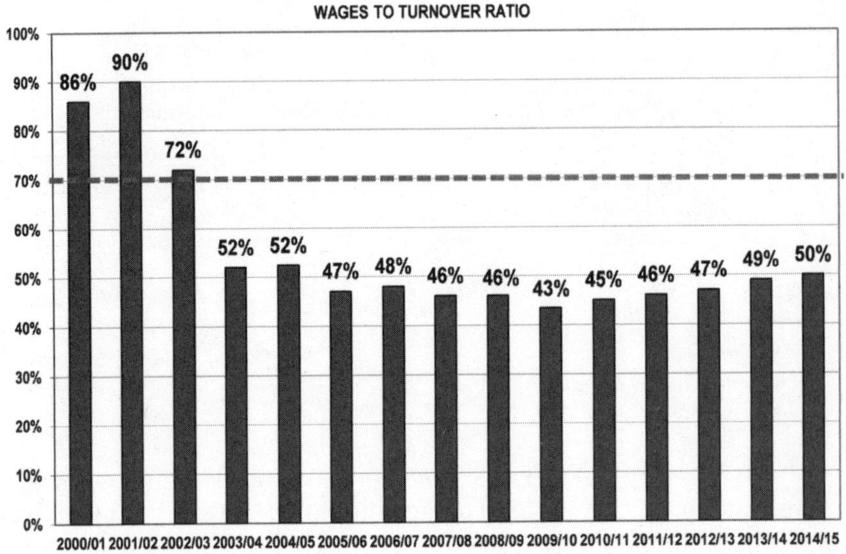

Because of Real Madrid's community values-centric approach in its sustainable economic-sport model, the club generates so much revenue that despite paying among the highest players' salaries in European soccer, those salaries are actually among the lowest when expressed as a percentage of revenues.

Lastly, the financial results demonstrate a sustainable economic model. "Sustainable" means that the model funds itself and doesn't constantly need equity injections or excessive borrowings to continue. In fiscal year 2015, which ended in June 2015, Real Madrid's revenues were €578 million ($641 million). Their EBITDA (Earnings Before Interest, Taxes, Depreciation, and Amortization), a simple proxy for cash flow, was €203 million ($221 million). Real Madrid has €96 million ($106 million) in net debt (total debt minus total cash). Net debt to EBITDA ratio is usually a very reliable indicator of the financial strength of a company. The net debt of €96 million divided by €203 million EBITDA equals 0.47. This is more favorable than the average balance sheets of the large companies in the S&P 500 (excluding financial institutions), which have an average ratio of 1.36.[40] Loan covenants for a typical corporate loan from a bank ("protections for the bank") usually stipulate that the debt-to-EBITDA ratio can't go above 4 or 5.

Table 2.2: Fiscal Year-End 2015 Real Madrid Financial Information

	June 2015
Revenues	€578m
EBITDA (before net gains on disposals)	€135m
EBITDA (as per accounting principles)	€203m
Wages to revenues	50%
Profit (Loss) before taxes	€56m
Net Debt	€96m
Net Debt / EBITDA	0.5x[41]

Moneyball vs. Organizational Culture

Moneyball. Sabermetrics. Big Data. These new ideas have revolutionized and modernized strategic thinking and decision-making—not just in sports management but more generally in organizational management. Managers have now been trained that success depends on "new school" thinking that involves sophisticated statistical analysis. Organizations and sports teams now have entire departments staffed with data scientists and analysts. The MIT Sloan Sports Analytics Conference, held in March every year in Boston, is the largest student-run conference in the world, attracting students from over 170 different schools and representatives from over 80 sports teams. Data analysts and data analytics providers have come up with increasingly sophisticated ways of monitoring and capturing ever-growing volumes of data in the search for better performance. It has become conventional wisdom that computer-generated analysis helps those charged with evaluating and selecting talent or making other important decisions to avoid succumbing to the tricky,

---

[40] Alan Gula, "Playing the Ratings Game." *Wall Street Daily*. http://www.wallstreetdaily.com/2015/11/23/credit-ratings-investing/.

[41] The calculation of ratio Net Debt/EBITDA is done with EBITDA as per the official accounting principles of soccer.

subtle biases or instincts that clutter human perception in order to lead
the organization to extraordinary success.

The 2011 film *Moneyball* (and the Michael Lewis book it was based
on) did such a good job of highlighting the concept of data analytics that
the word "moneyball" has become a catchall term for data analytics. In
reality, moneyball strategies are only a subset of analytics, but regardless,
the concept is so well established in public consciousness that *no one*
would dare question the importance of data analytics in winning. Well,
almost no one.

In February 2015, eleven-time NBA All-Star Charles Barkley took
issue with the conventional wisdom in an episode of TNT's *Inside the
NBA*. Barkley ranted about analytics, "Just because you got good stats
doesn't mean you got a good team…analytics is crap…all these guys
who run these organizations who talk about analytics, they have one
thing in common: they're a bunch of guys who ain't never played the
game [and] they never got the girls in high school." Known for speaking
his mind, Barkley also authoritatively declared his opinion that winning in the NBA is about talent and coaching staffs: "What analytics
did the Chicago Bulls have? [Referring to the six-time NBA champions Chicago Bulls with star players Michael Jordan and Scottie Pippen
and coach Phil Jackson.] What analytics do the Spurs have? [Referring
to the five-time NBA champions San Antonio Spurs with star players
David Robinson and Tim Duncan and coach Gregg Popovich.] They
have the best players, coaching staffs who make players better…The
NBA is about talent."

Money or talent or data analytics. Which is the most important ingredient for winning a championship? There is a long list of rich teams with
big payrolls and numerous superstars that don't win championships and
an equally long list of teams that now rely primarily on data analytics to
make decisions, and even have several superstars, but don't win either.[42]

Why has Real Madrid been able to win? Money, certainly. Talented
players, of course. Data analytics, without a doubt. But these are only
elements of the Real Madrid way. Real Madrid's executives believe that,

[42] Nick Cafardo, "John Henry says Red Sox will rely less on analytics." *Boston Globe*.
https://www.bostonglobe.com/sports/2016/02/24/john-henry-says-red-sox-will-rely-less-
analytics/95uy1OmoQw0ojxr7SRcOWO/story.html.

in the end, it is a team's culture that has the greatest impact on performance on and off the field. To them, culture means everyone working around a common mission in a selfless way and everyone knowing the goals and how to achieve them in a collaborative way. What makes Real Madrid such a fascinating case of organizational management is that their entire strategy both on and off the field is based in the adherence to the values and expectations of their community members—the community dictates the culture.

Real Madrid embraces data analytics. In fact, they utilize very sophisticated data collection and analysis tools both on the field and in business. It is hard to imagine what is not tracked. The club even has unique twists on the use of data that fit its culture. For example, more than evaluating players, Real Madrid employs data analytics to help examine and explain relevant and compelling questions, from in-game performance to front-office management. In contrast to most teams' data analysts and executives protecting their data and analysis like it was the Holy Grail of competitive advantages, Real Madrid seeks to make their data and data analytics available to their community. The club exposes and disperses information—possibly providing others a competitive informational advantage—to the community because the community passionately demands and consumes it and expects transparency. Real Madrid believes their community desires data and analysis for active and frequent updates, sharing, learning, understanding, clarifying, collaborating, storytelling, and infotainment. Serving the community's needs is Real Madrid's primary strategy. The club's management sees themselves as "community's values first." The club's leadership believes culture is the glue that holds a complex organization together, and when culture is drawn from shared values of their community it can forge extraordinary loyalty, inspiration, strength, passion, and identity.

Management consulting firm McKinsey & Company has highlighted the importance and value of culture.[43] The firm, through a survey of hundreds of companies in North America, Europe, and Asia, found 66.7 percent of business leaders felt culture provided their greatest source of competitive advantage. In addition, McKinsey & Company found that

---

[43] In full disclosure, I have worked with McKinsey & Company as a senior advisor and as a client.

companies with effective organizational culture outperformed peers significantly. In fact, those companies with high-performing cultures delivered significant performance improvement, 300 percent higher annual returns to shareholders than companies with undefined cultures.

Suggesting culture as the most important ingredient to winning on and off the field poses some challenges. Culture is hard to define, let alone analyze, measure, and compare, and it is difficult for the media to report on culture. It is much easier to reference and compare performance data and statistics for insights. However, Real Madrid is not the only successful sports franchise to emphasize culture. In the February 22, 2015, issue of the *Wall Street Journal*, Brian Costa wrote an article titled "Baseball Champions' CEO on Creating a Culture of Success: San Francisco Giant's Larry Baer Emphasizes Cooperation and Character" about the San Francisco Giants franchise that won the MLB World Series in 2010, 2012, and 2014. Similarly, in a July 24, 2015 interview with KNBR sports talk radio in San Francisco, five-time NBA champion San Antonio Spurs coach Gregg Popovich said about winning championships:

> Good fortune has something to do with it…It didn't take a whole lot of genius to draft Tim Duncan…Like any successful franchise whether sports or business…whatever it might be…it's about the people and the people you bring in…the character you build…the principles you live by…stick by in good times and in bad times…I think that camaraderie…that corporate knowledge is something that sustains us year after year…new people that come in…they get indoctrinated in the way we do things…The leaders [names some players]…they keep it going…[mentions players before them].[44]

---

[44] Eric Goldschein, "Whoa: Here's a Great 25-Minute Interview with Gregg Popovich on Becky Hammon, Gay NBA Players, Spurs Culture and More." *SportsGrid*. http://www.sportsgrid.com/nba/ whoa-heres-a-great-25-minute-interview-with-gregg-popovich-on-becky-hammon-gay-nba-players-spurs-culture/.

The Spurs have at least three players earning less money than they could make playing for other teams, demonstrating that the players are willing to personally sacrifice financially for the team to accumulate more money to get other good players with similar values. The actions of these players suggest the incredible impact of organizational culture, and challenge the idea that the only way to attract and retain talent is pay higher compensation than the competition.[45]

It is more straightforward to try to hire data analysts to assemble a theoretically competitive team by selecting undervalued players based on analytics. Maybe our fascination with fantasy league sports has made us lose sight of the fact that, at the end of the day, a real team has to be able to afford these theoretically winning players, which requires loyal and supportive fans and sponsors. It's also easy to forget that even the most talented superstars are real people from different backgrounds, at different stages in their lives and careers, who have to rely on one another and perform as expected, even when tired and injured after a long season, in actual high-pressure games, to win championships. What is the glue for this? Real Madrid believes it is culture.

Every winning culture has its own authentic personality and soul that can't be invented or imposed. In organizations, culture is an invisible but powerful force that influences the behavior of the members of that group. Most often the values of the founder or owner or a legendary top executive are instilled in the organization and shape its culture.

Even the skeptics that I spoke with about culture as the major factor for long-term success admitted that maybe the pendulum swung too far toward data analytics or, possibly, now that everyone essentially has the same data analytics, its competitive advantage has diminished. In February 2016, John Henry, the primary owner of MLB's Boston Red Sox, told reporters that a review of the organization, after a few years of disappointments on the field, led him to conclude, among other things, the Red Sox "perhaps overly relied on numbers" when it came to baseball

---

[45] Sean Deveney, "NBA Finals: Sacrifices of San Antonio's Big 3 help sustain Spurs dynasty." *Sporting News*. http://www.sportingnews.com/nba-news/4588746-nba-finals-spurs-heat-contract-salary-tim-duncan-tony-parker-manu-ginobili-lebron-james-dwyane-wade-chris-bosh.

Sam Amick, "Why David West left so much money on the table to join the Spurs." *USA Today*. http://www.usatoday.com/story/sports/nba/spurs/2015/10/13/david-west-spurs/73865012/.

Other players such as Tom Brady of the New England Patriots have made similar sacrifices.

decision making. He believes that there needed to be a change in philosophy defined by a shift in balance of attention from analytics to other areas, which he did not completely elaborate.[46] The skeptics believe it is time to think about something else as the new frontier, such as culture or team chemistry or human judgment and behavior. Some teams' data analysts are actually trying to identify and measure talents, attributes, and connective skills that make a team play much better than a group of talented individuals.[47, 48]

Culture is impossible to replicate. However, this book reveals ideas on the source of an organization's culture, how to codify it, and how to support and reinforce the culture and align it with a business strategy and identity. McKinsey & Company found that less than 10 percent of organizations have a very clear and consistently applied culture. At the very least, this book aims to stimulate ideas and provide inspiration for any sports team or organization seeking to maximize performance. Data analytics is more commonplace than when it provided early adopters a competitive advantage. The next frontier in competitive advantage, culture and values, should be more sustainable because it is more complex, and much more difficult to copy and commoditize.

The day after Barkley's rant, the often thought-provoking Keith Olbermann, then-host of ESPN's late night show *Olbermann*, said, "Analytics not only won in the NBA, MLB, NFL, and NHL, analytics

---

[46] Lee Igel, "What's On Deck After Boston Red Sox Send Sabermetrics, Analytics, and Moneyball To The Showers?" *Forbes.* http://www.forbes.com/sites/leeigel/2016/02/26/whats-on-deck-after-boston-red-sox-send-sabermetrics-analytics-and-moneyball-to-the-showers/?utm_source=#1e509d202ec5.

[47] Michael Schrage, "Team Chemistry Is the New Holy Grail of Performance Analytics." *Harvard Business Review.* https://hbr.org/2014/03/team-chemistry-is-the-new-holy-grail-of-performance-analytics/.

Eric Freeman, "Can team chemistry be quantified? Researchers are giving it an honest attempt." http://sports.yahoo.com/blogs/nba-ball-dont-lie/team-chemistry-quantified-researchers-giving-honest-attempt-031147093--nba.html.

[48] The idea of team chemistry existed at McKinsey & Company. When I was advising the firm, I was asked to take a Myers-Briggs Type Indicator (MBTI) test as shorthand for understanding my own individual preferences and team dynamic preferences. Whenever I met with my newly assigned McKinsey team internally for the first time to discuss a new client project, each team member introduced him/herself and disclosed his/her own MBTI results to the team to start discussing working styles and preferences. Then the team members assessed who might enjoy and excel at the various parts of the client project and how frequently and in what ways to interact to work better together. Since team members were unfamiliar with each other and then would have to work intensely together for months, the communication was ingeniously invaluable.

won so fast that most of the dinosaurs like Chuck [Barkley] don't even realize the war is over, the asteroid has darkened their sky, and their understanding of the games they cover has been dismissed as superstition."

Yet Barkley deserves credit for challenging what is now widely considered conventional wisdom. And there are reasons to challenge data analytics as the be-all and end-all. In soccer, for example, why are moneyball or soccernomics-fueled teams that rely largely on performance stats (for example, pass-completion percentage and scoring efficiency) to identify skilled but relatively cheap talent nowhere near as profitable or successful as Real Madrid? In a 2014 interview with Sean Ingle of *The Guardian*, Billy Beane conceded it is harder to implement moneyball in soccer because the game is more fluid and interdependent, which makes it more complicated to track and analyze.

A "moneyball disciple" was hired by the sabermetrics-loving Boston Red Sox owners after they bought the prestigious, but essentially bankrupt, Liverpool soccer team in the English Premier League in 2010 to find players with undervalued but useful—and, most important, measurable—skills. Liverpool thought the moneyball approach would maximize performance while minimizing the financial investment, but the team wound up losing tens of millions of dollars in 2011 and finished in eighth place. Since then, Liverpool has generally underperformed both on and off the field.

Tottenham in the English Premier League has also tried a moneyball-like strategy. In 2013–14, Tottenham used the £91 million ($120 million) from Gareth Bale's transfer to Real Madrid to acquire seven new players. A year later Liverpool used the £65 million ($99 million) from Luis Suárez's transfer to Barcelona to sign eight players, and loaned one of them to another team. Despite acquiring these fifteen new players, all selected for specific attributes revealed through statistical analysis—attributes that each team believed would collectively compensate for the loss of the star player and lead their respective teams to success—the teams have generally disappointed on the field. The "good" but not "great" players never seemed to blend together, and many have now been sold off.

Whether the negative experiences of Tottenham and Liverpool occurred because the application of data analytics to soccer is fundamentally flawed or because it was implemented poorly by people who were not as good at translating statistical data into predictions of future performance as they thought they were, or because of subsequent mismanagement of the newcomers, the results provide a warning that more may be required than data analytics, especially in sports like soccer that require players to be interdependent.

What is clear is that whether a moneyball-like strategy is used or not, most professional European soccer teams lose money, and a lot of it. Costs were so out of control, with teams spending vast sums for talent, that in 2010 UEFA imposed financial fair play (FFP) provisions prohibiting teams from repeatedly spending more than the revenues they generate. In May 2015, ten teams (including Inter Milan, Roma, and Monaco) had to sign "settlement agreements" to work toward achieving breakeven for the 2018–19 season.

In 2014, Manchester City and Paris Saint-Germain (PSG) were heavily sanctioned by UEFA for breaching FFP rules. Sheikh Mansour had bought Manchester City in 2008 for £210 million ($323 million) and has since accumulated annual losses of £535 million ($823 million), excluding approximately £200 million ($308 million) on facility upgrades, all of which was covered by its billionaire owner. Similarly, PSG was bought by Qatar's sovereign wealth fund, Qatar Investment Authority (QIA). In 2011–12, it spent massive sums for players. Although this spending at both clubs led to massive losses—especially excluding a related party sponsorship of up to €200 million ($264 million) a year by the Qatar Tourism Authority to PSG—it has led to success on the field: Manchester City has won two of the last three Premier League titles and PSG won consecutive French titles. Neither team, however, has reached the Champions League semifinals.

In 2015, UEFA found that Liverpool, despite losses of £49.8 million ($78 million) in 2012–13 and £41 million ($65 million) in 2011–12, did not breach FFP regulations, having signed a series of lucrative commercial deals over the previous eighteen months and being able to exclude some expenses.

What is little known is that only a handful of soccer teams, such as Real Madrid, Barcelona, Manchester United, and Bayern Munich, make money. As discussed, club members own Real Madrid, Barcelona, and Bayern Munich, and there is no billionaire to fund the losses. Public shareholders own Manchester United (it is traded on the NYSE) and probably expect profits.

Although there is a correlation of having the money to pay the best players to winning, it doesn't *guarantee* success, especially in the Champions League. Manchester United, for example, won their first European title in 1968 but would not win that title again until 1999. And although Manchester United had the highest revenues in soccer from 1997 (when Deloitte started their soccer team revenues rankings) to 2004 (when Real Madrid took over the top spot), and has been consistently one of the top five teams in terms of revenues, the team only won one Champions League title in the 2000s, in 2008, even with one of the greatest managers in history, Sir Alex Ferguson.

In the same 2014 interview with Sean Ingle of *The Guardian*, Billy Beane said, "When I first came into baseball, people didn't want to hear that a team was a business, but it is. And the better the business is run, the healthier the team on the field is going to be ... If I'm buying stock in a [soccer] team ... they've got revenues ... they pay down their debt. And ultimately in today's world that's the best way for a long-term success." Although he is referring to another soccer team, Real Madrid personifies what he is describing, which is essentially the link between on-field and off-field success.

I aim to demonstrate that there is much more to success on and off the field than data analytics and talent, and even money, and that those who do not include culture in building a winning organization are the real dinosaurs.

Interdependence (Ronaldo and Sixty Seconds)

Baseball is very different from basketball and soccer because baseball requires less team collaboration—for example, the too-much-talent effect (page 148) doesn't negatively impact baseball teams. There are other differences and nuances that add context to any lessons learned from comparing a baseball team (or applying moneyball concepts) to not only a basketball or soccer team but also generally to organizations. Most organizations require interdependence among team members. The key takeaway: the complexity and interdependence of soccer and organizations, in contrast to baseball, puts more responsibility on the management team to create an environment or culture that is conducive to teamwork. The analysis demonstrates how strong the connection is in soccer between teamwork and scoring goals, more than basketball and much more than baseball. Combine that connection with the limited scoring opportunities in soccer, and it is self-evident that teamwork becomes vital to winning in soccer, similar to most businesses.

Baseball is a team sport that is really an accumulation of individual activities. Throwing a strike or hitting a home run is primarily an individual achievement. Each play has a start and endpoint, with a focus on a battle between pitcher and hitter. Although the events in baseball are more discrete, some interdependence still exists (e.g., the quality of the infield defense behind a groundball-oriented pitcher, player chemistry), which can have a big impact on a player's statistics. There are nine players on the field on a baseball team. Regardless of what the other team does or a teammate does, each baseball player will come to the plate to bat around three to five times in a nine-inning game. A baseball team has at least twenty-seven different scoring opportunities. There are nine players, so each player has at least around 11 percent of the offensive opportunities to impact the game.

Contrast baseball with basketball. Basketball is a team-oriented sport requiring teammates to pass to each other and work together on the court. The five players on the court on a basketball team are interdependent and need to interact effectively under time pressure. A NBA game consists of four twelve-minute quarters, for a total of forty-eight minutes. In the NBA, there is a twenty-four-second shot clock. Instead baseball depends upon outs and innings, however long it takes.

Although interdependent, star players in the NBA can significantly impact a game. Stars LeBron James and Kobe Bryant each take, on average, 30 to 33 percent of their team's shots. If one includes assists, each is responsible for 52 to 57 percent of his team's shots. An NBA team, because of the shot clock, takes around 77 to 90 shots per game, so there are plenty of scoring opportunities. James and Bryant typically play 36 to 39 minutes (about 75 percent) of a 48-minute game. Each can be substituted for any reason as many times as he or the coach would like. They both touch the ball around 80 times and possess the ball for about 5 minutes per game, or around 10 percent of total playing time and around 13 to 14 percent of the time they play. James exemplified a star player's impact during the 2014–15 NBA finals. In the finals, the Cleveland Cavaliers' offensive rating was 93.8 points per 100 possessions. With James in the game the offensive rating was 97.3 points, and with James not in the game, it was 50.9. James only rested on the bench a total of 23 minutes over the six games, during which time the Cavaliers made only six field goals (shots). With athleticism and skill, star players can impact the game defensively as well, by shutting down one of the opposing team's top scorers, who probably possesses the ball a greater percentage of time than his teammates. In fact, Bryant and James have been elected to the NBA All-Defensive Teams twelve and six times, respectively. As a basketball team's performance emerges from a chain reaction of individual actions, one star player alone cannot dominate and beat the opposing NBA team. For example, Michael Jordan needed Scottie Pippen, and even the outside sharp shooting of players such as John Paxson or Steve Kerr to spread the floor and the unselfish rebounding of players such as Horace Grant or Dennis Rodman.[49]

This brings us back to soccer. Soccer is—like basketball, unlike baseball—a highly improvised and team-oriented sport, but even more so than basketball. Eleven soccer players form one of two teams on the field, interacting in a fluid, rapidly unfolding manner, similar to the way most nonsporting organizations work today. In soccer, a team's probability of scoring goes up as it strings together more and more successful passes. There is no shot clock, so a team can possess the ball as long as it would like and limit scoring opportunities. However, the teams face the pressure of a timed game, which consists of two forty-five-minute halves for a total of ninety minutes. Star players like Cristiano Ronaldo and Lionel Messi can significantly impact a game, as can NBA stars, but a soccer star's scoring is much more dependent on the player receiving passes from teammates at exactly the right time and place. Keep in mind that during the 2014 Champions League final, Ronaldo barely touched the ball in the entire first half. On average, Ronaldo and Messi possess the ball twenty times a game, three seconds each time, for a total of merely one minute

---

[49] In today's NBA, man-to-man defense can sometimes get overstated. The NBA has become a league in which the ability to switch defenders has become very important, as has being able to help teammates. Since the NBA has become so pick-and-roll dominated, help defense has become even more important. Any teams without teamwork on defense have suffered. At times, defense in the NBA is more interrelated than offense. It depends on the team; for example, the Cleveland Cavaliers are heavily reliant on isolations and LeBron James' play, while in contrast, the Golden State Warriors and San Antonio Spurs rely more on team play, such as passing, movement, etc.

per ninety-minute game. You read that right! Ronaldo and Messi touch the ball for around sixty seconds per game, around 1 percent of the game time.[50] Both stars have to work for their shots, as they are often fouled three to four times per game, reducing their twenty possessions to sixteen or seventeen. Goals mean a lot more in soccer than points do in most sports. Quality shot opportunities in soccer are very scarce, so making the most of them is critical. Within those sixteen to seventeen non-fouled possessions, Ronaldo and Messi typically attempt four to six shots per game.

Of Ronaldo's and Messi's four to six shots, 40 to 50 percent will be on goal and 40 to 50 percent of shots on goal (about 25 percent of all shots) will actually result in a goal, which is ridiculously high compared to other star soccer players. Ronaldo and Messi are responsible for around 50 to 60 percent of their team's total shot attempts when including assists, similar to the contributions of Bryant and James in basketball. Playing defense, however, Ronaldo and Messi have a more limited impact in stopping the opposing team's scorers. Thus, even with soccer stars like the duo, soccer teams are more interdependent than are baseball teams or even basketball teams. Moreover, unlike with basketball greats James and Bryant, soccer greats Ronaldo and Messi have no near equivalents. They are outliers in most relevant scoring categories. Whether one is better than the other, the data analysis demonstrates that those two players are significantly better than all other soccer players. Either Ronaldo or Messi has won the best player award, the FIFA Ballon d'Or ("the Golden Ball"), every year since 2008. In NBA basketball, unlike in soccer, no two players have won the player of the year award or have been statistically dominant scoring outliers year in and year out, over a seven-year period.[51] After discounting the individual effect of Ronaldo and Messi as outliers, soccer becomes much more interdependent than even basketball.

Because of the interdependence required in soccer, Ronaldo has to work on different goal scoring scenarios every day with his teammates. They know he has "one second, two seconds—and bang." They work on creating an image

---

[50] A very interesting 2006 movie titled *Zidane: A 21st Century Portrait*, by video artists Douglas Gordon and Philippe Pareno, uses seventeen cameras to follow Zidane in a soccer game. They follow the player only, not anything else in the game. You will see how extraordinarily little he touches the ball; how lonely he is; how focused and intense he is in following the ball; and how much he darts around without the ball.

[51] Michael Jordan won the NBA Points Per Game title for seven seasons (1986–93), but there wasn't a player who was second during all seven seasons.

of different situations and the desired outcome, asking themselves and each other, "Where am I positioned? Where's the ball coming from? Where is my teammate coming from? Where is he going? What is his speed? What is his preferred foot and angle? What opportunity do I have to get the ball there? Is the pass best in the air or on the ground? Where is the defense? Where's the goalkeeper likely to be? Where and what is the highest percentage for a finish?" Both the passer and Ronaldo have to almost instinctively know what the other is likely to do and when. Within seconds, they both have to analyze the situation and take action or the scarce opportunity is missed.

Soccer stars get no guarantee of possessions or shots, unlike baseball stars who get a minimum number of at bats, and opportunities in soccer are significantly fewer than in basketball. In addition, while in basketball it is very possible for a player to get an inbound pass underneath his basket from a teammate, dribble the length of the court without passing to another teammate, shoot, and score, the equivalent in soccer would be extremely difficult.

Table 2.3: Comparison of Baseball, Basketball, and Soccer

	BASEBALL	BASKETBALL	SOCCER
Duration of game	9 innings	Four 12-minute quarters = 48 minutes	Two 45-minute halves = 90 minutes
Level of interdependence on teammates (H, M, L)	Low	Medium	High
Total team scoring opportunities per game	At least 27 guaranteed. Average 38 plate appearances per team per game.	Average 83 attempted shots with a 24 second shot clock per team	Typically 6–7 shots on goal per team
Number of players	9	5	11
Substitutions	Unlimited, but can't reenter	Unlimited, can reenter	3, can't reenter
Individual star scoring opportunities	About 11% of total team scoring opportunities, or about 3 opportunities per player	Typically 23–30 shots per star player	Typically 1–3 shots on goal per star player

	BASEBALL	BASKETBALL	SOCCER
Defense	Pitcher involved in every play, players in traditional positions	Man on man, with help and switches	Cooperative, organized group defending
Primary team championship	World Series	NBA Championship	European Champions League
Finals playoff format	Best of 7 game series	Best of 7 game series	One game (knockout tournament to finals with 1 home and 1 away game using goal aggregates)
Other tournaments/ games during season	No	No	Numerous. Both for team and country/national team
Off-season national team tournaments prestige and frequency (L, M, H)	Low	Medium	Extremely high (FIFA World Cup, UEFA European Championships, qualifiers, friendlies)
Draft from high school/college	Yes	Yes	No
Academy/home grown talent	No	No	Yes
Relegation to lower league	No	No	Yes

Table 2.4: Comparison of Star NBA and Soccer Players

	BASKETBALL	SOCCER
Stars	Bryant / James	Ronaldo / Messi
Possession (time and percentage)	About 5 minutes per game (10%, ~13% when calculated on court), 80 touches in 38 minutes of playing time (2 touches per minute)	About 1 minute per game (<1%), 20 touches in 90 minutes of playing time (0.2 touches per minute)
Level of dependence on teammates to score (H, M, L)	Medium	High
Percentage of team's shots (# and %)	23–30 shots per game, 30–33%	4–6 shots per game, 2–3 on goal 25–33%
Minutes played per game/% of total	38–40/80%	90/100%
Percentage of team's shots and assists	52–57%	50–60%
Impact on defense (H, M, L)	High	Low
Plays for national team (H, M, L)	Medium	High

PART TWO

Galácticos 1.0
(1955–60)

Chapter 3

EARLY HISTORY (1902–60)

R EAL MADRID was founded in 1902. The club's origins can be traced to the introduction of soccer to Madrid by academics and students, including several graduates of Cambridge and Oxford. The founders' inspiration for selecting white as the color of the team's jerseys was a successful English amateur club, Corinthian FC. Real Madrid is often referred to as *Los Blancos* ("the Whites") or *Los Merengues* ("the Meringues," a dessert made from whipped egg whites) in reference to its jersey color. The first club crest had a simple design consisting of a decorative interlacing of the three initials of the club, "MCF" for Madrid Club de Fútbol, in dark blue on a white jersey. The first change in the crest occurred in 1908 when the letters adopted a more streamlined form and appeared inside a circle.

"Real" (which is pronounced re ' al) means "royal" in Spanish. King Alfonso XIII of Spain granted the title of Real to the club in 1920 and added a royal crown to their emblem, and around ten years later the club added a purplish band to its emblem.[52] Over time, the crest was modified for various reasons and it became full color, with gold as the most prominent color, and the purplish stripe becoming a little more blue.

Although today Real Madrid is closely associated with championships and was named "FIFA Club of the 20th Century," they were not a

---

[52] In 1931, the Republic forbade any sign related to the monarchy, and the crown was removed, and the purplish band was added, as a sign related to old Castilian flags and emblems. In 1941, the crown was restored to the emblem. Although the purplish band became more blue over time, purple is still recognized as a club color.

dominant team in their early years. Real Madrid won their first Spanish league La Liga title in the 1931–32 season, almost thirty years after their founding.[53]

The club won La Liga again the following season, but with the outbreak of the Spanish Civil War in 1936, professional soccer ceased to be played in Spain. After the war ended, Real Madrid was in very poor shape, while other clubs, such as Athletic Bilbao, Atlético Madrid, and Barcelona, had very good results on the field.[54] In 1943, forty-eight-year-old Santiago Bernabéu, a former Real Madrid player and captain, was elected president of Real Madrid—a position he would occupy until his death in 1978.

Santiago Bernabéu

Bernabéu's family had moved to Madrid when he was very young. He loved soccer and became a regular spectator at Real Madrid's games.[55] Like most Spanish children, he played soccer, but he started to demonstrate extraordinary ability, work ethic, and competitiveness at a young age. His skills in the playground reached such lore by 1909 that, at only fourteen, he was invited to the Real Madrid junior ranks. At age seventeen, he was promoted to the senior team, playing as a striker. Eventually, Bernabéu wore the captain's armband for a few years before retiring from playing in 1927. After his retirement, he continued to be associated with the club until 1935, first as a director, later as an assistant manager, and finally as coach of the first team.

---

[53] The first official league was in season 1928–29. Real Madrid won its first league in season 1931–32 (e.g., the fourth year of the official title).

[54] In the five years before the Spanish Civil War, Real Madrid won two Spanish League titles and two Copa de España cups, while neither Atlético Madrid nor Barcelona won anything at all. In the years immediately after the war, Barcelona won five Spanish League titles and four Copa del Generalísimo cups (later called Copa del Rey cups), plus international competitions such as two Latin Cups and three Eva Duarte Cups. In the same period Atlético Madrid merged with Aviación Nacional (sport section of the Air Force), adopted the new name of Athletic Aviación de Madrid, and won four Spanish leagues (being 1939–40 their first league title in their history), and no Generalísimo cups. In the same period, Real Madrid only won two Generalísimo cups (seasons 1945–46 and 1946–47). In 1947 the new stadium was inaugurated and Real Madrid were almost relegated to second division. In 1953 Bernabéu signed Di Stéfano and Gento, and the history of Real Madrid changed drastically.

[55] At the time, the club didn't have its own stadium, so the board of directors rented land on O'Donnell Street ("Calle de O'Donnell") in central Madrid.

Even with Bernabéu's charisma, once he became president, success on the field and in business did not come immediately. For example, Barcelona won La Liga in 1945, 1948, and 1949. At first, Bernabéu began to implement organizational changes, which took years to complete and produce results. He restructured the club at all levels, in what would become the normal operating structure of professional soccer teams in the future, giving every section and level of the club independent technical teams and recruiting people on merit who were ambitious and visionary in their own right.

In 1947, Bernabéu wanted to get the best players for Real Madrid. To pay for them, he did something innovative at the time. He took a huge financial risk and built the biggest soccer stadium to increase ticket revenues, predicting that the best-playing stars would not only win there but would also draw large crowds to the stadium to see them do it. To finance the stadium, which would one day be named after him,[56] he sold bonds to the club members and fans. At the time, many thought it was "too much stadium for so little a club." Bernabéu's gamble paid off, and with the larger ticket receipts, Real Madrid was able to afford better players. Real Madrid won La Liga in 1953–54 over defending champion Barcelona. It took Bernabéu ten years to win his first La Liga championship as president (the club's third Spanish title).

Not content with his success, in 1953, Bernabéu again did something on a scale that was unheard of at the time. He embarked upon an ambitious strategy of signing the best world-class players from abroad, the most famous being Argentine forward Alfredo Di Stéfano, and built the world's first truly multinational team. After Bernabéu signed Di Stéfano (1953) and his Argentine friend Héctor Rial (1954), in successive years he signed French midfielder Raymond Kopa (1956), Uruguayan defender José Santamaría and Argentine goalkeeper Rogelio Domínguez (1957), Hungarian striker Ferenc Puskás (1958), and Brazilians Canário and Didi (1959). The remaining players were talented Spaniards (including Luis del Sol and Francisco "Paco" Gento). It is important to keep

---

[56] The stadium was initially called the Nuevo Estadio Chamartin but received the name of the club president eight years later. At that time, Estadio Santiago Bernabéu consisted of two uncovered tiers that could hold just over 75,000 spectators. Capacity was further increased to 125,000 in 1954, when one of the long sides got expanded with a third tier.

Chamartin Stadium, located in Madrid, was inaugurated in 1947. In 1955 its name changed to Santiago Bernabéu Stadium.

in mind transfer fees, salaries, and bonuses of players in those days were very small in comparison with today. As a matter of fact, Di Stéfano was never considered wealthy by today's standards.

When Di Stéfano and Rial joined Real Madrid, they not only brought their remarkable skills, they added a "Latin American" style of play. In the 1960 European Cup Final, four of the eleven starters on Real Madrid were from Latin America—two from Argentina, one from Brazil, and one from Uruguay (two other Latin American players were regular contributors/substitutes).

Soccer's popularity spread rapidly during the mid to late 1800s as British sailors, traders, and soldiers introduced the sport to different parts of the globe. In the alleys of Argentina,[57] the immigrant neighborhoods of Uruguay, and the favelas and beaches of Brazil, the philosophy of *how* a soccer team won was as important as winning.[58] The constraints of pov-

---

[57] In the Barracas suburb of Buenos Aires, near the port where British sailors introduced soccer to Argentina, Di Stéfano (born in 1926) learned the game in what he called "the academy of the streets." He attended the same school as Pope Francis (born in 1936).

[58] Quotes from Brazilian soccer legend and 1982 World Cup Captain Sócrates explain the "beautiful game" (Portuguese: o jogo bonito): "Beauty comes first. Victory is secondary. What matters is joy.

erty promoted creativity, imagination, and invention. For example, they tied up newspapers and rolled up socks to make balls to play soccer. Also, their passion for and artistry in music and dance expressed in the natural rhythm and movements of tango, samba, and salsa seemed to transcend to their soccer. Latin American teams played an open, free-flowing, and attacking style of soccer. The players were artists and, in many ways, created with technical showmanship, flair, and a freedom of expression.

In contrast, at the time, European teams utilized discipline and order, denied the opposition space to move, encouraged direct passing, and emphasized a clinical and cautious approach. Their focus was simply on winning, and in some cases, not losing.

Di Stéfano used his elegant playing style, soccer intelligence, and leadership to integrate the players and teach them to value teamwork. His desire for self-improvement and professional pride set the team's standard and became essential values of Real Madrid. Together with his gifted teammates, Di Stéfano invented modern professional team soccer and embodied all that is magical about it.[59] The world-class players followed Di Stéfano's lead because he was the undisputed leader, and also because these highly skilled players learned that eleven men, when given paint (the ball), could go on to a canvas (the field) and paint a ninety-minute picture of imagination and beauty that expressed them.[60] Anything less than ninety minutes of full effort and beautiful, exciting, and attacking soccer with elegance, style, and class—whether the players were winning by several goals or losing—was considered an "unfinished painting" or disrespectful to the art and viewers.

The players had invented or perfected important moves used today, such as the "dry-leaf" dipping free-kick, which is a curling ball that drops precipitously, like a leaf picked up by a gust of wind that then suddenly stops and unexpectedly swerves downward, at a point near the goal; and

---

To win is not the most important thing. Football is an art and should be about showing creativity. If Vincent van Gogh and Edgar Degas had known the level of recognition they were going to have, they would not have done the same. You have to enjoy doing the art and not think 'will I win?'" https://docsocrates.wordpress.com/2014/08/03/famous-quotes-from-socrates-brasileiro/.

[59] The exact origins of the term "the beautiful game" are disputed. The origin has been attributed to Brazilian Didi, who played at Real Madrid in 1959-60.

[60] Rohit Brijnath, "Latin flourish vs European rigidity." *Sportstar*. http://www.sportstaronnet.com/tss2522/25220200.htm.

the quick, technically precise instep pass. Just three miles down the Paseo de la Castellana ("Castellana Street") from the Museo Nacional del Prado ("Prado Museum"), which housed some of the works from the greatest artists, Bernabéu showcased the greatest soccer players in the world playing in a mesmeric style never seen before in Europe. Their artistry fit perfectly because Madrid, the highest capital in Europe built on a vast elevated plateau in the center of the country, has a community rich in history and culture that could appreciate the beauty and artistry. Spain also had the natural advantage of the same language as, and a long history with, most of Latin America, so the Latin American players found it easier to communicate and assimilate. Di Stéfano and the others also had an honor, modesty, and elegance both on and off the field that *Madrileños*, natives or inhabitants of Madrid, respected and identified with. The Real Madrid community loved and passionately supported the club, in part because they wanted to be, and play like, them. Interestingly, the beauty, freedom of expression, and values resonated with so many people around the world beyond Madrid, that Real Madrid transcended Madrid and even Spain. As the team traveled around the world, had the best players from around the world whose countrymen followed, and was shown on TV, more people around the globe started to pay attention and passionately support the club. The best example of the players, their style of play, and fan reaction is described in the 1960 European Cup final on page 57.

Bernabéu's ability to build an international team with flair was even more astonishing because it was done under the relatively closed and restrictive dictatorship of General Francisco Franco and during years of extreme poverty in Spain.[61] Perhaps the freedom of expression conveyed by their style of play at a time of a dictatorship added to the appreciation of the team. Although Franco was not an exuberant fan of soccer, he

---

[61] Franco's Nationalists won the Spanish Civil War, and he ruled Spain for the next thirty-six years, from 1939 until his death in 1975. There is widespread folklore that Real Madrid is successful because of advantageous treatment from the Franco regime. When I analyzed the number of domestic trophies, it is difficult to see how any alleged advantageous treatment affected team performance. Examining the first decade of Franco rule from 1939–40 (when the Spanish League resumed after the Spanish Civil War) until 1949–50, Real Madrid did not win the La Liga even once. Barcelona, Atlético Madrid, and Valencia each won La Liga three times during the decade. In the following decade, from 1950–51 to 1959–60, Real Madrid won the league four times. Barcelona also won the league four times. From 1939 to 1960, Real Madrid won the Copa del Generalísimo twice. The big difference was Real Madrid's dominance of the European Cup, which was against many non-Spanish teams outside of Franco's Spain. Regardless, it is clear that Real Madrid struggled financially and drifted as early as the 1960s, when Franco still ruled Spain.

advantageously used Real Madrid's global fans and prestige as an ambassador of Spain (similar to a Spanish brand) in the time of political isolation of his regime, especially in the 1950s.

Bernabéu realized that to have the best team, he also needed to invest in infrastructure and the development of players. With his direction, the Ciudad Deportiva ("Sport City") training facilities were built on Madrid's outskirts so that the players could train without destroying the stadium's field.[62] Also, this allowed second team and youth players to train in the same location. They could share resources, but more importantly the star players would be an inspiration to the homegrown talent. The Ciudad Deportiva was a novel concept at the time. (Barcelona would not start an academy until 1970.)

In the mid-1950s, Bernabéu helped create the European Champion Clubs' Cup, simply referred to as the European Cup (later renamed as the UEFA Champions League), to showcase the team and build the Real Madrid brand beyond Spain. He wanted them to play in a tournament against the best teams from every country and teamed up with French magazine L'Equipe to put together the first European tournament. The idea gained momentum and during a meeting of nineteen European teams convened by the magazine in April 1955, it was agreed that a European Cup should be inaugurated. The first European Champion Clubs' Cup was held that autumn. Real Madrid won the first five European Cups from 1955 to 1960.

In 1952, Bernabéu, realizing the importance of rituals and traditions, personally oversaw the creation of the club's anthem, "Hala Madrid!"[63] By 1960, television coverage of the European Cup Final had made Real Madrid the world's best-known soccer club. Bernabéu took his

---

[62] I refer to the former facilities on Paseo del la Castellana, with an area of 12 hectares, as Ciudad Deportiva and the new facility with 120 hectares near the airport as Ciudad Deportiva Real Madrid. Ciudad Deportiva Real Madrid houses Real Madrid's training grounds of the youth academy, the first team, and the basketball team, as well as residences of both the first team and the academy. Di Stéfano and others would refer to the soccer academy portion of Ciudad Deportiva as La Fábrica.

[63] The creation of Real Madrid's anthem began on a train trip from Aranjuez to Madrid and came to life in the Green Frog restaurant through the writing of Luis Cisneros Galiane. The anthem's first audience heard it in a performance by José de Aguilar. Other people connected with its creation are Marine Garcia, Amora Farina, and Antonio Villena Sanchez. After its recording, Bernabéu declared, "It will become one of the symbols of Real Madrid!"

Santiago Bernabéu (right) transformed the history of Real Madrid by signing Alfredo Di Stéfano (left), considered one of the best soccer players in history.

star-studded club around the world to play friendly games to make more money as well as build the club's brand globally.

Fans saw soccer history unfolding during this time, but unbeknownst to them, they also were witnessing sports management history. Bernabéu's strategy seemed simple: sign the best players from around the world, such as Di Stéfano, Kopa, Santamaría, and Puskás, the first galácticos, that captured the imagination of fans and attracted new ones. It wasn't only the players people wanted to see but also their beautifully elegant attacking style of play. Equally important, Bernabéu had a strategy to pay for the players with the large number of stadium ticket receipts and international friendly appearance fees. He helped start a European tournament to showcase his club and build an international brand. He invested in infrastructure and the development of players. He established and culti-vated traditions and rituals to build loyalty and passion. His strategies on the field (get the best players in the world to play an attacking style), in the organization (have the best staff members focus on functional areas, investments in infrastructure and people), and in business (build a large stadium to fund the players, build a global brand) were highly innovative and unproven at the time. I refer to this period as Galácticos 1.0. I look at the period more holistically as an "economic-sport model" rather than just calling the players "galácticos." I refer to it as version 1.0 because in many ways Peréz and his executives draw from that era to innovate fur-ther in (what I also refer to as) the version 2.0 in 2000, the version 3.0 in 2009, and version 4.0 in 2015–16.

1960 European Cup Final

On May 18, 1960, Real Madrid's soccer players walk through the tunnel at Glasgow's Hampden Park Stadium and onto the field to the flash-ing lights, echoing screams, and haunting chants of 127,621 soccer fans, a European Cup final attendance record that has yet to be broken. In the record crowd is Alex Ferguson, an eighteen-year old forward with Queen's Park. The legendary Kenneth Wolstenholme will be calling the game for the BBC. With the temperature hovering around forty-one degrees Fahrenheit in the evening, all of the players have chosen to wear their all-white, long-sleeved jerseys. The jerseys only have the simple Real Madrid crest design over their hearts on the front (no spon-sor logos) and their numbers on the back (no names).

The four-time defending champions had beaten rival Barcelona in the semifinals to make the final against opponent Eintracht Frankfurt, whose starting players are all German.[64] In contrast, Real Madrid is a team of the best players from around the world (five of the eleven starters were born outside of Spain: four from Latin America and one

---

[64] The game being played was initially in doubt since the German football association had banned their clubs from taking part in games with any team containing Ferenc Puskás after the Hungarian had alleged the West German team had used drugs in 1954. Puskás had to make a formal written apology before the game could take place.

from Eastern Europe). The galácticos in the starting line-up include Di Stéfano, considered one of the greatest soccer players of all time. (Pelé once described Di Stéfano as "the most complete footballer in the history of the game."[65]) Di Stéfano, nicknamed "Saeta Rubia" ("Blonde Arrow"), was awarded the Ballon d'Or for the European Footballer of the Year in 1957 and 1959. He has a fearsome partnership with Puskás, a 1952 Olympic champion who joined the team in 1958 after having led his nation, Hungary, to the final of the 1954 World Cup where he was named the tournament's best player. "Paco" Gento, Santamaría (nicknamed "the Wall"), and del Sol, who did not miss one minute of action in any game that season, are the backbone support for Di Stéfano and Puskás. Domínguez, at six feet and three inches tall, is the imposing goalkeeper. The team is coached by Miguel Muñoz, a retired Real Madrid player who had scored Real Madrid's first-ever goal in the European Cup tournament, helping the team to a 2–0 away win against Servette FC in September 1955.[66]

With that background, the 1960 European Cup final commences. In the eighteenth minute of the 1960 European Cup final, Eintracht Frankfurt scores the first goal. Then, superstar Di Stéfano scores Real Madrid's first goal in the twenty-seventh minute to tie the game, and then scores again three minutes later to take the lead. The tireless Di Stéfano seems to be everywhere with speed and control. Puskás, too, is unstoppable. He scores from an impossible angle for his first goal, adding a second from a penalty kick, after Gento is brought down inside the penalty area, and then shoots a left-footed bullet from outside the penalty area for his third to give Madrid a five-goal cushion. The Hungarian scores on a header for his fourth goal and Real Madrid's sixth. Three minutes after Eintracht scores their second, Di Stéfano responds in the seventy-fifth minute for his third goal and Real Madrid's seventh, with an assist from Puskás. Eintracht scores the last goal of the game on a careless Real Madrid back pass in the seventy-sixth minute. Three total

---

[65] Louise Taylor, "Alfredo di Stéfano was one of football's greatest trailblazers." The *Guardian*. http://www.theguardian.com/football/blog/2014/jul/07/alfredo-di-stefano-real-madrid.

[66] Muñoz captained Real Madrid in two consecutive competition wins, in 1956 and 1957, and retired from playing soccer the following year at nearly thirty-six. He served a brief apprenticeship as coach of Real Madrid's reserve team before being appointed coach of the first team in 1959.

goals, a hat trick, by Di Stéfano, and four goals by Puskás help Real Madrid blow away Eintracht Frankfurt 7–3 in a night to remember for Real Madrid.[67]

The game is widely regarded as one of the best soccer games ever played and the one that opened people's eyes to what soccer could be. The flow of goals and graceful and beautiful play was breathtaking and had the Glasgow crowd completely awestruck.[68] The next day a *Daily Mail* article stated, "It's just a pity that the thousands of people at the game, and those who have to return to watching Scottish football, must have thought that they were dreaming." Jimmy Johnstone, the great Scottish soccer player who saw the game in person when he was sixteen years old, said, "The match remained the biggest single influence on my career. It was like a fantasy staged in heaven. I had never seen football like it, nor would I ever again. I'll recite the names of that Madrid forward line till the day I die."[69]

Real Madrid had won its fifth consecutive European championship. As a result, Muñoz became the first person to win the competition as both a player and a coach, Di Stéfano and Puskás became the first to ever score hat tricks in a final, and Di Stéfano became the only player to score in five consecutive European Cup finals. Also, Paco Gento, who appeared in all five of the European Cup finals for Real Madrid, would play in three more and win yet another in 1966. Three of the twenty-five Real Madrid players were graduates of the Real Madrid youth academy.

---

[67] Puskás and Di Stéfano are two of only three players to have scored a hat trick in a European Cup or Champions League final (Puskás is the only one to ever score four goals), with the other being Pierino Prati for A. C. Milan in the 1969 European Cup final. Puskás repeated the feat in the 1962 European Cup final.

[68] Cristian Nyari, "1960 European Cup Final–Eintracht Frankfurt's Run to the Final and the Game of the Century." *Bundesliga Fanatic*. http://bundesligafanatic.com/1960-european-cup-final-eintracht-frankfurts-run-to-the-final-and-the-game-of-the-century/.

[69] Andi Thomas, "The greatest Champions League hat tricks." *SB Nation*. http://www.sbnation.com/soccer/2014/11/28/7301701/champions-league-european-cup-hat-trick-messi-asprilla-puskas-muller.

Nostalgia for Galácticos 1.0

The 1959–60 Real Madrid team that won its fifth European Cup in Hampden Park, Glasgow, beating Eintracht of Frankfurt (7–3) in what has been considered the best final in European Cup history. Back row (left to right): Dominguez, Marquitos, Santamaría, Pachín, Vidal, Zárraga. Front row: Canario, Del Sol, Di Stéfano, Puskas, Gento.

It is important not to get lost in nostalgia about Real Madrid's on-field performance from 1955–60, during their five-time European championship run. Galácticos 1.0 became a legend, for good reasons, and this legend has been conveyed from generation to generation of the Real Madrid community and global soccer fans. A collective memory of it exists. However, it is critical to go back and understand what happened then. The club had the best players in the world and was beautiful to watch, but they did not win every game; they didn't win every Spanish league championship; and they had coaching turmoil.

Coaching

Bernabéu took over as president in 1943. Before he hired Muñoz in 1960, who would coach until 1974, Bernabéu changed coaches fourteen times in seventeen years. Only one coach, José Villalonga, lasted more than three years.

During the 1955–60 European Cup run, the club changed coaches six times: José Villalonga, Luis Carniglia, Miguel Muñoz, Carniglia (again), Manuel Fleitas, and Muñoz (again). Two coaches were fired right after winning a European Cup: Villalonga and Carniglia.

Table 3.1: Real Madrid Coaching Changes Between 1955 and 1960

Coach	Time Period	Championships during Tenure
José Villalonga*	December 1954–June 1957	Two La Liga trophies, Two European Cups
Luis Carniglia	June 1957–February 1959	One La Liga trophy, One European Cup
Miguel Muñoz	February–April 1959	
Luis Carniglia*	April–July 1959	One European Cup
Manuel Fleitas	July 1959–April 1960	
Miguel Muñoz	April 1960–January 1974	Nine La Liga trophies, Two Copa del Rey, Two European Cups, One Intercontinental Cup

* Fired shortly after winning a European Cup.

In the 1956–57 European Cup first round, Real Madrid beat Rapid Vienna at home 4–2. Two weeks later, Real Madrid was losing 3–0 away at Rapid Vienna at halftime, therefore Real Madrid was 5–4 down on aggregate and facing early elimination in their first defense of the trophy. According to a Di Stéfano interview, Bernabéu was not pleased. At halftime, he made his displeasure known in the locker room, practically pushing coach José Villalonga to the side and delivering his own pep talk to remind the players that "we haven't come here on holiday" and that they wore "the shields of Real Madrid" on their jerseys.[70] Back on the field for the second half, Di Stéfano scored in the sixtieth minute to keep Real Madrid in the running for the European Cup. Real Madrid would win the playoff game a few weeks later and then go on to win their second of the club's five consecutive European Cups. But Di Stéfano only secured that crucial win by disregarding coach Villalonga's instruction to remain higher up on the field. He said, "Villalonga told me to stay up in

---

[70] Miguel Delaney, "Power to the president." *ESPNFC*. http://www.espnfc.com/blog/espn-fc-united-blog/68/post/1840578/power-to-the-president.

attack, but we knew it was not working." Villalonga was fired by Bernabéu in 1957, a mere few weeks after coaching Real Madrid to their second European Cup (he coached in both of them) and fifth La Liga trophy (he coached in two of them).

In the summer of 1958, Bernabéu signed Puskás. Villalonga's replacement, coach Luis Carniglia, was understandably upset that Puskás arrived overweight and out of shape. Puskás hadn't played professionally in almost two years because he refused to go back to Hungary during the Hungarian Revolution. Legend is that Carniglia told Bernabéu, "I don't know what I'm supposed to do with this guy. He's so overweight." Bernabéu supposedly shot back, "That's your job. You're here to make him prettier." Puskás got back into shape and became one of the greatest players in Real Madrid history. Carniglia, however, still left Puskás out of the 1959 European Cup final starting lineup at the last minute because he didn't get along with him. Carniglia was soon fired by Bernabéu, even though Real Madrid won the game under Carniglia, and he had won the European Cup as coach for Real Madrid once before.

La Liga Results

Even with the best players in the world, Real Madrid was not dominating every game.[71] Real Madrid won the Spanish domestic competition (La Liga) twice during the five year span, the same number of times as Barcelona. In fact, Real Madrid's best statistical year and highest points in La Liga was not between 1955 and 1960; it was the 1960–61 season. The 1960–61 Real Madrid team dominated the league by winning twenty-four of thirty games (80 percent), beating the second place team by twelve points and finishing with a goal difference of sixty-four points (second place had twenty-two). The great 1960–61 team lost to Barcelona in the first round of the European Cup, 3–2 on aggregate. Di Stéfano and Puskás didn't score a goal in the series after leading La Liga during the season in total goals (del Sol also finished fifth, while no Barcelona player finished in the top five). Barcelona finished fourth in La Liga that year, twenty points behind Real Madrid, after qualifying for the European Cup as La Liga champions the prior year.

---

[71] During the 1930s, 1940s, and 1950s, there were strict limits imposed on foreign players in La Liga. In most cases, clubs could only have three foreign players on their teams, meaning that at least eight Spanish players had to play in every game. During the 1950s, however, naturalizing foreign players circumvented these rules.

Table 3.2: La Liga Results 1955–56 to 1960–61 (Thirty-game seasons)

Season	La Liga Champion	#1 Points	La Liga #2	#2 Points	European Cup Results	RM Coach
1955–56	Athletic Bilbao	48	Barcelona	47	Real Madrid	Villalonga
1956–57	Real Madrid	44	Seville	39	Real Madrid	Villalonga
1957–58	Real Madrid	45	Atlético	42	Real Madrid	Carniglia
1958–59	Barcelona	51	Real Madrid	47	Real Madrid	Carniglia
1959–60	Barcelona**	46	Real Madrid	46	Real Madrid	Muñoz
1960–61	Real Madrid	52	Atlético	40	Barca was runner-up to Benfica*	Muñoz

* Barcelona beat Real Madrid in the European Cup 4–3 on aggregate in the first round. Barcelona finished fourth in La Liga with 32 points. Barcelona's La Liga record was 13 wins, 6 ties, and 11 losses. Real Madrid's record was 24 wins, 4 ties, and 2 losses.

** Barcelona won on goal differential (58–56).

The closest season in contemporary times to their La Liga dominance in 1960–61 was Real Madrid's 2011–12 season. The 2011–12 season has been often termed by some newspapers as "La Liga de los Récords" ("the League of the Records") as Real Madrid broke several long-standing records throughout the season, including 100 points in a single season, a record 121 goals scored with a goal difference of +89, and a record thirty-two overall wins (88 percent versus 1960–61's 80 percent). However, Real Madrid lost in the semifinals of the Champions League in a penalty kick shoot-out to settle the tied score.

During the five thirty-game seasons between 1955 and 1960, Real Madrid averaged a 48-goal differential (goals scored minus goals allowed), or 1.61 times more goals scored than allowed. Since 2011, Real Madrid has averaged a 74-goal differential in a thirty-eight game season, or 1.95 times more goals scored than allowed, 21 percent better than Galácticos 1.0. Although statistics are useful and interesting (and used here to provide context), I am sure the Real Madrid community would agree the bottom line are the titles, and the way the club wins them.

Winning La Liga Doesn't Correlate to Champions League Success

Real Madrid is well known for its European championships, but in order to put Real Madrid's on-field performance into perspective, I analyzed the club's performance in the Spanish league to see if there was a correlation. Only twice, in 1957 and 1958, has Real Madrid won La Liga along with winning that year's Champions League. In fact, the club's last four Champions League wins were accompanied with a third-place or lower position in the Spanish league. The only year Real Madrid won both the Champions League and Copa del Rey tournaments was 2014.

**Table 3.3: Real Madrid Domestic Results the Year
It Won the Champions League**

Year	Champions League	La Liga Position	Copa del Rey Result
1956	W	#3	SF
1957	W	#1	QF
1958	W	#1	RU
1959	W	#2	SF
1960	W	#2	RU
1966	W	#2	QF
1998	W	#4	R16
2000	W	#5	QF
2002	W	#3	RU
2014	W	#3	W
2016	W	#2	R16

Examining years in which Real Madrid won La Liga by five points or more, with the exception of 1957, Real Madrid has not even made the Champions League final. In addition, in only one year, 1986, did Real Madrid win both La Liga and the Copa del Rey.

**Table 3.4: Real Madrid Champions League Results the Year
It Won La Liga By >5 Points**

Year	La Liga Position	Champions League Result	Copa del Rey Result
1957	#1 (+5)	W	QF
1961	#1 (+12)	R16	RU
1963	#1 (+12)	R16	SF
1967	#1 (+5)	QF	QF
1969	#1 (+9)	R16	R16
1975	#1 (+12)	QF	W
1978	#1 (+6)	DNQ	R16
1986	#1 (+11)	SF	W
1988	#1 (+11)	SF	SF
1990	#1 (+9)	R16	RU
2001	#1 (+7)	SF	R64
2008	#1 (+8)	R16	R16
2012	#1 (+9)	QF	SF

Copa del Rey Results

Real Madrid did not win the Copa del Rey at all from 1955 to 1960. Barcelona, Atlético Madrid, and Athletic Bilbao won it twice each. In the Copa del Generalísimo (as it was referred to during Franco's time) 1960 final, played that June (one month after Real Madrid's incredible 1960 European Cup final), Atlético Madrid beat Real Madrid 3–1 at Bernabéu Stadium with Di Stéfano, Puskás, Gento, and Santamaría all in the starting lineup for Real Madrid.

Chapter 4

COPYCATS AND
FINANCIAL STRUGGLES

ONCE BERNABÉU proved the sustainable economic-sport model works, other clubs quickly copied elements of it. Barcelona, for example, began construction of a new stadium called Camp Nou on March 28, 1954, which was much larger than Real Madrid's stadium (Barcelona's 106,146 capacity versus Real Madrid's 75,145 in 1957).

So, although Real Madrid won the first five European Cups (from 1955–56 through 1959–60), the other teams eventually caught up. Real Madrid would only win one more European championship in the 1960s with an all-Spanish team that had three of the starting eleven players as graduates of the Real Madrid youth academy. After that, the team would not win another European Cup until the late 1990s. The shift is glaringly evident when examining the number of players Real Madrid and Barcelona had in the top three for the Ballon d'Or award.[72] From 1956–60, a Real Madrid player placed in the top three eight times (Di Stéfano in 1956, 1957, and 1959; Kopa in 1956–59; and Puskás in 1960), while Barcelona had one (Luisito in 1960). None of Real Madrid's players that placed in the top three were Spanish. Over the next seventeen years, from 1961 to 1978,

---

[72] The FIFA Ballon d'Or is an annual award given by the sport's governing body, FIFA, and the owners of the French publication France Football (Amaury Group) since 2010. It is awarded based on votes from international media representatives and national team coaches and captains. Prior to 2010, the top individual soccer awards were the Ballon d'Or and the FIFA World Player of the Year award. The original Ballon d'Or, also known as the European Footballer of the Year award, had been awarded by France Football since 1956. From 2005 to 2009, the winners of the Ballon d'Or and FIFA World Player of the Year award were coincidentally the same, and in 2010 the two awards were merged.

Real Madrid had one player in the top three (Amancio Amaro from Spain in 1964), and Barcelona had four (1973–75 and 1978).

Table 4.1: Real Madrid and Barcelona Players Placing in the Top Three for the Ballon d'Or Award (1956–78)

	Real Madrid		Barcelona	
Year	**Player**	**Country**	**Player**	**Country**
1956	Alfredo Di Stéfano (2nd) Raymond Kopa (3rd)	Argentina France		
1957	Alfredo Di Stéfano (1st) Raymond Kopa (3rd)	Argentina France		
1958	Raymond Kopa (1st)	France		
1959	Alfredo Di Stéfano (1st) Raymond Kopa (3rd)	Argentina France		
1960	Ferenc Puskás (2nd)	Hungary	Luis Suárez (1st)	Spain
1961–63				
1964	Amancio (3rd)	Spain		
1965–73				
1973			Johan Cruyff (1st)	Netherlands
1974			Johan Cruyff (1st)	Netherlands
1975			Johan Cruyff (3rd)	Netherlands
1976–77				
1978			Hans Krankl (2nd)	Austria

Over the decades, Bernabéu's strategy started to slowly drift. Due to copycats, rising salaries,[73] aging players, a smaller stadium capacity (after new safety regulations forced Real Madrid to make modifications and

---

[73] Players' salaries were increasing due to a 1995 European Court of Justice decision in favor of Belgian soccer player Jean-Marc Bosman. Prior to the Bosman ruling, professional clubs in some parts of Europe (though not in Spain) were able to prevent a player from joining a club in another country, even if the player's contract had expired. The Bosman ruling meant that a player could move to a new club at the end of his contract, without the old club receiving a fee. Players can now agree on a pre-contract with another club for a free transfer if the player's existing contract will expire in six months or less. The Bosman ruling also prohibited domestic soccer leagues in EU member states, and UEFA, from imposing quotas on foreign players to the extent that they discriminated against nationals of EU states. Salaries were also rising because more billionaires, who could afford personal losses, were investing their private personal fortunes in soccer clubs.

decrease capacity) reducing revenues,[74] and lack of new revenues without further innovations, Real Madrid was struggling financially, and this impacted the strategy on the field. With financial constraints, the team moved away from signing the best global star players that demanded the highest salaries to signing the best Spanish players that it could afford. When Real Madrid beat Partizan Belgrade in the 1966 European Cup final, every starting player on the team was Spanish. Miguel Muñoz (who coached from 1960–74) added young Spanish players such as José Martínez ("Pirri"), Manuel Velázquez, Manuel Sanchís,[75] and Ramón Grosso to play alongside an established great Spanish player, Amancio Amaro, nicknamed El Brujo ("The Wizard"). This team became known as the Yé-yé.[76] In the 1960s, Real Madrid won eight La Liga championships and one European Cup. In the 1970s, Real Madrid won five La Liga championships, but without the best players in the world, and with other clubs catching up and copying elements of Real Madrid's strategy, the club won no European Cups.[77]

When Bernabéu passed away in 1978, he had been the club's president for thirty-five years, during which time Real Madrid won six European Cups and sixteen Spanish league titles. In the later years of his presidency, Real Madrid failed to continue to innovate or tweak the model and found itself struggling financially. During this time, Ajax, Bayern Munich, Benfica, Inter Milan, and Liverpool were starting to have consistent success in the Champions League, sometimes taking elements from the Galácticos 1.0 model. For example, Inter Milan won the 1965 European Cup, for the second year in a row, with the Italian team having

---

[74] In the 1990s, UEFA required the stadium to become an all-seating stadium (no standing attendance), which would have reduced capacity to 50,000 seats. Real Madrid therefore started an extensive redevelopment program that included extending the third tier over the entire stadium, the creation of corporate facilities, and building four access towers in each corner of the stadium. Work started in 1992 and was completed two years later.

[75] Manuel Sanchís Martínez (1966) and his son, Manuel Sanchís Hontiyuelo (1998 and 2000), both won the European Cup for Real Madrid.

[76] The name "Yé-yé" came from the "Yeah, yeah, yeah" chorus in the Beatles' song "She Loves You" after four members of the team posed for a Spanish national daily sport newspaper *Marca* and impersonated the Beatles. "Yé-yé" was also what youngsters were called in Spain in the sixties when Beatlemania was catching on around the world.

[77] The two decades between 1961 and 1980 are often referred to as the "Madrid Years." Real Madrid dominated La Liga, winning the championship fourteen times out of twenty. This included an incredible five in a row from 1961 to 1965. During this era, only Atlético Madrid offered Real Madrid any real threat, winning four times.

two starters from Spain and one from Brazil. Inter Milan players finished second and third in voting for the Ballon d'Or in 1965 and had two more in the top fifteen. Unlike Inter Milan, Real Madrid did not have a player in the top ten and only one in the top fifteen (thirty-eight-year-old Puskás).

By the early 1980s, Real Madrid had lost its grasp on the Spanish league title and no longer had the resources to sign even the best Spanish players, impacting strategy. The club's new strategy was to develop and promote players from within (from the academy). A new cohort of homegrown stars brought domestic success to the club with the nick-name *La Quinta del Buitre* ("Vulture's Cohort"), which was derived from the nickname given to the most charismatic and prominent player of the group, Emilio Butragueño (*El Buitre*, "the Vulture"). The other four members were Manuel Sanchís, Martín Vázquez, Míchel, and Miguel Pardeza; all five were graduates of Real Madrid's youth academy. With *La Quinta del Buitre*, Real Madrid was one of the best teams in Spain and Europe during the second half of the 1980s, winning five domestic championships in a row, though the club failed to win the European Cup. Emilio Butragueño finished in the top three for the Ballon d'Or award in 1986 and 1987; the last Real Madrid player to do so was in 1964. In the early 1990s, *La Quinta del Buitre* split up as the members left the club or retired, and Real Madrid did not have a player finish in the top three in voting for the Ballon d'Or.

In 1995, Lorenzo Sanz, who had been a board member from 1985 to 1995 during the presidency of Ramón Mendoza, became president of the club. Mendoza resigned after admitting the club had undisclosed large debts. Sanz tried to turn around the club by bringing in star players such as Brazilian left-back Roberto Carlos, Croatian striker Davor Šuker, and Montenegrin striker Predrag "Peda" Mijatovi to play with homegrown star striker Raúl. Real Madrid went from having no players in the top three voting for the Ballon d'Or to having Roberto Carlos (second in 1997) and Davor Šuker (third in 1998) place among the top. The club borrowed more money to sign the new players but was not successful in creating an economic model or financial strategy to pay off the debt. Generally, it was assumed that if the club won, it would make money. The assumption was wrong. The club won on the field, but it did not lead to off-the-field financial success. Financially, the club sank deeper into trouble.

Between 1997 and 2000, Real Madrid's net debt doubled, reaching €162 million ($150 million) on recurring revenues of only €118 million ($108 million). The club teetered on the brink of bankruptcy, despite impressive on-the-field success in the Champions League. Real Madrid won their seventh European title in May 1998, breaking a thirty-two-year drought, and won its eighth in May 2000.

PART THREE

Galácticos 2.0
(2000–06)

Chapter 5

FLORENTINO PÉREZ ELECTED IN 2000

F LORENTINO PÉREZ sat at his desk in his study at home in Madrid late into the evening in June 2000. Born in 1947, Florentino is a self-made man, the son of a hardware store owner. *Forbes* estimates his net worth at over $2 billion. He is almost always seen in a conservative suit and tie and wearing glasses. As much as he is disciplined, meticulous, persistent, and driven, he is friendly, jovial, and self-effacing. He shuns television interviews and feels much more comfortable in a small group, preferably with longtime friends. Typically, papers from his company, Grupo ACS, would be neatly organized into piles on his desk as the chief executive officer read and analyzed various company reports and communications at home after work. However, this night he had the Real Madrid annual report open on his desk. Florentino has been a club member of Real Madrid since he was fourteen years old and has attended most home games since childhood. He lives and breathes Real Madrid. It is his only passion—one could say obsession. He dedicates any leisure time to watching, supporting, and talking about Real Madrid.

As a club member, he had access to the annual reports with financial statements and the coming year's financial budget. Although he only had studied civil engineering at one of the top universities in Spain, he developed into a very sophisticated and experienced executive. He had the capability to review Real Madrid's complex financial statements and their respective footnotes. A lot of complexities arise in sports accounting because of the gains and losses in buying and selling players and assets; determining revenues from sponsorships, image rights, transfers of broadcasting rights or other deals; and recognizing debt. Even the timing as to when salaries and bonuses are paid and recognized can paint a completely different picture. Florentino examined the numbers carefully and believed they didn't add up.

Contrary to the official annual reports, Florentino believed the club was losing a lot of money and was heavily in debt. In the 1999–2000 season, the official annual report indicated revenues of €164 million ($152 million) and profit before taxes of €2.4 million ($2.2 million). Florentino believed the club was improperly accounting for revenues by taking credit for premiums on options for the transfer of broadcasting rights and advertising. If the option contracts and anticipated revenues had been accounted properly, then the financial result would have been much different. Florentino believed the real recurring revenues were around €118 million ($109 million), a whopping €46 million ($43 million) less than reported, and instead of a slight positive profit before taxes, as reported, the real pre-tax profit was instead a loss of €23 million ($21 million)—a €25 million ($23 million) negative swing. The net debt had doubled in the last three years, reaching €162 million ($150 million) in June 2000. And with the losses, Florentino knew the debt would only get larger. He could see that a train wreck was coming.[78]

This really troubled him. As previously discussed, Spain's Sports Law 10/1990 requires all clubs that can't prove they are financially viable based on audited annual financial statements to be converted to a Sociedad Anónima Deportiva (SAD), to increase financial accountability.[79] This law was enacted because so many Spanish soccer clubs were essentially bankrupt. In Real Madrid's case, the club would have been unavoidably converted into a SAD by exchanging debt for shares in the club, falling

---

[78] Later, Deloitte completed an independent audit. They reported that during the 1996–97 to 1999–2000 seasons, Real Madrid improperly accounted for revenues amounting to €96 million for premiums on options for the sale of broadcasting rights and advertising. This later led the ICAC (Institute of Accounting and Accounts Auditing) to a qualification in the audit opinion of the financial statements. In the 1999–2000 season, the official annual report indicated revenues of €164 million, EBIT of €14 million, and profit before taxes of €2.4 million. If the above-mentioned option contracts and anticipated revenues had been accounted properly, the result would be financial statements totally different than reported, showing recurring revenues of €118 million, negative EBIT of €11 million, and losses of €23 million.

[79] This is discussed in the "Ownership Structure" sidebar on page 23.

under the control of the creditors, among which were some of the largest TV broadcasters. In these cases usually one majority owner would emerge.

This was incomprehensible for someone who has been a socio since 1961 and who was born and bred in Madrid. To Florentino and most socios, Real Madrid belonged to the members, who were the only ones to decide the future of the club. They couldn't even imagine a scenario where a corporation, a TV broadcaster, or a billionaire would own the club.

Emboldened by having won two Champions League trophies in three years, the incumbent president, Lorenzo Sanz, confidently called the presidential election earlier than expected. Florentino feared that too many members would overlook the poor financial state of the club or, wrongly equating trophies with profits, would simply not believe the team could be in poor financial shape if it was winning European championships. Most experts thought it was a foregone conclusion that the president who delivered trophies, with a proven track record of winning the most prestigious trophy, would easily beat any challenger. Most experts discounted any concern by the club members about the financial situation. Few experts considered that community members actually might not be completely happy with winning this way.

Florentino took off his glasses and placed them on the Real Madrid reports. He went to bed worried about the long-term stability of the club and contemplated running for president.

Florentino had run for president of the club in 1995 on a platform of concerns about mismanagement and the club's mounting debt. He knew he had the experience and skills to execute a turnaround. In fact, in 1983, he and a group of engineers had acquired a financially troubled midsized construction company in the Cataluña region of Spain and turned it into the multibillion-dollar Grupo ACS. Florentino lost the 1995 election by 699 votes out of a possible 80,000. His partners and investors in Grupo ACS, concerned the club would be too much of a distraction for an already overburdened executive, were actually relieved that Florentino lost. Since 1995, the club's financial situation had only gotten worse, while Florentino's company and his commitments had grown much larger.

When Florentino woke up the next morning, one thing in particular (besides the club's debt) was on his mind: In the 1999–2000 season, the club had failed to sell out Bernabéu Stadium for seventeen of their eighteen home league games.[80] The team was on its way to winning the Champions League again after taking home the trophy two years earlier, yet the club couldn't regularly sell out the stadium. This signaled to Florentino that something deeper was wrong beyond the club's precarious financial situation.

He thought that polling the club members on their attitudes and expectations might provide some clues about what was going on. In addition, he asked them which player they most wanted to play for Real Madrid. The feedback he got from club members revealed what was important to them: transparency, accountability, the will to win, sportsmanship, excellence, teamwork, a beautiful attacking style on the field, and economic responsibility. They wanted the team to be true to its heritage of the 1950s and respected globally, and not simply for winning trophies. They wanted everything, from the facilities to the management team to the players, to be world-class. Also, more community members than Florentino originally anticipated shared his concern about the debt and long-term stability of the club, regardless of the wins. The player they wanted most was Portuguese winger Luís Figo, who happened to play for archrival Barcelona. Figo was quick, elegant, and highly skillful. He could provide accurate curling crosses to teammates that resulted in goals. He routinely beat defenders with his dribbling ability and quick stepovers. Real Madrid already had homegrown superstar scorer Raúl. Pairing Raúl with Figo was an exciting idea because the Real Madrid community cherished beautiful attacking soccer. The prospect of getting Barcelona's best player made it even sweeter.

In Spain, each player has a "clausula de rescisión," which is an official price at which his team has to sell a player. If the money is deposited with the league, the player's team (the selling team) can do nothing to stop it. The *clausulas* are purposely set exorbitantly high. In 2000, Barcelona would never have sold Figo to Real Madrid, but Florentino knew negotiations between Figo and Barcelona to renew Figo's contract were contentious and the buyout clause, set when Figo

---

[80] Richard Fitzpatrick, "Luis Figo to Real Madrid: The Transfer that Launched the Galacticos Era." *Bleacher Report*. http://bleacherreport.com/articles/2496426-luis-figo-to-real-madrid-the-transfer-that-launched-the-galacticos-era.

had signed his previous deal, was 10 billion Spanish pesetas (around €60 million or $64 million). It was a world-record transfer price for a player at the time, but manageable, if he could pull off a few other things he planned to do if he took over the presidency.

Sid Lowe in *Fear and Loathing in La Liga* and others reported that Florentino offered Figo a guaranteed 400 million pesetas (around €2.4 million or $2.5 million) just to sign a contract legally requiring him to sign with Real Madrid in the highly improbable event of Florentino winning. If Figo renounced the deal, he would have to pay Florentino 5 billion pesetas (around €30 million or $32 million) in compensation. If Florentino lost the election, Figo would stay at Barcelona. To Figo and his agent, it seemed like free money, and it might provide leverage in contract negotiations with Barcelona. Regardless, when news of the deal between Florentino and Figo became public it sent shock waves throughout the soccer world.

News of the Figo deal leaked on July 6, 2000, during incumbent president Sanz's daughter's wedding to Real Madrid right-back Míchel Salgado. Figo went into damage control mode. In an interview, Figo said, "I want to send a message of calm to Barcelona's fans...I want to assure [them] that Luis Figo will, with absolute certainty, be at [Barcelona's stadium]...to start the new season." He added: "I've not signed a pre-contract with a presidential candidate at Real Madrid." The media suggested that he was trying to torpedo Florentino's chances of winning so he could keep the 400 million pesetas and stay at Barcelona. Sanz joked, "Maybe Florentino will announce that he's signed Claudia Schiffer next."

However, if what was reported was true, Figo's agent had been outmaneuvered because the deal was airtight. Figo had to go to Real Madrid if Florentino won the presidency. The only way Barcelona could rescue Figo was to reimburse Figo for the penalty clause of 5 billion pesetas to re-sign their own player.

To convince the Real Madrid socios that the Figo deal was authentic, Florentino promised to personally pay the membership fees of all club members during the season if he was elected and Figo did not play for Real Madrid. How would Florentino pay for it? With the 5 billion pesetas that Figo legally agreed to pay as a penalty for not showing up.

So Barcelona would effectively be paying Figo more money to offset what Figo would have to give to Florentino, which Florentino would then give the Real Madrid fans to go to Real Madrid games for free.

What people did not know is that Florentino was taking an enormous personal financial gamble with the Figo deal if he did win the election. Florentino couldn't have been sure that Real Madrid had the money to pay for Figo. As part of the Sports Law 10/1990, the elected president and board of directors of a member-owned club have to personally pledge 15 percent of total expenses and assume 100 percent of all losses. This legal provision was added in order to increase the financial accountability and responsibility of the member-owned clubs. (Many people wrongly assume that this is a Real Madrid club rule when, in fact, it is a Spanish sports law.) At the time the Spanish law was enacted, budgets were small. For example, at the time of the implementation of the law in 1990, the budget for Real Madrid was around €30 million ($33 million), and the corresponding 15 percent may have been €4.5 million ($5 million).

In 2000, by contrast, to stand for election, Florentino had to provide a personal pledge of €18 million ($19 million or 3 billion pesetas at that time), equivalent to 15 percent of budget expenditures of the club of the 1999–2000 season.[81] Florentino had received a letter of guarantee from a bank. According to Spanish sport laws, when the club reports cumulative pre-tax profits corresponding to the seasons that the president and the board of directors had been directing the club, which are greater than the pledge provided by the president and the board of directors at the beginning of their mandate, there is no obligation of providing a bank guarantee by the incumbent president and board of directors. Even though the club's slight pre-tax profits in 1999–2000 were a result of unaccepted audited accounting by mixing recurring revenues with the sale of options contracts on Real Madrid rights, Sanz, unlike Florentino, was not required to provide a guarantee.

---

[81] The president is elected as the head of an electoral group that also includes the board of directors. The Real Madrid Statutes (the documents that govern the functioning of the club) state that the president must be Spanish (at the time of election) and a member of the club for ten or more consecutive years. To be eligible to run for election, the candidate must give a substantial bank guarantee. A bank guarantee is a promise from a bank or other lending institution that if a particular borrower defaults on a loan, the bank will cover the loss.

In 2000, the total cost for Figo's "clausula de rescisión" was €60 million ($64 million). If Real Madrid didn't have the cash, Florentino would have to put up the money or guarantee a loan for the amount, plus Florentino would be on the hook for the €18 million ($19 million) for budget expenditures. However, if Florentino didn't take this personal financial risk, there would not be a Figo deal.

On July 18, 2000, Florentino was elected Real Madrid's new president by a slim margin. His gamble had paid off.

On July 24, the twenty-seven-year-old Figo flew into Madrid on a private jet from a holiday with his wife and daughter on the Italian island of Sardinia and was presented his new jersey bearing the number 10 by Di Stéfano in the trophy room of Bernabéu Stadium. Still looking a little stunned by this turn of events, Figo had just become the world's most expensive soccer player in a €60 million ($64 million) transfer price deal. At the press conference, Florentino said, "[Figo] is, in my opinion, the best player in the world. As Real Madrid is the best club in the world, it's normal for the best player in the world to play for the best club in the world."

The irony of Figo standing alongside Di Stéfano was that when the magical Argentine forward first opted for a move to Spain, he appeared to be destined not for Real Madrid but for their rival Barcelona. The end result was Di Stéfano signed with Real Madrid. In his first El Clásico, Real Madrid won 5–0, and Di Stéfano scored four of the five goals. The Di Stéfano and, in a smaller way, Figo moves had much the same impact on the two teams and on the history of the sport as Babe Ruth being traded from the Boston Red Sox to the New York Yankees.

A few days earlier, mostly unnoticed because of the Figo excitement, Florentino announced that Real Madrid had agreed to sell French striker Nicolas Anelka to Paris-Saint German for £22 million ($23 million). Real Madrid needed the cash, but the Anelka transfer had even greater significance as a harbinger of things to come. After Anelka's transfer to Real Madrid in the summer of 1999 for £22.3 million, he started out well but soon fell out of favor with fans, fellow players, and the coach, at one point receiving a forty-five-day suspension for refusing to train. The talented player returned and scored vital goals in the semifinals against Bayern Munich in the Champions League and started in the finals, but he really didn't fit with the Real Madrid community's values and expectations, which meant that he did not fit with Florentino's vision of a new direction for the club. Therefore, his departure was not only financially advantageous but also culturally desirable.

What the 2000 Election Reveals about the Real Madrid Community

Astonishingly, even with the club's incredible success on the field, the number of socios quietly declined over the years from 66,744 in 1995 to 61,450 in 2000 as the club was winning its two European championships.

Table 5.1: Socios Membership in Selected Years

Date (June 30)	Socios (Members)	Season Ticket Holders	Membership Cost	Season Tickets Range
1995	66,744	30,210	€117	€81 to €652
1998	66,483	46,460	€133	€90 to €787
2000	61,450	50,554	€136	€117 to €914
2015	91,846	61,287	€149	€370 to €2,384

This signaled that something deeper was wrong beyond the club's precarious financial situation. The identified sense of mission and shared goals went beyond simply winning trophies at any cost. Supporters wanted more. They wanted to win with the best players, team philosophy, beauty, style, and class. In addition, the community members had the impression that management was not holding itself to the highest standards of accountability, transparency, and trust.[82] They were concerned that the management team was financially irresponsible and putting the long-term viability of the club at risk. In many

---

[82] In addition to other issues, two of Sanz's sons were signed by Real Madrid while Sanz was president, one on the soccer team and the other on the basketball team. Neither could be characterized as stars. Regardless whether their skill merited being on the first teams or not, the perception of members was that people were getting positions at their member-owned club as favors instead of merit.

ways, the socios wanted to go back to sustainable economic-sport model days of Bernabéu and Di Stéfano (or, as I refer to it, Galácticos 1.0).

Real Madrid's community cares more about *why* the team exists, *how* their sports team wins, and *whom* it wins with versus "just winning" (*what* is the result). The why and how are the critical parts and what inspire passion and loyalty. This is a fascinating idea because many sport organizations seem to rationalize actions, including the signing of players with off-field or on-field issues, under the premise of trying to give the fans what they want, which they assume is winning championships. Remarkably, the lessons learned in the election about the Real Madrid community stand in stark contrast to the conventional wisdom that winning is all that matters to fans.

Lastly, it is worth mentioning the backdrop in Europe and Spain around the time of the election in 2000. In 1999, the Euro currency was born virtually, and in 2002, physical notes and coins began to circulate. The creation of the European Union added more wealth and sophistication in Spain and an attitude that the old ways of doing things should be improved and modernized. A successful and respected businessman inside and outside of Spain who embraced innovation, accountability, transparency, corporate governance, organization, meritocracy, and cross-border business, Florentino reflected a new dynamic that the entire Spanish society was experiencing in the late 1990s and early 2000s.

Real Madrid's 2000 Finances Are Worse Than Expected

Sorting out Real Madrid's financial mess after Florentino won the club's presidential election was something of a challenge. Florentino hired Deloitte & Touche, the accounting and consulting firm, to review the club's financial statements and get to the bottom of what was going on. The independent auditor's results showed the situation to be as bleak as Florentino had feared.

As illustrated in Table 5.2, in 2000, Real Madrid had €118 million ($109 million) in operating revenues, €23 million ($22.1 million) in losses, and €162 million ($150 million) in debt. An August 2000 letter from a group of Deloitte & Touche auditors expressed concerns about Real Madrid's ongoing existence: "The budget that has been provided to us for the year 2000–01 has an excess of expenses over revenues...[which raises] important doubts about the ability of Real Madrid to continue its operations so that it can...meet its obligations...in the normal course of its business."

Table 5.2: Fiscal Year-End 2000 Real Madrid Financial Information

	June 2000
Revenues	€118m[83]
EBITDA (before net gains on disposals)	€10m
Wages to revenues	66%
Profit (Loss) before taxes	(€23m)
Net debt	€162m
Result	Auditor's opinion: unsustainable model

Time would be of the essence. Florentino's highest priority was to increase liquidity and pay down the debt as quickly as possible. He had some quick fixes in mind to stabilize the situation, and he assembled an executive team to develop and execute a strategy.

In Florentino's first year, Real Madrid ranked number five in total revenues among soccer teams according to the Deloitte Football Money League, published annually.[84] The €79 million ($73 million) difference (57 percent higher) between number one Manchester United at €217 million ($200 million) and number five Real Madrid at €138 million ($127 million) is staggering.

---

[83] The figure of revenues of €138 million does not correspond with the €118 million reported revenues. The €20 million difference reported as revenues corresponds to options for selling broadcasting rights of future seasons.

[84] The Deloitte Football Money League is a ranking of soccer teams by revenue generated from soccer operations. It is produced annually by the consulting and auditing firm Deloitte and released in early February of each year, describing the season most recently finished.

Table 5.3: Deloitte Football Money League Rankings (2000–01)

Rank	Team	Revenues (€ million)	Country
1	Manchester United	€217.2	England
2	Juventus	€173.5	Italy
3	Bayern Munich	€173.2	Germany
4	AC Milan	€164.6	Italy
5	Real Madrid	€138.2	Spain

As mentioned earlier, Florentino had to give a pledge of €18 million ($19 million), 15 percent of the budget by Spanish law, to run for president. The club had no money and huge debt. However, it had immediate working capital needs. To get the banks to agree to lend Real Madrid an additional €78 million, Florentino had to personally guarantee the amount. The club signed seven new players, including Figo, Conceição, Makélélé, and Solari, at a total cost of €151 million. To borrow to pay for two of those signings, Makélélé and Conceição, Florentino personally guaranteed another €39 million to the banks. (Real Madrid sold some players, including Redondo and Anelka, and received €67 million, otherwise the club would have had to borrow more.) Finally, when the budget for the 2000–01 season was approved, the expenditures were higher than the previous year's budget, and, by law, Florentino had to personally guarantee an additional €12 million. So in 2000, after becoming president of the club, Florentino personally guaranteed €147 million ($155 million) in total [18+78+39+12]. Only €30 million [18+12] of the €147 million was required by law. Without Florentino's additional €117 personal guarantees, the club wouldn't have been able to afford the necessary investments required to start Galácticos 2.0. The personal financial risk was so large that it would be fair to say that Florentino's passion really was both an obsession to save the club and conviction of the strategy he was to apply.

Chapter 6

THE TURNAROUND PART 1

Real Madrid's Mission and Values Statement

Soon after winning the election in 2000, Florentino Pérez went into his home office, closed the door, sat at his desk, and started to reread the results of the informal surveys from the club's community members. He jotted down notes from the answers to the questions asked, such as:

- What values do we want to serve as the foundation for our club?
- What attitudes and beliefs about competition and team do you hold?
- What are the goals that you want to pursue?
- What do you expect from management and the team?
- How do you want to be treated and communicated with?
- How often do you want to be communicated with?
- What kind of atmosphere and experience do you want when you attend the games?
- What players (former or current) represent your ideals?
- What player do you most want to join Real Madrid that is not already on the team?

He highlighted and circled words and drew lines connecting phrases and ideas. He was starting to work on a mission and values statement for Real Madrid. A mission statement's aim is to provide focus for management and staff. Typically, it defines the company's business, its objectives, and its approach to reaching those objectives. The purpose of a values statement is to describe the desired culture and provide a behavioral compass or set of behavioral expectations for the organization. In many corporations, senior management, sometimes with the input of employees or consultants, typically writes the mission statement. In this case, Florentino was writing a mission and values statement based entirely on what the community members had said, which was a highly unorthodox approach. He believed that since the club members owned the team, they should be the ones to guide management's thinking on strategic issues, provide focus and common goals, help define performance standards, guide employees' decision making, and help establish a framework for behavior. He believed that if the club closely followed the mission and values, the club members would be even more passionate and loyal because the club would be a reflection of what was important to them.

Florentino understood the value of a mission and values statement in running a large multinational company. Grupo ACS is a business organization that appreciates and rewards autonomy, responsibility, and initiative with the aim of promoting excellence. Florentino had built Grupo ACS through acquisitions, and he had found that it worked best to leave each company with its own brands/identity and decision making, but to have them all follow a single codified, written strategic mission and set of values.

When Florentino took over the presidency of Real Madrid, there was no documented mission statement and no written values. Although having such a statement or set of governing principles is relatively common practice for the best-performing businesses, in sports it was highly unusual. Conventional thinking in sports was that the single mission and value of every team was simply to win—nothing complicated about that.[85] What Florentino was tapping into was *why* the club exists and *how* community members wanted to win on and off the field.

Real Madrid's employees and community members seemed to know implicitly what the answers were, but they had never formally written them down. Florentino wanted to spell them out explicitly so that everyone in the community could read them and the club could be held accountable to them, especially as the organization grew. After board approval, he included them in the first annual report Real Madrid published during his presidency.

---

[85] At least this is how most fans think about it. Some owners have the mission of breaking even or making money.

Florentino Pérez, president of Real Madrid, in front of the tenth European Cup won in 2014 and Real Madrid's other nine European Cups. Real Madrid's eleventh trophy would be added in 2016.

Mission

To be an open and multicultural club that is both appreciated and respected throughout the world both for its sporting successes and for the values it disseminates, which, based on the search for excellence both on and off the field of play, contribute toward fulfilling the expectations of its members and followers.

Values

WILL TO WIN. Real Madrid's main objective is to strive, to the best of its abilities, to win all of the competitions it enters while showing its commitment, its belief in hard work, and its loyalty to its supporters at all times.

SPORTSMANSHIP. Real Madrid is a worthy and fair opponent on the field of play, upon which it competes with goodwill and respect toward all rival clubs and their respective supporters. Away from the field of play it is Real Madrid's overriding desire to maintain relations with all other clubs based on fraternity and solidarity and to collaborate with them and with the Spanish and international sports authorities on a permanently ongoing basis.

EXCELLENCE AND QUALITY. Real Madrid aspires to have the best Spanish and foreign players within its ranks, to imbue them with the values to which the Club aspires, and to repay the support of its fans with a sporting project based on quality, discipline, and sacrifice for the common cause. With respect to the management of its activities, the Club adheres to the principles of good governance and strives for excellence at all times.

TEAM PHILOSOPHY. All those who form part of Real Madrid, be they sportspeople or other professionals, make a commitment to working as part of a team and to give the best they have to offer for the good of the whole without putting their personal or professional aspirations first.

TRAINING. Real Madrid constantly devotes a great deal of effort to the discovery and instilling of new sporting values. This involves channeling the necessary attention and resources into the youth teams of all its sporting disciplines and nurturing not only the sporting development of its youth players but also their social, ethical, and civic education.

SOCIAL RESPONSIBILITY. Real Madrid is aware of the high social repercussion of its activities and it is for this reason that it dedicates all the resources within its power to complying with the very highest standards of good corporate governance and the promotion of the best sporting values, to strengthening its relations with its members, former players, fan clubs, and supporters, and to the development and implementation of solidarity projects in favor of the needy both within Spain and beyond its borders.

ECONOMIC RESPONSIBILITY. Real Madrid is aware that it manages tangible and intangible assets of exceptional value and importance, and it is for this reason that it pledges to administer them responsibly, efficiently, and honestly in benefit of its members.

Every employee and player was to adhere to the mission and values, which sponsors were to implicitly support. The mission and values pervaded every corner of the organization, from the marketing department to the player development staff, to the coach and to the players on the field. For the club members and fans, winning wasn't everything: They wanted to win with values.

Why Is Your Organization Purposeful and Meaningful?

A company's values are the core of its culture. Values expressed in a mission offer a set of guidelines on the behaviors and mindsets needed to achieve that vision; it acts as a filter for decision making. Companies that have written mission and/or values statements have a better sense of where they are going, and this leads to better performance. Jim Collins, a former McKinsey & Company consultant and professor at Stanford Business School, and Jerry Porras, a professor at Stanford Business School, determined in their research for *Built to Last: Successful Habits of Visionary Companies* (New York: HarperBusiness, 1994) that organizations driven by purpose and values outperformed the general market fifteen to one and outperformed comparable companies without one six to one. Harvard Business School professors John Kotter and James Heskett studied firms across twenty different industries and found that companies with cultures based on shared values significantly outperformed those without a mission statement. They demonstrated that revenues of these companies grew more than 400 percent faster than companies in similar industries.

McKinsey & Company has been voted the most prestigious management consultant firm for all fourteen years that Vault.com has been running its survey. Similar to sports organizations, McKinsey & Company is in the "attract, retain, and manage the best talent we can find and afford" business. Also similar to a sports team, it needs to get the best talent to work together to outperform the competition. The firm has a clearly articulated set of values that are prominently communicated to all employees and involve the way that firm promises to serve clients, treat colleagues, and uphold professional standards.[86] McKinsey & Company believes its values inform both its long-term strategy as a firm and the way it serves its clients on a daily basis. The firm puts aside one day a year to reflect as a group on what its values mean to both its work and employees' lives.

Conventional wisdom is that the mission of a sports team is simple and obvious: "Win a championship." However, there is a difference between a "goal" and a "mission with values." A mission statement is a statement that is used as a way of communicating the purpose of the organization. Properly crafted mission statements (1) serve as filters to separate what is important from what is not, (2) clearly state who the organization serves and how, and (3) communicate a sense of intended direction to the entire organization. A mission is different from a goal in that the former is the cause and the latter is the effect; a mission is something to be accomplished, whereas a goal is something to be pursued for that accomplishment. Neel Doshi and Lindsay McGregor, former McKinsey & Company consultants and authors of *Primed to Perform* (New York: Harper Business, 2015), proved through their research that "the highest performing cultures are built on the simple truth: *why* people work affects how *well* they work." With a common mission and values, an organization can work more effectively across functions to address dynamic challenges with purpose. I don't believe every organization has to have a written mission statement. I believe it certainly helps make the organization more scalable and transparent to its stakeholders. Most importantly, I believe it can be something the organization can turn to in difficult times to remind themselves who they are, why they exist, what their purpose is, what do they stand for, and why they are meaningful.

---

[86] McKinsey & Company Mission Statement and Values is an example for a talent-oriented, client-services business.

Similar to Florentino, one of the first actions Steve Ballmer, the former CEO of Microsoft from 2000 to 2014 and graduate of Harvard College and Stanford Business School, took after he purchased the Los Angeles Clippers was to develop a mission statement. Along with coach Doc Rivers, Ballmer developed the "Clipper Credo." It's a one-page document about teamwork and integrity.

"It doesn't say we're going to win," Ballmer explained.[87] It says: "The Clippers will stand for doing things the right way, giving 100 percent at all times, the highest degree of conviction and integrity, respect towards fans, community, teammates, and opposition. Hardcore and tough."[88] Similar to Florentino, Ballmer polled 1,000 people in Los Angeles about the Credo. In an October 2014 article about Ballmer's new life with the Clippers, Ballmer said, "It polled well, as authentic and important with the audience. We've got to walk that walk. We've got to walk it on the court. We've got to walk it off the court. We've got to walk it in community."[89] Since both Ballmer and Florentino are highly successful and respected business executives who came to sport management as outsiders, I think their prioritized action of developing a mission statement when they assumed leadership is revealing.

The Chicago Bulls had the top-selling team jersey in the NBA in 2015.[90] They have not won the NBA championship since 1998 with Michael Jordan. The fifth most popular NBA player jersey is Derrick Rose's—the team's current star player. The Cleveland Cavaliers, Los Angeles Clippers, and Oklahoma City Thunder have more than one team member in the top-fifteen-selling player jerseys, and yet the Bulls still beat them out. I looked to see if they have a mission statement, and they do:

The Chicago Bulls organization is a sports entertainment company
dedicated to winning NBA Championships, growing new basketball
fans, and providing superior entertainment, value, and service. We aim
to achieve our mission by working hard to emphasize the following core

---

[87] Ashlee Vance, "Steve Ballmer's New Life with the Clippers." *Bloomberg.* http://www.bloomberg.com/bw/articles/2014-10-16/steve-ballmers-new-life-as-owner-of-nbas-most-expensive-team.

[88] The Fred Roggin Show on The Beast 980. October 16, 2014.

[89] Vance, "Steve Ballmer's New Life."

[90] "LeBron No. 1 in jersey sales; Bulls are top-selling team." *NBA.com.* http://www.nba.com/2015/news/04/14/nba-most-popular-jerseys-2014-15-season-lebron-james-still-reigns/.

values: Mutual respect for each other, and a commitment to excellence,
innovation, integrity and quality in everything we do.

The Bulls have also started their new #SeeRed (the Bulls' colors are red and black) campaign, which is aimed to make fans feel like a part of the team and involve them in the team rather than just relegating them to spectators. The team app includes fan-friendly features such as lineup announcements and up-to-the-minute team news. All of this has been aimed at increasing the connection to fans and, ultimately, the value of the Bulls' brand. They demonstrated their dedication to their mission statement through social media and the #SeeRed campaign for the play-offs, trying to get the community involved and rally behind the team's goals.

As previously mentioned, the Green Bay Packers have the top-selling NFL team jerseys. Star player Aaron Rodgers's jersey ranks fifth in the player rankings. I looked to see if they have a mission statement, and they do:

The Green Bay Packers' mission is to be a dominating force in professional
football's competitive arenas. On the field, the Packers will continually
strive to present their fans with the highest level of performance quality
available. In their operating activities and relations with the NFL, the
Packers will also continually strive for excellence. On-the-field and
operating personnel will, at all times, maintain the highest ethical
and moral standards in their actions, recognizing that they are all
representatives of the Packers franchise and traditions. Overall, the
Packers will commit themselves to doing their part in representing the
State of Wisconsin with competitiveness, respect, and dignity.

No one can definitely say why the Packers or the Bulls have the top-selling jerseys in their respective leagues. The Packers are a small market team and last won a Super Bowl in 2010. The city of Chicago is the third largest city in America, and the Bulls haven't won the NBA Championship in almost twenty years.[91] Personally, I believe the Packers' community ownership, mission, tradition, rituals, and values are appealing to fans and lead to high levels of

---

[91] This is discussed further in chapter seven sidebar "Community Brands and Identity in American Sports."

passion and loyalty, which lead to the commercial success of selling jerseys. The Chicago Bulls seem to be trying to tap into mission and values as a differentiator and supporting that with technology/social media and active and frequent engagement.

Something I discovered in my research that fascinated me was a coach who had a mission statement. The challenge is that the coach has to buy into the statement and then get the players to buy into it, too, even if they don't believe it helps them individually. If the mission for the coach is not solely winning, which is how most coaches are judged and hired/fired, then what could it possibly be? Upon accepting the Green Bay Packers' head coach position in 2006, Mike McCarthy issued the following mission statement:

> *The foundation for the new direction of the Green Bay Packers will be constructed with three key components of obtaining "Packer People," creating "stable structure," and concentrating on "character and chemistry." A positive environment will be created with "leadership" that keeps its eye on the target of establishing a championship football team. The direction will be fueled with constant communication to ensure everyone is on board. We will attack the voyage with energy and enthusiasm to overcome the obstacles that we will encounter. This vision is enhanced with the resources and tradition that stands in the forefront of professional sports organizations.*

Mike McCarthy has a reputation for living by these words and trying to stay true to his vision. McCarthy is supported by a Packers organization that has a reputation for making an effort to draft and sign "Packer People" and inculcating them with the history, rituals, prestige, humbleness, and team-orientation of being a Green Bay Packer.

Lastly, I thought I would provide a sport analogy of the purpose of a mission and values statement. Every professional sports team's coaching staff is investing an enormous amount of time and effort to approach the next game. The goal is to win. But the first thing the team needs is the plan on how to do it. So the coaches provide the players with a written playbook to study, memorize, and practice in order to execute the game plan as a group. Not having a mission and values statement is like showing up to play a game with the goal of winning, using a stick to draw up a few plays in the dirt or trying to wing it by remembering what the team did last week, and expecting the players to be able to execute as a unit. An organization is a team, just like a soccer club. The mission and values statement is an "organizational play-book" so all team members clearly understand their individual roles as well as their organization's purpose. Without this mission, the team can't maximize its performance.

The Executive Team Goes to Work

In July 2000, Florentino's first objective was to professionalize the management of Real Madrid. The president and board of directors, elected every four years, are supposed to define organizational objectives and monitor management. Before Florentino's election, there was no clear definition of managerial responsibilities, and the board of directors tended to interfere with the day-to-day operations of the club. The employees' compensation system mimicked the players', which included a basic salary and bonus based on the team's performance, regardless of the employee's role, responsibilities, or individual performance. Florentino restructured the organization into four main units that corresponded to strategic priorities: a unit responsible for the stadium, marketing/brand management, corporate, and sport. He recruited four key executives and appointed a new board member:

- Jorge Valdano as Sports Director General, responsible for soccer and basketball from the academy teams to the first team;
- José Ángel Sánchez as Marketing Director General, responsible for developing the commercial actions for the brand exploitation;
- Manuel Redondo as Presidency Director General, responsible for members, ticketing, and infrastructure departments;
- Carlos Martínez de Albornoz as Corporate Director General, responsible for all the corporate matters (financial, HR, legal, purchasing, information systems/technology) and the internal organization of the club, as well as transforming the

Executive management team of Real Madrid at the celebration party of the ninth European Cup in Glasgow, May 2002. From left to right: José Ángel Sánchez, Carlos M. de Albornoz, Florentino Pérez, Manuel Redondo, Jorge Valdano.

club's governance, management, and reporting as if it were a conventional corporation; and

- Pedro López Jiménez as board member.

Jorge Valdano is an Argentine former soccer player who had been part of the Argentina national team (with Diego Maradona) that won the 1986 FIFA World Cup. He scored four goals in the tournament, including the second goal against West Germany in the final. He played for Real Madrid from 1984 to 1987 and coached Real Madrid's youth team in 1990–92 and the first team from 1994 to 1996.

Jorge commands the respect of players and coaches alike. He knows what it means to be both a Real Madrid player and coach. He understands Real Madrid's youth academy. While Jorge's playing history with Real Madrid might lead many to consider him an insider, in some ways he is not. Florentino respected Jorge's soccer knowledge, but the characteristics he most admired were his intellect and his willingness and ability to think about soccer as something beyond a game played on a field. Jorge's nickname is *El Filósofo* ("The Philosopher") because of his thoughtfulness in most matters. For example, when he was playing for Real Madrid in the late 1980s, he wrote a column in a Spanish newspaper criticizing Ronald Reagan's policies in Latin America. He is also known to quote Shakespeare and Argentine writer Jorge Luis Borges. Above all, Florentino valued Jorge's ability to motivate, provide leadership, resolve conflicts, and nurture talent.

Jorge and Florentino were aligned on a vision. Both men saw soccer as a metaphor for life, one that helps us understand who we are. They understood that the power of the metaphor is that it gives us the chance to be associated with something larger than ourselves because the soccer world is one of exaggeration and excess. It produces powerful images and analogies to which we can all relate. Jorge and Florentino believed that the key to a turnaround for Real Madrid was for the values and expectations of the community to be reflected by the club overall and played out on the field—excellence; championships; winning with elegance, style, and class; beautiful, exciting attacking soccer; romanticism; respect; never giving up; and more.

José Ángel Sánchez grew up a Real Madrid fan and socio. He was working at Sega, the multinational video game developer. A mutual acquaintance of Florentino and José Ángel, who knew that Florentino was looking for a head of marketing, thought the then-thirty-three-year-old José Ángel would be an excellent candidate and made an introduction. Florentino admired José Ángel's contagious passion and curiosity. He respected the way José Ángel bucked the traditional Spanish system by going into the business world with a college degree in philosophy (this was very unusual in Spain). Believing that technology would be a key to strengthening and building the connection with and passion of the community, Florentino also saw José Ángel's ties to the digital world as a very valuable asset.

José Ángel, Jorge, and Florentino all had a romantic notion of soccer but realized that their ideas would only work if they were grounded in reality. The reality was that soccer was becoming part of international commerce. They asked themselves: What does a team need to do to be a major global force? They realized that even in this age of international growth, they could only conquer the market through the strength of their own authentic community identity and values. And they knew that the values of Real Madrid were not only beautiful but also universal, with appeal that went far beyond Madrid and Spain. Television and technology were globalizing the sport in a marriage of convenience. José Ángel would figure out innovative ways to bundle the authentic, universal values of the Real Madrid community as content to be marketed around the world to generate revenues. Media companies that develop content and focus on making people happy, such as Disney, inspired him.

Manuel Redondo was appointed Presidency Director General, responsible for members, ticketing, and infrastructure departments. His priorities were twofold: reorganizing all matters related to club members, fan clubs (*peñas*), season tickets, VIP areas, and venue organization; and revamping the infrastructure of Bernabéu Stadium and launching the infrastructure of the new Ciudad Deportiva Real Madrid ("Real Madrid Sport City," the club's training facility).

The Real Madrid executives wanted to make sure that the players represented the values and identity of the community and acted accordingly, which they felt was a critical part of their success. This was the vision, but, just like Benabéu's Galácticos 1.0, it had never been done before. No one could say for sure what the marketing revenues would or could be.

Real Madrid didn't have the money or time to invest up-front in an untested theory and wait to see if it produced the anticipated results. The team was heavily in debt and losing money. The outcome of Florentino's personal financial gamble for the club was at stake. The players would need to be paid up-front, and the projected theoretical marketing dollars would come later. It was left to Carlos (the non-soccer fan at the time) to help Florentino sell the future—in particular, the future marketing dollars—in much the same manner that they raised equity for the infrastructure projects they were involved with as construction and engineering executives, only in this case, the future income would be collected in ticket and merchandise sales rather than highway and bridge tolls.

Carlos, an engineer as well, had worked alongside and served on boards with Florentino and had made a name for himself successfully managing the leading Spanish steel company and its integration into Arcelor, and turning around the largest Spanish shipbuilding company with nine shipyards. Carlos also had business experience outside of Spain that could prove useful as Real Madrid focused on global growth. Florentino figured the levelheaded, dispassionate executive, who had to be talked into the job, wouldn't be caught up in the excitement of professional sports and its stars. Florentino also knew Carlos could execute and get things done.

Florentino had both credibility as a successful businessman and the connections to get meetings with corporations and bankers. He was skilled in selling a vision and getting buy-in, not just from his executives but also from employees and other stakeholders. However, no precedent existed for estimating what Real Madrid's new strategy would yield over the next ten to fifteen years from marketing, licensing, and sponsorship revenues. Carlos contributed to developing a stand-alone legal entity (named "Sociedad Mixta") to own and manage the future marketing, licensing, and sponsorship, player-image rights, and online business revenues of Real Madrid, and developing a credible financial model with projections for the next eleven years. The Sociedad Mixta, managed by the club's marketing division, handled all such interactions with current and potential customers and partners.

Florentino and his team went to meeting after meeting with various companies to explain the concept and the financial model and its underlying assumptions. The idea was for the companies to pay up-front for a percentage of Real Madrid's future revenues based on the potential financial return they would get. The challenge was that with no historical track record, this strategy required investors to take a big leap of faith. Carlos' reputation as a successful, financially sophisticated and responsible executive added credibility to the executive team's ability to execute the plan. Once projections and assumptions were agreed upon, the parties had to negotiate the discount rates to present value-projected future cash flows that would reflect the risks to come up with a valuation—but there were no good comparable precedents. Finally, in October 2000, Caja Madrid (a Spanish savings and loan institution that would later become part of Bankia) paid €78.13 million ($72 million) for a 20 percent share. In February 2001, Sogecable (the leading pay-TV group in Spain) signed a €39.07 million ($36 million) deal for a 10 percent share. There were risks on both sides—Real Madrid didn't want to sell too low and the investors didn't want to overpay—which were mitigated by establishing put-and-call arrangements at various prices and times for protection. By October 2000, Real Madrid had sold a total of 30 percent of the rights for eleven years for a total of €117.2 million ($108 million), which gave the club some financial liquidity for operations. In the end, the venture was a financial success for both sides. Real Madrid got the immediate financial stability it needed, and the investing companies saw an 11 percent annualized return by 2014.

In order to improve Real Madrid's operations and start to address accountability, transparency, and trust, the management team implemented an effective tool that had never been used in sports management at the time (but had been used at large companies like General Electric). Carlos implemented Harvard Business School professor Robert Kaplan's Balanced Scorecard. When Carlos arrived at Real Madrid, he saw there was no consistent tracking and alignment in each of the different functional areas between revenues and expenses. Carlos changed this so that each department had to budget and control its revenues, if any, and its expenses, if any. Carlos and Florentino were accustomed to data, metrics, and analysis to measure performance and hold managers accountable. Carlos had successfully implemented the Balanced Scorecard at the other companies he managed. It enabled Real Madrid's managers to align business activities to the vision and strategy of the organization, improve internal and external communications, and monitor the organization's performance against strategic goals. Florentino and his band of outsiders implemented internal control and audit procedures to improve transparency and accountability. They installed performance management software and data analytics to get the right performance information to the right people at the right time. Automation and data analytics added structure and discipline, helped transform disparate corporate data into usable information and knowledge, and helped communicate performance information. In addition, they added financial oversight committees to review and analyze financial data and to ensure open,

fair, and competitive bidding of work Real Madrid needed (any companies with conflicts of interest were disqualified). Lastly, they dramatically increased the transparency and reporting of financial data to club
members. Today, this may seem basic, but when the new management
team took over, there was very little in terms of systems, procedures, and
controls (and this was true for most European soccer teams at the time,
not just Real Madrid). Similar to Bernabéu, Florentino wanted to focus
on organizational changes right away as they set the tone.

In addition to improving performance measurement, Carlos also
overhauled the compensation structure. Non-sports employees' bonuses
were no longer linked to the soccer team's performance. Pay was determined by the achievement of financial and nonfinancial targets aligned
to departmental and company business plans in the Balanced Scorecard
framework. Everyone had to commit to the mission and values of the
club and part of their reviews and compensation was based on that.

In 2000, Real Madrid had 120 permanent staff, 280 players in all
leagues including youth teams, 150 part-time staff for venues of soccer
and basketball, and 30 other associates for a total of about 580 employees. This total number would grow to 703 in 2014 (see Appendix C for
a Real Madrid organization chart).

Lastly, Florentino nominated business partner and fellow civil engineer Pedro López Jiménez (whose son, my friend Fabio, introduced me
to Carlos) to the board. Pedro has the gift of telling it to you straight,
without holding back. He has known Florentino since the 1970s.

In July 2000, Florentino nominated Di Stéfano to be honorary president. Florentino believes the Argentine forward is the most important
player in the history of Real Madrid and the best soccer player of all
time. Florentino wanted Di Stéfano to get the recognition he deserved
and create a link back to history and traditions of Galácticos 1.0 with Di
Stéfano as a regular presence at games and club events. Di Stéfano died
in July 2014 at eighty-eight years old. In December 2015, Florentino
nominated Paco Gento to be honorary president. Gento played for Real
Madrid from 1953 to 1971 and won an unprecedented six European
Cups and twelve La Liga titles.

Strategic Sale of Real Madrid's Ciudad Deportiva

Bernabéu kicked off his economic-sport strategy (Galácticos 1.0) by building the largest stadium in Spain in 1947, totally financed by its club members. At the time, it was built in the middle of open fields and pastureland in the outskirts of Madrid. In 1963 Bernabéu developed the Real Madrid training facilities (Ciudad Deportiva) in an area of 120,000 square meters not far from its stadium but even farther in the outskirts.

In 1996, then-president of Real Madrid Lorenzo Sanz sold 15,000 square meters of the old Ciudad Deportiva to the Community of Madrid and 15,000 square meters to the City Hall of Madrid for €13.5 million ($15 million) each. After the transaction, the regional and the City Hall governments controlled almost 25 percent of the property. This would give the governments a stronger position in a future negotiation for finding a solution to the urban planning problem that was arising.

Eventually, the city would grow around Real Madrid's stadium and Ciudad Deportiva. By 2000, the old Ciudad Deportiva had become not only obsolete for Real Madrid's needs but also a problem for the urban planning and socioeconomic development of Madrid, as stated by the city urban authorities. The Ciudad Deportiva was adjacent to the financial district that the city wanted to develop in the coming years as Madrid grew and expanded. Removing the Ciudad Deportiva from that location became a historic opportunity to improve and modernize the entire configuration of the north area of Madrid.

Florentino instinctively knew Ciudad Deportiva was now prime real estate and the asset that could be monetized to provide liquidity, reduce debt, finance the needed improvements to Bernabéu Stadium (which the community desperately wanted), and pay for new and larger world-class training facilities (which Florentino believed were necessary to attract, retain, and train the best players and to win). Florentino's understanding of, and connections in, construction, zoning, and development would come in very handy to Real Madrid.

In 2000, the area of the Ciudad Deportiva was zoned for non-commercial purposes. In addition, at the time, skyscrapers were not allowed to be built in Madrid. Rezoning the land for commercial purposes and to allow skyscrapers to be built would increase the value of the land dramatically, not only for Real Madrid but also for the Community of Madrid and the City Hall of Madrid. In 2000, Real Madrid agreed to cede an additional portion of the land of Ciudad Deportiva to the local governments, if the land was rezoned for commercial purposes and to allow skyscrapers. Therefore, the government had an even greater economic incentive to make changes. Then, in May 2001, the planning agreement was signed with the Community of Madrid and the Madrid City Council for the transformation. Although commonly believed to be a direct transaction in which Real Madrid sold the land to the Madrid City council, this is not in fact what happened. In public project bids, both Real Madrid and the government sold their portions to four corporations: Repsol, Mutua Automovilística de Madrid, Sacyr Vallehermoso, and Obrascón Huarte Lain (OHL). These corporations constructed four skyscrapers on the site that became their headquarters. The Community of Madrid and the city council of Madrid sold their stakes—a combined €27 million ($25 million) in 1996—for a combined €211 million ($194 million) a few years later. Real Madrid, as owner of the largest part of the land of the old Ciudad Deportiva, made a net total of €474 million ($545 million), which permitted the club to enlarge and modernize the facilities of Bernabéu Stadium (€240 million has been spent since 2000) and to pay for the land and subsequent construction and development of all the facilities at the new Ciudad Deportiva Real Madrid (€186 million has been spent since 2000). In total 90 percent of the €474 million has been invested in building new facilities and reforming old ones (around half was spent in the first six years). With regards to the attention to the stadium, the field is meticulously maintained. For example, sun lamps are used to ensure exactly equal sun for each part of the field.

With the remaining €48 million from the real estate sale, the new management team recaptured exploitation rights sold off to various operators and licensees in the past to raise cash. Before Florentino arrived, most assets that had value, like VIP boxes, for example, had been sold to raise capital. The VIP boxes had been sold under ten-year contracts. The new management team bought the boxes back for €16 million and refurbished them for 20 million. In addition, they added new boxes.

Presently, Bernabéu Stadium has 243 VIP boxes[92] with 2,980 seats, plus 1,776 VIP seats distributed around the field at different levels. During the 2014–15 season, more than 17,500 VIP tickets were sold, compared to 14,000 the previous year. With revitalized community engagement based on values, the total annual income from the boxes in 2014–15 was €35 million ($42 million). The management team bought back the rights that were sold for electronic signage (which was on the perimeter of the field visible for TV broadcasting) that generated €3 million ($3 million) per year and, with leveraging the community engagement based on values, resold it for €9 million ($9 million) per year.

The management team also looked to maximize the revenue potential of the stadium instead of being utilized and generating revenues only on game day. Therefore, they made the stadium a tourist destination in its own right, keeping it open most days. The Real Madrid Museum and a stadium tour were developed to show the history and achievements of the most honored sports team in the world; presently, with more than one million visitors per year, it is one of the main tourist attractions in the city of Madrid. The Real Madrid official store was also developed and presently receives more than two million visitors per year thanks to its unique location at Bernabéu Stadium. Another initiative was the restaurants. In 2000, there was no space leased to restaurants with views of the stadium. At present there are four restaurants (Puerto 57, Asador de la Esquina, Real Café, and Zen Market): one international, one grill, one international/Real Madrid themed, and one Asian. The aim was twofold: leverage the profits of the infrastructure of the stadium seven days a week and then use the restaurants as a VIP area on game days, selling them as VIP seats.

---

[92] The Dallas Cowboys' AT&T Stadium has an estimated 342 luxury suites (the most in the NFL), ranging from $224,000 to $900,000 per season of eight home games, and 15,000 club seats. The New York Giants and Jets' MetLife Stadium has 218 luxury suites, ranging from $150,000 to $500,000, and 10,005 club seats. The Green Bay Packers' Lambeau Field has 168 luxury suites, ranging from $90,000 to $175,000.

With the Sociedad Mixta, strategic sale, change of Real Madrid's Ciudad Deportiva, and recapturing the exploitation rights, Real Madrid's management had addressed the immediate desperate financial situation. The culture of trust and collaboration of the executive team as well as their experience and credibility were essential in execution.

Chapter 7

THE TURNAROUND PART 2

Zidanes and Pavones

After Florentino Pérez's election and signing the player the community most coveted, Figo, in 2000, Real Madrid started to bring in the best players from around the world who fit the Real Madrid values and expectations. It was a part of the sustainable economic-sport model, a strategy inspired by Bernabéu's Galácticos 1.0 in the 1950s and desired by the community. Having stabilized the financial situation, Real Madrid methodically signed at least one of these special players the summer of every year while keeping true to the mission statement, as detailed in the previous chapter.

In 2001, the club signed Zinedine Zidane, the star attacking midfielder of the French national team, paying a record fee of 150 billion Italian lire (about €75 million or $69 million) to Juventus. The signing of Zidane, nicknamed "Zizou," epitomized the notion of a multicultural club and what Real Madrid's members and fans wanted.

Zidane had world-class talent. He was renowned on the field for his elegance, vision, ball control, and technique, and is considered one of the greatest soccer players of all time. Before joining Real Madrid, Zidane had won the Ballon d'Or in 1998 and FIFA World Player of the Year in 1998 and 2000 (and would win it again in 2003 with Real Madrid); he was also named one of World Soccer's 100 Greatest Players of the 20th Century in 1999. When the technical team recommended Zidane, the marketing team discovered that he was the most respected player by Real Madrid fans in all five geographic zones that the club surveyed.

Zidane himself is multicultural. He was born in southern France. His parents immigrated to France from a Berber-speaking region in northern

Algeria in 1953 before the start of the Algerian War. His father worked as a warehouseman/night watchman at a department store, often on the night shift, while his mother was a housewife. The family lived in a neighborhood that was notorious throughout Marseille for its high crime and unemployment rates. Although he didn't seek the role, he became a symbol of, and inspiration for, French progress toward racial/socioeconomic/religious harmony. He fit Real Madrid's mission perfectly.

Zidane became a global sensation by leading France to its first FIFA World Cup in 1998 on its home soil. France defeated defending champion and heavy favorite Brazil 3–0. Zidane scored two goals, both headers, in the first half of the final, held at the Stade de France in Paris. During the victory parade on the Champs-Élysées in Paris, a huge picture of national hero Zidane was projected on the Arc de Triomphe along with the words "Merci Zizou."

Florentino promised to build a team full of the best players in the world like Zidane and Figo and talented Real Madrid academy graduates such as Raúl, Iker Casillas, and Francisco Pavón. Before the media used the phrase "galácticos" to describe Real Madrid's players or strategy, they referred to it as *Zidanes y Pavones* ("Zidanes and Pavones").

Born in Madrid, Pavón progressed through the academy ranks at Real Madrid, starting with the youth team in 1998 until he established himself with the second team in 2000. The center-back made his La Liga debut as part of the first team in October 2001 at twenty-one years old. Although Pavón was a very good player, he never reached legendary status, so the nickname for the era lost enthusiasm. However, the idea was to pair excellent academy players with outside stars, and that stayed a consistent focus for the executives. The epitome of an excellent academy player was Raúl.

Raúl was a working-class kid from Madrid and actually was enrolled at Atlético Madrid's youth academy until Atlético's president decided that his team didn't need a youth team. So Raúl transferred to, and graduated from, the Real Madrid academy. He started his professional career in the 1994–95 season with Real Madrid C; he scored thirteen goals in just seven games and was promptly promoted to the first team, replacing another Real Madrid academy graduate and legend, Emilio Butragueño, in a symbolic "passing of the crown." Raúl became the youngest player—17 years and 124 days—ever to play for Real Madrid's first team at the time. Remarkably, Raúl wasn't particularly quick or strong and didn't have a booming shot. What he did have was an incredible will to both score and win, and a talent for always being in the right place at the right time. He was second in the Ballon d'Or voting in 2001 and ranked third in the 2001 FIFA World Player of the Year. By the end of his career, Raúl had scored 323 goals for Real Madrid, breaking Di Stéfano's long-standing club record. The fans adored him, and at his retirement he was often mentioned as the second-greatest Real Madrid player of all time behind Di Stéfano. To Real Madrid fans, Raúl personified the traditional values of Real Madrid. As a testament to his values and how he played and led, Raúl holds the distinction of never having received a red card[93] throughout his seventeen years at the professional level.

Although the media would move from *Zidanes y Pavones* to use the word "galácticos" after a few more high-profile signings, Florentino and his team of executives never drifted from the idea of pairing excellent Real Madrid academy players with the best players from around the world. They thought incorporating academy players would benefit both the team's and community's culture and identity. Florentino had learned with his experience at Grupo ACS that when he hired the best external talent for the company, he needed to surround them with internal "culture carriers" who had spent most of their careers at Grupo ACS to help assimilate the new talent into the firm's culture and best practices.

The media speculated that using academy players was purely a financial decision because the club didn't have any more money to pay large transfer fees. At the beginning, especially with the financial turnaround, saving money was always a consideration, and economic responsibility is in the values statement. However, one of the first things Real Madrid did with the proceeds of the real estate deal was to invest in and upgrade the academy. Florentino believed that—just like a world-class company investing in training and facilities for its people to bond, learn, and improve—Real Madrid should be a world-class leader in investing in

---

[93] Yellow and red cards are used as a means to discipline players for misconduct during the game. A yellow card is used to caution players, while a red card results in the player's dismissal from the field of play. Thus, yellow cards are used to punish milder forms of misconduct than red cards. However, if a player receives two yellow cards in one game, he gets an automatic red card.

its players, training, and facilities. To be discussed in more detail later, the academy and its players would become a larger focus of emphasis for cultural reasons.

Although players and player selection get a lot of attention in the media, Florentino and his management team focused on strategies to make sure the community's values and expectations were transmitted through the organization to the playing field. They thought the strategies also needed to be uniquely suited to their sustainable economic-sport model, which has the element of featuring the best players in the world.

Equal Treatment

The club philosophy, published along with Real Madrid's mission and values, emphasizes the good of the whole over that of the individual. Equal treatment for all has been a guiding principle since the days of Bernabéu. With a firm grasp of this principle, Florentino and his management team have made difficult and potentially unpopular decisions with confidence that they are acting for the good of the entire community.

Real Madrid goes to great pains to treat players as equally and consistently as possible. Every member of the team must feel important, especially when superstars are involved, and the best way to convey that is by treating all of them in exactly the same way. In the Real Madrid locker room, for example, all players have the same exact lockers and are strictly ordered by number. If all the players sat down simultaneously on the wooden bench in front of their lockers, they would be shoulder to shoulder. In the US, in contrast, teams commonly provide star players with special, larger lockers and cushioned chairs or preferred locations in the locker room. Similarly, no Real Madrid player receives special or different travel accommodations. In the US, in contrast, teams commonly provide star players with larger hotel rooms and other amenities. Also, no Real Madrid player receives special seating for family members. A player that wishes special seats or box seats must pay for the difference in cost. In the US, in contrast, star players' families are often provided VIP seating. Real Madrid's players' contracts are standardized, each including the same provisions and codes of conduct.[94] The only real difference between one contract and another is the euro amount. Real Madrid management found that sticking to this policy removes any unfair disadvantage or treatment when negotiating contracts with different players, reducing negotiating time and confrontation because "it is what it is."[95]

Of course, every player knows compensation will differ depending on demand, technical skills, and performance, but Real Madrid believes treatment outside of that must be consistent. Real Madrid management believes exceptions can negatively impact teamwork and team spirit and create future challenges and distractions. Over time, the managers have learned to be even more focused on making sure they do not "rationalize" incremental exceptions. Real Madrid's strategy means that talented employees may leave the organization because leadership is unwilling to compromise the community's goals and core values. Players who put their personal or professional aspirations first (going against the stated team philosophy, including economic responsibility or fairness) may choose to leave if their contract demands are not met. Management may be criticized by the press and fans for letting players walk, when management is actually acting in concert with the community's values and expectations. Determining which players to sign, or re-sign, and which to let go, and even how much to pay each player, is part art and part science, balancing financial considerations with cultural ones, economic responsibility with talent needed to win, all with relative fairness and in alignment with the organization's core values.

Equality doesn't just impact those on the field; it impacts the entire organization. Real Madrid, for example, treats the person who is an

---

[94] The Code of Conduct requires the players to adhere to and support the club in its commitments with sponsors, advertisers, social actions, etc., providing the players a proper and adequate image. In any public appearances of the club, the players representing the same need to respect agreements with sponsors while transmitting an image of Real Madrid according to its sport and institutional values. They must show respect to the institution they represent, through both verbal and nonverbal communication, an essential part of which is the dress and behavior.

[95] Research by organizational culture expert Vega Factor and shared in *Primed to Perform* by Neel Doshi and Lindsay McGregor has proven that *why* people participate in an activity determines how well they perform. When people are motivated by emotional pressure (such as prestige chasing) or economic pressure (the desire to win a reward or avoid a punishment), their performance declines. Policies like this keep players focused on the motives that have been proven to truly drive performance: play (love of the game), purpose, and potential. Athletes driven by these last three have been proven to have higher levels of grit and lower burnout.

assistant in the marketing department just like a player on the team and expects very similar behavior from both. Business employees and players alike have access to top management. Everyone from the boardroom to the locker room feels valued and goes in the same direction.

Lastly, Carlos and the management team drastically deviated from convention in one more way. Conventionally, players receive all revenue from their image rights. But at Real Madrid, unlike most teams, players personally benefited from the club's investment in community engagement, identity, and brand. Real Madrid management believed the club, then, should receive a return on the investments benefiting the players. To do so, the club standardized the players' contracts by putting in a provision for the club to receive 50 percent of the players' image-rights fees. The club required fee sharing for all players, regardless of popularity. As can be imagined, the requirement initially shocked the best players, but the club would not budge for anyone. As a result, the club now has a vested interest in helping market each player's image. So, if a player receives a $10 million sponsorship deal while signed with Real Madrid, the club receives $5 million. The management team demonstrated that by being a part of Real Madrid, players would often receive more lucrative sponsorship offers and more of those offers. The data implied that, because of Real Madrid's strong following, starting players typically receive 200 to 300 percent more in sponsorship revenue. For players who do not regularly start, Real Madrid's brand increased sponsorship revenue by, in some cases, more than 500 percent. Some sponsor contracts actually stipulate that if the player were to no longer be on Real Madrid's team, the sponsorship amount paid to the player would be less. The players have learned that the arrangement with the club is value-added to them. In addition, with Real Madrid controlling the marketing, the club is better able to oversee the quality and consistency of sponsors as well as ensure that the marketing obligations don't distract the players from their training, playing, and winning.

Captains Appointed by Seniority

Real Madrid has a captain and a vice-captain. They appoint team captains according to seniority, not by election. The captain and vice-captain have played the most and second-most years at Real Madrid, respectively. Most, if not all, teams in the US—unlike Real Madrid—elect their captains through player votes, which can sometimes turn into popularity contests, or the head coach appoints them. Real Madrid's approach differs from some other teams in La Liga as well. For example, the members of Barcelona's first-team squad elect their captains.

Real Madrid believes that a captain with seniority and considerable experience on the field garners credibility from both players and management. Real Madrid's approach also ensures that the team captain has been around long enough to have absorbed Real Madrid's history, tradition, rituals, and values, and is able to model them on and off the field. When I questioned whether this approach could lead to a mediocre (by Real Madrid standards) talent becoming captain and jeopardizing his ability to lead a superstar, Real Madrid responded that, essentially, if a player has been at the club that long, then he must be an exceptional talent, and if he could survive the intense competition, scrutiny, and pressure for that long, he has everyone's categorical respect and admiration.

Homegrown Talent

Real Madrid's youth academy houses, educates, and develops promising players starting at age seven. The fourteen teams that make up the academy range from under-10s to Real Madrid Castilla, the second team right under the first, main team. In 2014, seven teams won their respective championship and three were runners-up. The youngest team (consisting of under-ten-year olds) is called Prebenjamín, and for these kids, the academy is mostly about educating players, academically, athletically, and technically. At the academy, players don't just learn about soccer, they learn about life and values. Players face intense competition to advance through the teams. Players live at the youth academy an average of three years.

Approximately 300 players are enrolled in the academy, including four of Zidane's sons. The cost to have a player board and attend the academic school is around €35–40,000 annually; this excludes the costs of soccer training and running the facility. Ideally, players get developed into starters on the first team, saving the club millions of euros in transfer fees. Even if a player cannot make the first team, Real Madrid can sell the developed player to another team to recoup its investment. However, the main target of the academy is not financial; it is seen as a crucial part of the club fulfilling the values and expectations of the community members.

Since 2000, typically around five to eight of the twenty-two to twenty-five players (around 25 percent) on Real Madrid's first team were developed by the club's own academy. During Bernabéu's Galácticos 1.0 era between 1955–60, the rate of academy graduates on the team was around 10 to 15 percent. Real Madrid executives believe that for cultural reasons the percentage needs to be higher today.

Table 7.1: Number and Percentage of Academy Players in the First Team (2001–15)[96]

Year	# of Academy Players	Total # of Players	% of Academy Players
2000–01	5	25	20%
2001–02	6	22	27%
2002–03	8	22	36%
2003–04	12	25	48%
2004–05	8	22	36%
2005–06	8	23	35%
2006–07	8	24	33%
2007–08	7	25	28%
2008–09	7	25	28%
2009–10	4	22	18%
2010–11	6	24	25%
2011–12	5	23	22%
2012–13	5	22	23%
2013–14	9	23	39%
2014–15	7	23	30%
2015–16	7	21	33%

[96] The maximum number of players registered in the first team is twenty-five. However, the Spanish Football Federation authorizes players registered in the teams of the academy to play with the first team in both League and King's Cup games, if they are under twenty-three years old. The same applies for UEFA Champions League if those players have been in the Real Madrid Academy teams at least the previous two years. The table shows just the players registered in the first team, both from academy and total number. The total number is therefore always equal to or below twenty-five. However, in every season of the table, there were more players from the academy that occasionally played in the first team in the three competitions.

Academy graduates on the first team—having grown up with Real Madrid's values and mission—reinforce the club's values. Their presence alongside imported star players yields the greatest benefits. Homegrown talent Raúl and record-breaking transfer Figo, for example, formed an incredible bond both on and off the field that helped embody and perpetuate community values.

Like the experienced captains who know and exemplify what Real Madrid means, the academy players promote the values that unify the club, set examples, and create the right atmosphere to achieve the club's goals and mission. Members and supporters very much like to see academy players on the first team and especially as starters. It creates a sense of pride, enhancing the passion of the fans. This was part of the special allure of the legendary *Quinta del Buitre* in the 1980s and the community's love for Raúl.

Homegrown talent helps fuel the passion.[97] According to Florentino, "The world-class players we have signed have increased our prestige in world football, but we will combine them with our own players from Real Madrid in what can be an explosive mix."[98] Academy players embody the stated values. In an interview, Florentino explained: "Real Madrid constantly devotes a great deal of effort to the instilling of values. This involves channeling the necessary attention and resources into the youth clubs and nurturing not only the sporting development of its youth players but also their social, ethical, and civic education."

Inspiring Passion and Loyalty

In many ways, the mission of Real Madrid is to nurture and project the Real Madrid values and brand around the world. The management team believes the brand value drivers are:

- Size and characteristics of the community/audience;
- Frequency with which the community/audience is engaged with the brand;

---

[97] The unheralded success of Real Madrid's academy in comparison to Barcelona's is discussed in chapter eleven, "*El Clásico*—Real Madrid vs. Barcelona."

[98] "Perez works a quiet revolution at Real Madrid." *Rediff*. http://www.rediff.com/sports/2001/oct/17foot1.htm.

- Bridges to link the identity of the brand with the community/audience.

With values universal to a wide fan base of different ages, incomes, and geographies, Real Madrid's continues to grow globally. The key is giving its positive message as often as possible not only to its fanatics and loyalists but also to casual, social viewers. Real Madrid is very successful in getting star-struck spectators (followers of a superstar rather than a team) to transfer their fanaticism to the team before the star retires or moves to another team. Real Madrid aims to fill a part of the everyday lives of its community (part of the fabric of life), so the club's continuous engagement through content, events, and traditions is very important.

"We" Won

The Ballon d'Or is an individual award presented to the best soccer player in the world. For the Real Madrid community it means more. I experienced this in person during Cristiano Ronaldo's first home game after winning the Ballon d'Or in January 2015. I happened to be at the game at Bernabéu Stadium the week I was teaching my course in Madrid. When I arrived at my seat, waiting for me, as for every other spectator, was a gold foil sheet. When Ronaldo was introduced and lifted the gold trophy above his head, everyone in the stands held up their gold foil sheet high above their heads as if they were lifting the gold trophy together with him. All of the community members in the seats were united, participating, experiencing, and belonging. Even a casual fan would feel out of place if he or she didn't lift the foil. Everyone is engaged and part of the fun. The atmosphere was electric, the crowd deploying a golden mosaic that set the atmosphere for the clash before the players had even shaken hands. With Ronaldo lifting the trophy and the fans holding up the gold foil, the crowd launched into Real Madrid's "La Décima" song—singing is a common ritual and tradition.[99] Florentino commissioned the special

---

[99] During halftime and before games, the "Hala Madrid" anthem is played at Bernabéu. In 2002, on the 100-year anniversary of the club, a new anthem, "Himno del Centenario" ("Hymn for the Centenary"), was created and performed by Placido Domingo, who is also a Madridista.

song to be written to celebrate Real Madrid's Décima,[100] just like how Bernabéu commissioned the "Hala Madrid" anthem in the 1950s. The entire team sang when the song was recorded, and its music video of the players recording the song went viral. It was meant to be simple and easy to remember so that fans could quickly learn to sing it to support the club.

Similarly, fans felt part of Real Madrid's victory at the Copa del Rey. I happened to watch the final on TV in April 2014 when Real Madrid beat Barcelona 2–1. Real Madrid's top scorer of the season, Cristiano Ronaldo, missed the final due to knee and thigh injuries. The winning goal came with five minutes to go when Gareth Bale picked up the ball just inside his own half on the left wing, kicked it down field, unbelievably sprinted around the Barcelona center-back by going several yards out of bounds, caught up with the ball, kept control of the ball while running at incredible speed, and slotted a left-footed goal past the goalie. It was one of the most remarkable displays of strength, determination, speed, skill, and finishing in a pressured game and situation. After the game, the TV broadcast showed Plaza de Cibeles, the focal point for celebrations of Real Madrid. Thousands of fans had gathered at the Cibeles Fountain, an iconic Madrid landmark depicting the Roman goddess sitting on a chariot pulled by two lions, on the square in central Madrid immediately after the final. Supporters were chanting, "*Campeones, campeones!*" ("Champions, champions!"). Real Madrid scarves and jerseys filled the square with color, and the crowd sung to celebrate: "*Así, así, así gana el Madrid,*" ("Like that, like that, like that, Madrid wins") and "*Sí, sí, sí, la Copa ya está aquí*" ("Yes, yes, yes, the Cup is here").

One of my Madridista friends called me at around four or five in the morning Madrid time when the team appeared on an open-top white bus with the slogan "Campeones Copa del Rey." I could hear him screaming "We won" over the lively clapping, dancing, singing, and music. His identity is the team's identity. To him, the club winning is equivalent to his own victory.

---

[100] Composed by RedOne, with lyrics by Manuel Jabois, the song is called "Hala Madrid y Nada Más" ("Hala Madrid, Nothing More"). Florentino said, "It's going to be a song that forms part of Real Madrid's history."

Real Madrid players and Zidane (then assistant coach) in the locker room celebrating the 2014 Copa del Rey victory over Barcelona 2-1. Gareth Bale scored a magical late game winner.

Florentino recognized and leveraged the unifying power and strategic potential of rituals and traditions like wearing the club color on game day, singing marches and chanting slogans, or celebrating victories at Cibeles Fountain. Although many believe Florentino builds the brand or makes the decisions, the community members are, in fact, the coproducers, who advocate and evangelize the brand to their network. Florentino said:

> As the president of Real Madrid I have a priority: that you continue to be the only people in charge of the club's future. Because your wishes for the future are legitimate and sacred. Real Madrid will be what its members continue to want it to be. You are the only leaders and nobody else.[101]

---

[101] Florentino Pérez, "The Board of Directors is going to propose Francisco Gento as honorary president of Real Madrid." *Realmadrid.com*. http://www.realmadrid.com/en/news/2015/12/florentino-perez-the-board-of-directors-is-going-to-propose-francisco-gento-as-honorary-president-of-real-madrid.

Complementing traditions and rituals is a strong sense of winning championships with values (winning with class) with some of the best (and most inspirational) players in the world. Aligning this sense of community as a strategy, identity, and brand impacts consumer behavior patterns such as attendance, media consumption, merchandizing sales, and loyalty. These community members will fill the stadium, shop at the Real Madrid Adidas stores, drive cars made by Real Madrid sponsor Audi, and use Real Madrid sponsor Samsung's Galaxy phones—hence, the sustainable economic-sport model.

Real Madrid's car sponsor, Audi, exemplifies this alignment. Audi is a classy, distinctive, and aspirational brand. In John Carlin's book *White Angels: Beckham, the Real Madrid and the New Football* (Bloomsbury USA, 2004), he quotes an Audi executive: "Real Madrid represents values we ourselves identify with. The idea of being the leader, the best, plus that unique sense of style. To be a Real Madrid fan or to own an Audi car is to show discernment, class. That is why we pay Real Madrid good money: to make that identification between them and us explicit." (The amusing thing to me is that this epiphany came in part from civil engineers, known for building structures and products, not communities, brands, or a sense of belonging!)

Embracing Rivalries

Real Madrid smartly embraces the rivalries that make the community. Although organizations typically prefer to avoid conflict, Real Madrid's management team respectfully accepts and embraces the rivalries common in a thriving community.[102] Communities need a way to define themselves that fosters unity and cohesiveness. Conflicts and rivalries provide just that. For example, just as Microsoft or Harley-Davidson enthusiasts may show disdain for certain competing technologies or motorcycles, Real Madrid fans and members express disfavor for Barcelona and/or Atlético Madrid. An "us vs. them" or "insider vs. outsider" mentality serves to hold a community together and helps transmit their values to the next generation. Real Madrid's management team is extremely sensitive to ensuring that the mentality is respectful, in keeping with

---

[102] Fournier and Lee, "Getting Brand Communities Right."

the values. For example, although there is a big buildup of the Real Madrid–Barcelona rivalry, both clubs' executives show good relations and respect. By tradition, the Real Madrid and Barcelona directors eat together before their clubs play against each other in their regular season games.

For all the passionate rivalry between the two clubs, Real Madrid's community will show respect that rises above the rivalry. In 2005, Ronaldinho, a star player for Barcelona, scored two magnificent goals in a 3–0 defeat of home team Real Madrid at Bernabéu Stadium. Many Real Madrid fans gave the opposing star a standing ovation. The same happened for Barcelona's Andres Iniesta in 2015 when Barcelona beat Real Madrid at Bernabéu Stadium. The community of Real Madrid respects beautiful, stylish soccer and effort, even if it is from the opposing team.

Interestingly, the socios have a formal process to self-regulate in case any members are not following club rules, including misbehavior during rival games. The club has a Disciplinary Committee in accordance with its bylaws to discipline members who are not following the rules. Usually the issue is related to resale and misuse of season passes and game tickets, but discipline is also handed out for breaking club rules related to respect, violence, racism, xenophobia, and intolerance in sport. The five members of the Disciplinary Committee are elected every four years by the General Assembly at the proposal of the board of directors.

A Place of Worship

When Florentino became the president of Real Madrid, he launched a "master plan" to improve the comfort of Santiago Bernabéu Stadium, sometimes referred to by supporters as "the White House," and the quality of its facilities. He wanted to make Bernabéu Stadium into a cathedral for community members to be proud to watch their team; he wanted it to reflect their high standards. He recognized that for many fans, this was their personal interaction with the team. Also, with socios occupying the majority of the seats, Florentino thought that they should feel like they are going to a special place that they are proud of because the stadium represented them. He was convinced that this attention to them would maximize revenues from the stadium. Real Madrid has the advantage of owning their stadium, and it is located in the center of Madrid where there are economic opportunities for shops and restaurants to be used during regular days. It is easy for tourists and fans to get to.

Real Madrid invested €129 million ($154 million) in five years (2001–06) by adding an expansion to the east side of the stadium, as well as adding a new façade on Padre Damián street, new boxes and VIP areas, a new press area (also located on the east side), a new audio system, new bars, integration of heating in the stands, panoramic lifts, new restaurants, escalators in the tower access, and implementation of a new multipurpose building.

In 2003, Real Madrid opened the Real Madrid Museum and stadium tour. A tangible sense of history and tradition is evoked from the hundreds of polished, sparkling trophies and an array of documents, plaques, photos, jerseys, balls, and cleats. Real Madrid Museum is literally a treasure chest and is often credited with being the second most-visited tourist site in Madrid after the Prado Museum.[103] More than 60 percent of visitors to Bernabéu Stadium are from outside Spain, mainly the UK, France, Germany, US, Japan, United Arab Emirates, China, and Brazil.

I have been to many "stadium museums and tours," which are essentially collections of sports memorabilia such as trophies and jerseys in glass cases. I have never seen anything like this. The museum space is hard to describe because, besides displaying the most important trophies won in Real Madrid's history, it is technologically advanced in its use of digital screens, video, images, audio, and interactive technology. In the museum, you can point, click, and drag images and videos on screens. In the background, you can hear the sounds from exciting games, and wherever you look, you see the colors or crest of the club. Utilizing the physical space of the stadium and museum builds webs of interpersonal connections and evokes passions. As museum visitors see and listen to the inscriptions and videos, they reflect on the stories and people behind those stories. People who meet at the stadium or museum soon find themselves comparing and pointing to favorites, and before long they're engaged in conversation and storytelling. Visitors find a powerful force and strength in community together. The museum and the shared stories

---

[103] In the 2013–14 season, approximately 1.2 million and 2.2 million people paid for a tour of the stadium and attended a game at the stadium, respectively.

ensure that the players and history are not forgotten. The images, colors, and sounds evoke memories of not only the players and club but also the community, to continue to make it more powerful and purposeful.

The 1.5-hour, nonguided tour includes a panoramic view of the stadium, "Best Club in History" room, "sensations" room, photomontage room, the field, the presidential box, the Real Madrid locker room, the tunnel and dugouts the players use, the press room, and the official store. The sheer beauty and size of the stadium captivates visitors. Fans will feel it is a special place that can create an intimidating and intense atmosphere for visiting teams. The entire tour is organized to maximize photo opportunities. The attention to cleanliness is remarkable. On the tour visitors will see the impressive sight of eleven replica Champions League trophies lined up in a row. Also, visitors will see the relatively spartan locker room where every locker, regardless of a star's status, is exactly the same size and in numerical order. Visitors can sit on the same leather sports car "racing seat" bench on the field as the players do for the games. When visitors look up from the bench it is hard not to be overawed because the stadium seems to just keep going up and up. Visitors will also see how meticulous the club is about the field, which is essentially the "altar" of the cathedral. No one on the tour is allowed inside the lines on the grass. Even while giving me a tour, Carlos, a senior executive, wouldn't dare step inside the lines.

Mini-Communities

Real Madrid invests significant energy and resources in helping community members start and support official fan clubs. It has 2,311 official fan clubs spread throughout the world, the greatest number of official fan clubs of any sports franchise. There are 153 official fan clubs registered abroad, with Switzerland boasting the highest number with fifteen, US with twelve, Morocco with ten, and Belgium with eight. Supporters join to be brought together by the same feeling, the same passion, and the same source of pride: being a Real Madrid fan.

Official supporters clubs must have a minimum of fifty people and a headquarters to host meetings. Each fan club is registered and even has its own distinctive name. These fans attend or watch games together. In support, Real Madrid gives them discounts on games or merchandise. At every game played outside Madrid, Real Madrid organizes player auto-graph sessions and invites local members and supporters clubs. Also, senior management, including Florentino, Pedro, and Emilio, meet with fan clubs on club road trips, typically at the hotel the club is staying, to get feedback from the community.

In 1920, fans at a bar in Madrid created Real Madrid's oldest fan club where they would listen to games on the radio. Even with TVs, technology, and social media, the members still meet up at least once a month to chat about the team, celebrate the club's birthday, and raise money for charity. In an interview, the president of that fan club said, "Whilst I am alive, we will be here serving and supporting Real Madrid. When I can no longer be in charge, my son will take over. He is another lifelong Real Madrid sup-porter." Another member added, "Passion and devotion for Real Madrid are passed down like an heirloom." Real Madrid believes these fan clubs are an important part of the fabric in binding the community.

Lastly, Real Madrid celebrates long-time community members. Each year Real Madrid holds a ceremony and presents special insignias to those reaching membership milestones of twenty-five, fifty, and sixty years. In 2014, the club presented 1,512 insignias. Members of the Real Madrid 100 Club, comprised of the 100 most senior members, receive personalized service and special privileges, in appreciation of their loy-alty and service.

Technology/Social Media

José Ángel Sánchez's experience with cutting-edge game technology at Sega empowered him to embrace and experiment with new technology to send information to members, enrich their experiences, and connect. Whether using mobile technology or digital broadcasting technology, Real Madrid thinks about how to deliver more "content" to the com-munity members, whether that is news, video highlights, injury updates, statistics and analysis, or messages from players. For the global club, technology and social media provide the fastest and most scalable ways to connect to their community.[104]

---

[104] Technology, including the Microsoft partnership and the Real Madrid App, is discussed in "Digital Ecosystem Transformation" in chapter twelve.

Color and Sound

Watching or attending a game, people are surrounded in an arousing and intense stimulation of color and sound. The sensation of watching Real Madrid's beautiful attacking style of action is framed by bright visuals and high-fidelity audio. Colorful flags of white, blue, and purple are waving; scarves in team colors are being worn and raised by fans; large banner flags with messages or images are pulled over a section of fans; banners hang from rafters; rhythmic clapping and chanting reverberate throughout. All of this and more add to fans' experiences and active participation. If the play on the field is like a movie, the anthems, chanting, and clapping act as a soundtrack, adding to the emotion and feeling. From the games to the tour, there is an ever-present sense of color and sound. The club focuses on club anthems to create a common identity among members. It is a source of pride and cultural significance for members and creates allegiance and loyalty to Real Madrid, like a country. The songs provide a link and serve as a reminder of significant games. The stadium, the color, and the sounds are firmly entrenched as defining links between Real Madrid and their community.

Media/Publications

Keeping in mind Real Madrid's main objectives such as worldwide reach and closeness with the fans, the club utilizes the official media outlets in order to provide the latest and most important information. Along with this information, Real Madrid tries to provide appropriate access to the players, initiate ideas for stories, and develop content around the world in order to keep Real Madrid topical and relevant. In 2015, the club processed 14,000 press credentials, and the club's soccer and basketball players appeared in more than 1,700 interviews and press conferences. The media caters to an insatiable appetite for coverage of Real Madrid. The local daily papers, in particular *Marca* and *AS*, dedicate pages and pages to Real Madrid every day. Typically, these papers publish close to a half a dozen pages on the team every single day, but in all honesty, no sports team—in any field, be it soccer, baseball, basketball, and so on—creates that much news on a daily basis. But with papers to move and readers to attract, actual news is bulked up with stories based on unsubstantiated rumors and unnamed sources. To feed the frenzy, crises are crafted and sold in the papers. It must be totally and utterly mentally exhausting for the executives and players to be trapped in the ebbs and flows of the turmoil of manufactured drama. Training is open to the press for fifteen minutes the day prior to any game, and to the general public one day per year, so it is not just a case of being judged on the day of a game. If a player underperforms in a few training sessions, he is just as likely to be the subject of criticism.[105] The pressure and scrutiny is extraordinarily intense because the community passion is, too. The attention itself keeps people talking about the club and feeds the appetite of the community and attracts the awareness of potential members.

Real Madrid has thirteen publications with different formats, which are published throughout the year. Its leading publication, Hala Madrid, has an annual circulation of 824,000. The editions provide club members (as well as official supporters and other magazine subscribers) with images of the club's success. In 2014–15, each edition included a special gift consisting of a commemorative poster of each title won. The children and young people's edition, Hala Madrid Junior, has an annual circulation of 200,000 copies sent to fans between seven and fourteen years of age.

Other quarterly publications include the newsletters Hala Madrid online and eMadridistas, which the club sent to 342,921 users in Spanish and English. Two publications play a key role in the games played by Real Madrid at the Santiago Bernabéu: Grada Blanca and the Press Kit. Grada Blanca is distributed throughout the stadium (30,000 copies) and the Press Kit is provided to all the professionals covering the game.

More Than Soccer

Real Madrid's community members expect the club to be about more than just winning trophies; they expect the club to give back to their global community. The Real Madrid Foundation was created in 1997 to

---

[105] Michael Owen, "Champions League final 2014: Real Madrid ruled by Europe so they dare not lose to Atletico Madrid." Telegraph. http://www.telegraph.co.uk/sport/columnists/michael-owen/10852545/Champions-League-final-2014-Real-Madrid-ruled-by-Europe-so-they-dare-not-lose-to-Atletico-Madrid.html.

promote the club's values through sport and education, teaching children human values such as commitment, responsibility, and teamwork, which will be central to their success in their future lives. The foundation spreads Real Madrid's values to children around the world.

The executives at Real Madrid are following what the community emphasizes and expects: give back to society by assisting the most vulnerable people, at-risk children and youngsters living in precarious conditions or exposed to violence, poverty, drugs, and crime. The organization runs regular sports camps for children around Spain, while also working in prisons and hospitals, and with immigrants and individuals with physical or learning difficulties. Florentino told attendees of the club's annual general meeting in September 2015 that the club currently operates 388 projects in 69 countries, which help more than 60,000 people on five continents.

Funding for the projects comes from the club, including the proceeds from "legend" games featuring former Madrid stars such as Butragueño and Zidane. Corporate partnerships are also a major source of the foundation's resources. For example, Microsoft has provided computer software worth a reported $1.38 million in conjunction with the Real Madrid Foundation as an initiative to reach 20,000 children in Argentina, Brazil, Colombia, Ecuador, and Mexico.

While skeptics might say that the club's budget for development-type activities is not too significant when put beside the multimillion euro salaries paid to their star players, Real Madrid management prefers to focus on the positive influence that the foundation can bring to the lives of those they help while meeting the expectations of their community members.

Game Day for Real Madrid

The coaches of Real Madrid typically speak to the team in Spanish, which is what they also use in the locker rooms, but when one player talks privately with another player of the same nationality or native language, the two typically speak their common language. Most of the players speak several languages, including English, but on the field during the game they communicate mostly in Spanish. Just over 50 percent of the team members over the last few years were born in Spain; this is due in part to the high percentage of academy players.

The day before a home game, the players leave their cars at the Bernabéu Stadium, and together they go by bus to the residence of players at Ciudad Deportiva Real Madrid training facility near the airport. On game day they come to the stadium by bus and at the end of the game they go home in their cars. Real Madrid TV[106] records the departure and arrival to the stadium, images that do not harm the privacy of the players.

The media is not allowed in the locker room after games, unlike with most North American sports. All players must exit Bernabéu Stadium to get to their cars in a private underground parking lot through Zona Mixta (mixed zone), where they meet the media. The club's rules make it mandatory for all players to go through the Zona Mixta, but they are not required to talk to the media.[107] Players don't have to stop if they don't want to. The mixed zone has sponsors' logos on the walls, so if pictures are taken, the logos are present.

After La Liga games, one player on the field meets a TV reporter representing the TV network that holds transmission rights.[108] Another player, or sometimes two players, in the zone before Zona Mixta, meets with four TV reporters, representing the four TV networks that hold transmission rights. Two players meet with all TV reporters in the Zona Mixta. The coach attends all media in the pressroom. Finally, the spokesman of the club meets a TV reporter representing the TV network that holds transmission rights in the presidential box. The club can provide whichever players and representatives of the club they would like but are sensitive to providing the personnel that the media requests.

Almost as soon as the game is over, data analysts, technical staff, and coaches start to analyze data for evaluation of strategies and players, to make midseason adjustments, and pregame preparation for the next game.

---

[106] Real Madrid has a TV channel called Real Madrid TV, which broadcasts anything related to Real Madrid, including interviews, training, group activities, old matches, etc., except for the matches whose TV rights are the property of UEFA and La Liga. These matches are broadcast after a certain period of time from when they are played.

[107] In UEFA games, only the players who participated in the game are required to speak.

[108] Presently there are two TV networks (Movistar Plus and Vodafone/Orange) that hold the live TV rights in Spain for La Liga, and two TV networks (Antena 3 and beIN Sports) for the UEFA Champions League. One operator broadcasts some matches, and the other broadcasts the rest. The same applies for UEFA Champion League games.

Not All about the Numbers: Real Madrid Basketball

Real Madrid is, effectively, a not-for-profit social trust. Florentino and his management team know that they need to make money on a sustainable basis to meet the values and expectations of the community members, which include signing the best players in the world. Florentino and his team are highly efficient in allocating resources, tracking data and performance, and holding everyone accountable. But they also satisfy their community members as it relates to basketball.

As mentioned earlier, the club also owns a basketball team. The basketball team was added in 1931 and has won a record twenty-five Spanish Cup championships and an unprecedented nine Euroleague championships (a tournament of the best professional basketball teams from each European country's premier league).[109] Real Madrid's basketball team has an incredible legacy of championships, but when reviewing the financial information, it becomes obvious that the basketball team actually loses money.

The club receives approximately €10 million ($11 million) in revenues related to the basketball team (ticketing: €3.6 million, broadcasting: €1.4 million, marketing: €5 million). However, the direct costs for the €10 million in revenues are around €31 million ($34 million), primarily because of the costs of the players. The television revenues suffer because NBA basketball is available now on pay TV in Spain and the rest of Europe; and many European basketball fans, instead of solely watching European teams, are increasingly watching many of the best stars and teams that compete in the NBA.[110]

Basketball teams supported by billionaires are willing to pay whatever it takes for talent and there are no financial responsibility or fair play regulations in basketball. The players cost too much relative to the revenues their content creates. Economically, it does not make sense to

---

[109] Real Madrid's 2014–15 basketball season was the best in European history. The team won all four possible titles, including its ninth European title. The basketball team also has an academy ranging from under-14s to EBA (the team under the first team). Real Madrid's basketball academy won the under-18, under-16, and under-14 Spanish championships in 2014–15. Real Madrid players who moved to the NBA and were inducted into the Naismith Memorial Basketball Hall of Fame include Arvydas Sabonis (Portland Trailblazers) and Dražen Petrovi (Portland Trailblazers, New Jersey Nets).

[110] Major League Soccer in North America faces the same challenges because American pay TV offers European league games, such as the English Premier League and La Liga.

have a basketball team. But Real Madrid is a club and the community wants Real Madrid to have a championship-level basketball team.

Community Brands and Identity in American Sports

When Florentino described his ambition that Real Madrid so closely reflect the values and expectations of the community members that it would be difficult to see the line between the identity and life of the community members and the club, I thought of the NFL's Pittsburgh Steelers' notoriously hardworking, hardnosed, blue-collar front four defensive line in the 1970s, nicknamed "The Steel Curtain," reflecting and taking on the identity of the hardworking steelworkers of Pittsburgh. The players identified with the town and the town identified with them, and the town loved it. The Steel Curtain analogy continued to ring true to me because so many people, within Pittsburgh and beyond, identified with being hardworking, hardnosed, and blue collar that the Steelers developed a national following. As Pittsburgh has lost its steel mills, their clear brand image has drifted in some ways. However, the work ethic of the team led by tough, hardworking, and respected coaches, and more importantly the work ethic of the city, still hits home with a lot of fans around the country. They have won the most Super Bowls of any team and win consistently. They are still very popular nationally but, perhaps, in a different way and context than they were in the 1970s. I am not commenting on the culture or values of the team or if the difference is for the better or worse, simply that there was an identity built on a community. This may or may not have been a conscious strategy, and the same for the other examples below.

The Dallas Cowboys created a national following by positioning themselves as "America's Team" with the help of a key player and a blue star as its logo. The Cowboys had a star quarterback, Roger Staubach, aptly nicknamed "Captain America" from 1969–79. He epitomized the importance of the players fitting with, reflecting, and supporting the values and expectations of the community or fans. He attended the US Naval Academy where he won a Heisman Trophy as the best college football player, and after graduation he served in the US Navy, including a tour of duty in Vietnam. He led the Cowboys to two Super Bowl victories and was named Most Valuable Player of Super Bowl VI, becoming the first of four players to win both the Heisman

Trophy and Super Bowl MVP. The community and following of the Cowboys went beyond Dallas or Texas; it was national, as many people identified with what Staubach and his Dallas Cowboys represented—an American ideal. Just like how the elite scorer Cristiano Ronaldo follows Di Stéfano's legacy, every quarterback for the Dallas Cowboys, such as Troy Aikman, follows Staubach's legacy. Just as there is an epic rivalry between Real Madrid and Barcelona, the Cowboys have a rivalry with the Steelers.

Community values can also embrace the values of an owner. Think of the late maverick owner, Al Davis, of the NFL's three-time Super Bowl–winning Oakland Raiders with his "Just win, baby" motto. In many ways, the Raiders' culture and values are a stark contrast to Real Madrid's "champions and gentlemen" and stem from the values of an owner rather than a community, but they are just as distinctive and highly successful. Interestingly, similar to Bernabéu who helped create the Champions League, Davis helped make the Super Bowl what it is. In addition, like Real Madrid, Steelers, and Cowboys, the Raiders' values and expectations resulted in lots of championships. Different from Real Madrid, Davis took players who were perceived as rebels, misfits, and outcasts who thumbed their noses at convention. Many of the players would not be welcomed on most NFL teams. Players on the Raiders relished bone-crushing hits, clothesline tackles, and knocking their opponents out of games. While they might have been a wild, fun-loving bunch, they worked hard and played to win, and the Raiders' fan base loved them. The Raiders' black-and-silver uniforms and pirate-like logo reflected an outlaw image. Davis created a counterculture image for his franchise that to this day is still among the most recognizable in all of sport. The team didn't appeal only to a local fan base but to a national "Raider Nation" that identified with Davis's/the team's values and culture (Davis and the team seemed inseparable) and bought lots of black-and-silver Raider merchandise. The nickname "Raider Nation" refers to die-hard fans of the team who attend home games, arriving at the stadium early and dressing up in facemasks and black outfits.

Another thing worth mentioning: the Packers, Steelers, and Raiders each have had one controlling ownership of family/shareholders essentially from the beginning. I believe that consistency of ownership can help the consistency in the values and culture needed to develop a community.

After writing the passages above, I looked up the top jersey sales in the NFL. I wasn't terribly surprised by what I found. According to the NFL, in 2015 the four top-selling team jerseys in order are: 1) Green Bay, 2) Pittsburgh, 3) Oakland, and 4) Dallas. Green Bay is the definition of a small-market team and has the smallest "local" community, but it consistently dominates NFL jersey sales.

I think jersey sales are a very important metric because they reflect how people think of a team. If people are passionate enough to spend money on something to actually wear, then they are consciously choosing to identify themselves with a team. Fans all over the world show their support for their favorite teams in a variety of ways, including getting tattoos, spending a small fortune on tickets, and buying the top satellite packages to watch all the games. It would be difficult to tally tattoos, which would be a very strong indicator of alignment of identity and brand. People may be willing to go to a game or anonymously watch on TV at home for entertainment. But wearing a team jersey is much more. It says something about the person wearing it, and the person wants others to see him/her wearing it.[111]

Table 7.2: Top-Four Selling NFL Jerseys (2015) by NFL Sales[112]

Rank	Team
1	Green Bay Packers
2	Pittsburgh Steelers
3	Oakland Raiders
4	Dallas Cowboys

Community members own Green Bay, and I believe that many people relate with their unique brand and proposition, similar to Real Madrid. Pittsburgh and Oakland are small-market teams but have unique identities: people have a sense of what they stand for and what wearing the jersey means, which extends their community beyond their local markets.

The glaring omission on the list is the New England Patriots, who have recently dominated in the NFL play-offs and have a large regional following.

---

[111] In US sports, revenue sharing can significantly impact a team's revenues and values. Also, box seats, stadium naming rights, and local TV contracts, which can be outside of revenue sharing, can be significantly impacted by local or regional factors (e.g., media market size, other teams, etc.).

[112] Levi Damien, "Raiders again among NFL's top selling jerseys." *Silver and Black Pride.* http://www.silverandblackpride.com/2015/5/27/8672651/oakland-raiders-again-among-nfls-top-selling-jerseys.

The Patriots have a mission statement: "We are building a big, strong, fast, smart, tough, and disciplined football team that consistently competes for championships." The Patriots have created a culture to achieve their goal. However, for a team that has accomplished so much success on the field and with a marketable star quarterback, it is remarkable that the Patriots have not become "America's Team" and do not have even greater commercial success. I believe part of the issue is that people outside of New England are not willing to overlook the perception of the team playing too close to the line of what is right and wrong (rightly or wrongly portrayed in the media with "2007 Spygate," "2015 Deflategate," or "2015 Headsetgate"). Therefore, people outside of New England are not passionate enough about, or identify enough with, the team to buy as many of their jerseys as one would expect for an organization that consistently wins so much.[113] It seems that winning alone is not enough to generate nationwide passion, loyalty, and identity.

To illustrate my points, I asked one of my classes of graduate students at Columbia University, "What do you think of when you see someone wearing a Real Madrid jersey?" They answered, "History, trophies, class, scoring, great players, and El Clásico." The students knew what the brand and values stood for, how the team plays, mentioned an important rivalry, and didn't associate the team with any geography.

I continued, "Steelers jersey?" They answered, "Tough, hardworking, blue collar, consistent success, and Terrible Towel." Once again, they mentioned a brand and values, a recognition of the way they play, a team symbol, but no geographic association.

Raiders jersey? "Outlaws, Raider Nation, rebels, black and silver, costumes, pirate logo." In this case, they identified a brand, values, colors, and logo associated with the brand, and not only was there no geographic association, there was recognition of a "nation."

Packers jersey? "History, Lombardi, cold, cheese heads, Midwestern values, title town, Lambeau Leap." They understood a brand and specifically mentioned values, a person that embodied the brand, and even a ritual.

Lastly, I asked, "Jacksonville Jaguars jersey?" The answer: "You're from Jacksonville." The students had no understanding of the team's brand or values

---

[113] The 2015 Harris Poll lists the New England Patriots as America's second-favorite team, tied with the Packers, based on polling (http://www.theharrispoll.com/sports/Americas-Favorite-Football-Team-2015.html). However, I believe jersey sales are a strong indicator of the passion, loyalty, and identity of a team.

or the team's style of play, only a geographic association. I don't want to single out Jacksonville; I have gotten the same answer asking about many other NFL teams. The Jaguars' first season in the NFL was 1995 and they have made the play-offs six times since; the Raiders (first season in 1960) and Cowboys (1960) have been to the play-offs three and nine times since 1995, respectively. The Cowboys last won the Super Bowl in 1995. As the examples suggest, it takes time to build a brand, identity, and sense of community values, but also that once developed they can maintain themselves even when the team hasn't won a recent championship. This is important because winning a championship is rare, so it is difficult to rely solely on the result. Organizations make short-term decisions because they feel many pressures (competitive, regulatory, organizational, and technological). Organizations need to understand that staying true to the mission and identity takes time but produces powerful results. In addition, the most an organization can hope for is to create the possible conditions for success.

When I questioned the students, they also identified players who they thought represented the values of each team, such as Raúl, Zidane, and Ronaldo for Real Madrid; Jack Lambert, "Mean Joe" Green, and James Harrison for the Steelers; Jack "The Assassin" Tatum and Gene Upshaw for the Raiders; and Aaron Rodgers, Reggie White, and Brett Favre for the Packers. It indicates that perceived values of the players help define the values of the team. Sadly, no one could name any Jacksonville players (I mentioned Mark Brunell and Fred Taylor).

Surprisingly, the Cowboys were the number four jersey-selling team in the NFL, lower than expected. I have a hypothesis about this. The Dallas Cowboys have been exceptional in maintaining such a prestigious image of being "America's team," have a big "star" on their helmet (since grade-school teachers put stars on the best test results, who doesn't want a star?) and are known as "champions." It is incredibly important for the Cowboys to continue to promote and emphasize this image because it gives them a much wider fan base than Dallas or Texas. Fans who identify and buy into the image live across America and even internationally. However, this can be risky in two ways. One is to lose. The last time the Dallas Cowboys won the Super Bowl was 1995. And it is not due to a lack of resources or support or competitiveness from its highly respected owner, Jerry Jones. Even not winning a Super Bowl in twenty years, the team's valuation and revenues are the highest in the NFL and keep growing, but that also has something to do with the team's local and regional community and market and stadium.[114] More importantly than not winning, when winning is a part of the brand identity,[115] the second threat is that players and coaches do not live up to the core brand and identity. Players like Roger Staubach help define the Cowboy's brand, identity, and values. A few personnel mistakes could confuse or tarnish the values and brand identity, which over the long term can have negative effects. In 2015, the Cowboys drafted a "high-risk/high-reward" prospect who fell from being a projected top-ten pick to sixtieth overall in the NFL draft. Also in 2015, the Cowboys signed an incredibly talented player who had received numerous game suspensions due in part to domestic violence accusations that included guns (the criminal charges were dropped due to a lack of cooperation of the accuser in the investigation). The rationalization that "if you're a good enough player, no one cares what kind of person you are" could put the Cowboys brand image and identity at risk and alienate community members and/or sponsors over the long term.[116] It may be one reason why Dallas doesn't lead the NFL in jersey sales.[117]

There are a few NBA examples of championship teams and their styles reflecting their communities. The Detroit "Bad Boy" Pistons in the late 1980s/ early 1990s played a style that reflected the tough, no-nonsense community going through a recession. And to overcome the challenges of Michael Jordan and his Chicago Bulls in the play-offs, the team came up with a defensive system called "the Jordan Rules."[118] The Los Angeles "Showtime" Lakers in

---

[114] Even if winning championships is a part of the values and culture, not winning a championship for a period of time does not necessarily negatively impact the community. While winning is a part of their brand and image, the Oakland Raiders have not won the Super Bowl since 1983, and their jersey sales still are among the leaders.

[115] Trophies and winning don't necessarily have to be a part of the identity to inspire a passionate and loyal community. The Chicago Cubs have an incredible community, and, unfortunately, have not won a World Series since 1908.

[116] Michael David Smith, "Michael Irvin on Greg Hardy: I don't mean to be insensitive, but he's too good not to sign." NBC Sports: Pro Football Talk. http://profootballtalk.nbcsports.com/2015/10/13/michael-irvin-on-greg-hardy-i-dont-mean-to-be-insensitive-but-hes-too-good-not-to-sign/.

[117] The 2015 Harris Poll lists the Dallas Cowboys as America's favorite team based on polling (http://www.theharrispoll.com/sports/Americas-Favorite-Football-Team-2015.html). However, I believe jersey sales are a strong indicator of the passion, loyalty, and identity of a team.

[118] The Jordan Rules were a defensive strategy employed by the Detroit Pistons against Michael Jordan in 1988 in order to limit his effectiveness on offense. The Pistons' strategy resulted in physically challenging Jordan to throw him off balance. In a May 2007 interview with Sports Illustrated, then Detroit Pistons coach Chuck Daly described the Jordan Rules as: "If Michael was at the point, we forced him left and doubled him. If he was on the left wing, we went immediately to a double team from the top. If he was on the right wing, we went to a slow double team. He could hurt you equally from either wing—hell, he could hurt you from the hot-dog stand—but we just

the 1980s played an exciting and entertaining run-and-gun style of basketball that reflected its Hollywood-celebrity community. The most important component of the Lakers' Showtime offensive system was quick outlet passes and the fast break. Both teams embraced bitter rivalries that helped define and increase the passion and loyalty of their respective communities.

In this book I consciously stay away from examples from American collegiate sports primarily because of the differences in ownership structure and the management of student athletes versus professional players. There are many good examples where a college team's values and playing style reflect the values and identities of its supporting community (also there are rivalries to help define the community). It is not surprising because in many ways college team communities, including the students, alumni, and local town, "own" the college sports teams and have deep ties and shared experiences.

The Cardinal Way

The St. Louis Cardinals have become one of baseball's model franchises on and off the field. Since 2000, on the field, the Cardinals have won two World Series titles (only the Red Sox and Giants have won more, each with three), four pennants (which ties for the most with the Yankees and Giants), and qualified for the postseason twelve times (only the Yankees have more). They have won even while being economically responsible. The team's 2014 payroll was thirteenth highest in the MLB. They had the second highest attendance in the MLB each of the past two years, behind the Los Angeles Dodgers but ahead of the San Francisco Giants and New York Yankees. The team has had at least three million fans attend games for ten straight years, despite playing in the twenty-first biggest media market in the United States. The Cardinals also had the highest local TV ratings in baseball in 2014.

wanted to vary the look. And if he was on the box, we doubled with a big guy. The other rule was, any time he went by you, you had to nail him. If he was coming off a screen, nail him. We didn't want to be dirty—I know some people thought we were—but we had to make contact and be very physical." https://web.archive.org/web/20121020061711/http://sportsillustrated.cnn.com/2007/writers/jack_mccallum/05/28/daly.lebron/1.html.

The Cardinals attribute their success to "the Cardinal Way." The Cardinal way has never been officially and completely defined for the general public,[119] but pitcher Adam Wainwright once explained:

> *CliffsNotes version is, this is a way of thinking that we have in St. Louis and in our clubhouse and throughout our organization—an expectation of winning, an expectation of professionalism that comes with that winning, and doing things the right way…And that's been taught and bred over the years from guys like Red Schoendienst, like Stan Musial, Bob Gibson, Lou Brock, Ozzie Smith. All of these great Hall of Famers that you've grown to love, they're still in our clubhouse hanging out…We are very blessed in St. Louis to have those guys in the red jackets around, and we still feel their presence there. We still feel their lessons.*[120]

The manager of the Cardinals is Mike Matheny, who played twelve years in the major leagues, won four Rawlings Gold Glove Awards, and holds several MLB records. The Cardinals hired him even though he had no previous professional manager experience. In addition, he was the youngest manager at the time. He was hired because of his ties to the organization during his playing days (he played for the Cardinals from 2000 to 2004), as well as for intangible qualities such as his presence as a leader. He is known for having a calm and supportive style. Matheny said in the same interview:

> *As far as kind of the expectation and the culture within the Cardinals, it's such a rich history. We hold ourselves to such a high level of expectation of how we play—not just wins and losses, but how you go about your business. And I think it's been something that's just been passed down…It was something, when I came here as a player, that was very clear, and it was obvious and something that I feel is a responsibility to continue. And we have a group of guys that buy into it.*

---

[119] See Howard Megdal's book, *The Cardinals Way: How One Team Embraced Tradition and Moneyball at the Same Time* (New York: Thomas Dunne Books, 2016).

[120] Mike Bauman, "Current Cards carry torch of 'The Cardinal Way.'" *MBL.com*. http://m.mlb.com/news/article/63344846/.

The players seem to want to stay in the culture and benefit from it. Over the last ten years, forty players have had at least 500 plate appearances or pitched at least 100 innings before leaving, and the performance levels dropped for two-thirds of those players after they left.

When the Cardinals draft a player, they provide him with an eighty-six-page handbook that outlines the team's expectations of each player in areas ranging from infield and outfield positioning, base running, bunting a runner over to another base, and the manner in which the player is expected to conduct himself off the field. Off the field, the team's executive management focuses on a long-term approach of investing in scouting, drafting, and player development. Coaches and managers receive the unabridged version, which is 117 pages. These "organizational manuals" are the result of several years of work to collect the lessons from former players and coaches. The handbook discusses living the Cardinal Way, respecting the Cardinal Way, and realizing what it means to abide by the Cardinal Way.

Lastly, the Cardinals' fans treat their players and opposing players with respect. Compared to most other teams' fans, the Cardinals' fans have a reputation for being more patient with and supportive of struggling players, and recognize excellence in opposing teams and players. This economic-sport model has created a loyal customer base that has an emotional attachment to the brand. The success of the Cardinal Way is at least as worthy as the attention paid to the success of the Oakland Athletics described in *Moneyball*.

Galácticos 1.0 Meet Galácticos 2.0

The 2001–02 UEFA Champions League was the forty-seventh season of the European championship and the tenth since its rebranding from the "European Champion Clubs' Cup" or "European Cup" in 1992. To get to the final, Real Madrid beat defending champions Bayern Munich in the quarterfinals and then Barcelona in the semifinals. Real Madrid and Barcelona had not met in the European Cup since the quarterfinals in the 1960–61 season. Real Madrid's opponent in the final was the German team Bayer Leverkusen, which beat all three English teams in the tournament on their way to the final, including Liverpool in the quarterfinals and Manchester United in the semifinals. The final was played at Hampden

Iker Casillas celebrating the ninth European Cup on the balcony of the former City Hall of Madrid in Plaza de la Villa, May 2002.

Park in Glasgow, Scotland, in front of 52,000 fans on May 15, 2002. It was relevant because Hampden Park was also the site of one of Real Madrid's most famous European Cup victories, in 1960, and the fifth of its famous Five-Peat, and just like in 1960, Real Madrid was playing a German team. With Galáticos 1.0 serving as an inspiration to many of Florentino's strategies, it was fitting that Galácticos 2.0 was following in Galácticos 1.0's footsteps on the same field. Bayer Leverkusen appeared in the final for the first time, whereas Real Madrid appeared in its twelfth final.

Real Madrid was regarded as the favorite before the game. Real Madrid's coach, Vicente del Bosque, was able to start the team he wanted for the final. Figo and French midfielder Claude Makélélé had been in doubt to play because of injuries but were diagnosed as fit enough to play.

Game time. Real Madrid is looking to take the game to its German opponent from the first whistle. GOAL! In the eighth minute, Madrid's hometown hero Raúl reacts fastest to an angled long throw in from close to the halfway line by Brazilian full-back Roberto Carlos. Like always, Raúl has an uncanny way of being at the right place at the right time. He times his break perfectly and sends the ball left-footed past Bayer Leverkusen's keeper. As Ray Hudson describes, "…the German's defense was stretched out like spandex at Miami Beach...once again the pure genius of Raúl to anticipate the throw-in...the throw-in is perfection...sublime...and the finish is the personification of grace under pressure..." The goal is Raúl's thirty-fourth overall in the Champions League—the highest record for the competition at the time. After scoring, Raúl takes off running to celebrate and kisses his wedding ring as an acknowledgment to his wife. The early goal seems to justify Real Madrid's status as favorites. However, the German squad bounces back quickly, taking only five minutes before equalizing to make it 1–1.

In the forty-fifth minute, just before the stroke of halftime, it looks like the teams will go into their respective locker rooms tied at the break. GOAL! Zidane receives a high, arching cross from Roberto Carlos on the edge of the penalty area, and volleys a left-footed shot seventeen yards out into the top corner with exquisite balance, timing, and technique. The shot is so sensational that the goalkeeper has no chance. It is considered one of the greatest goals in Champions League history. Ray Hudson is jumping up from a chair screaming: "...aaaaahhhh...excuse me for being excited...I think I just saw a ghost...a flash of 1960 Di Stéfano or Puskás...that goal has just woken the spirit of Bernabéu himself...astonishing and mesmerizing skill and grace..." The halftime whistle is blown but almost no one in the crowd can hear it. Fans are still buzzing about Zidane's goal.

When the second half starts, Madridistas are still singing "Viva España." Real Madrid begins the second half confidently, with Raúl and Zidane in particular crafting openings with fluid passing and movement. Real Madrid dominates the beginning of the second half. English Steve McManaman substitutes in for Figo, still recovering from injury, on the left side of the midfield. In the sixty-eighth minute, César, Real Madrid's steady goalie, is injured and replaced by twenty-one-year-old substitute goalkeeper Iker Casillas, a graduate of the Real Madrid youth academy. A few minutes later, Real Madrid replaces Makélélé, also recovering from injury, with Brazilian Conceição in central midfield. The action becomes end to end as Bayer Leverkusen starts to play with more desperation as time ticks down. With the young Casillas between the posts, Real Madrid manages to hold their ground. The referee decides to add seven minutes of stoppage time because of the substitutions and players taking time after fouls and being injured. Casillas makes three spectacular

acrobatic saves in the final minutes as Real Madrid frantically holds on
to keep the game from going into extra time. The final whistle could not
come quickly enough. The referee calls it—and Real Madrid wins 2–1,
their ninth Champions League cup. Rain fails to dampen the mood. The
thrilled Real Madrid captain Fernando Hierro, who had been at Real
Madrid since 1989, raises the trophy. The jubilant players parade the
Champions League cup around the stadium as Raúl clutches a Spanish
flag.

Once again, Glasgow belongs to Real Madrid. Zidane's goal would
have comfortably graced the magical 1960 final. It is a fitting climax to
Real Madrid's centenary season and connects the dots from Galácticos
1.0 to Galácticos 2.0 with impressive style. Zidane's goal and the flowing
attack and speed of Real Madrid on the field shows that the flair of Di
Stéfano and Puskás[121] are alive and well at Real Madrid. Galácticos 2.0
is a true and worthy heir to the rich legacy of Galácticos 1.0.

Celebrating a Century

Real Madrid was one of the founding members of FIFA[122] and in 2000 Real
Madrid was elected "FIFA Club of the Century." 2002 was the actual centennial year for the club. Real Madrid published books, commissioned a centennial song sung by the Spanish tenor Plácido Domingo, licensed special
souvenirs, organized gala evenings, and had artfully managed to wipe out the
bulk of its massive debt while getting two of the greatest players of all time,
Figo and Zidane.[123] Centennial celebrations were not just held on March 6,
2002 (the official date), but stretched out to include a host of different parties
and events that took place throughout the year. One of the highlights was on
December 18, when Real Madrid faced a FIFA World Select XI team (a group
of global all-stars) at Santiago Bernabéu.

---

[121] In October 2009, FIFA announced the introduction of the FIFA Puskás Award, awarded to the
player who scored the "most beautiful goal" over the past year.

[122] On May 21, 1904, Real Madrid was the only soccer team in the foundation of FIFA, together
with six countries: France, Belgium, Denmark, Netherlands, Sweden, and Switzerland.

[123] Christopher Clarey, "Champions League: Real flamboyance beats Bayern grit." New York Times.
http://www.nytimes.com/2002/04/12/sports/12iht-soccer_ed3__8.html.

Chapter 8

CRISIS ON THE FIELD, SUCCESS OFF THE FIELD

Too Much Talent? Aging Stars? Too Many Changes?

In 2002 and 2003, not content to rest on the club's laurels, Florentino Pérez continued trying to ensure that Real Madrid had the best possible person, who fit the club's values, at each position throughout the organization—both on and off the field. In September 2002, Real Madrid paid €46 million ($43 million) to Inter Milan to get Brazilian striker Ronaldo, popularly called *El Fenomeno* ("the Phenomenon"). He is one of only four players to have won the FIFA World Player of the Year award three times or more, along with Zinedine Zidane, Cristiano Ronaldo, and Lionel Messi. When he signed with Real Madrid, his first-day jersey sales broke the record at the time. Even while he was sidelined from injury until October, the fans kept chanting his name.

On June 18, 2003, Real Madrid paid Manchester United a transfer fee of £24.5 million ($40 million) for the 28-year-old international superstar, England captain and midfielder David Beckham.

On June 24, 2003, two days after winning La Liga, Real Madrid announced that, with a unanimous decision of the board, they made the difficult decision of not re-signing coach Vicente del Bosque, whose contract had expired, and releasing thirty-five-year-old team captain Fernando Hierro. Coach del Bosque grew up in Real Madrid's youth academy and was a former player and captain. As a coach, he collected seven trophies in four seasons. He was offered a job on the technical staff but, after thirty-five years of loyalty, he respectfully turned it down. Jorge Valdano, who guided the board on the hiring of players and coaches, conceded that it hadn't been an easy day: "Two people who have been standard-bearers for the club have gone," he said. "But we believed that it was time for a change in direction before things stagnate at the club." The press was shocked. And when Claude Makélélé, thought to be one of the best defensive midfielders, asked for more money, Real Madrid, unable to reach an agreement with him, sold Makélélé to Chelsea on September 1, 2003. Russian billionaire Roman Abramovich had just bought Chelsea in July and was spending big money to get players, highlighting the possibility of market disruptions with owners with lots of resources. At the time, there were no financial fair-play rules and the member-owned clubs like Barcelona and Real Madrid had to compete with billionaires willing to spend whatever they personally wanted.

With the signing of Ronaldo and Beckham in 2003, five of the top-ten players being considered for the World Player of the Year award competed for Real Madrid (and the team had Casillas and Figo, who were world-class players).

Table 8.1: 2003 Soccer Player of the Year Award Voting Results

Rank	Player	Born	Age	Team	Country	Points
1	Zinedine Zidane	1972	31	Real Madrid	France	264
2	Thierry Henry	1977	26	Arsenal	France	200
3	Ronaldo	1976	27	Real Madrid	Brazil	176
4	Pavel Nedvěd	1972	31	Juventus	Czech Republic	158
5	Roberto Carlos	1973	30	Real Madrid	Brazil	105
6	Ruud van Nistelrooy	1976	27	Manchester United	Netherlands	86
7	David Beckham	1975	28	Manchester United Real Madrid	England	74
8	Raúl	1977	26	Real Madrid	Spain	39
9	Paolo Maldini	1968	35	AC Milan	Italy	37
10	Andriy Shevchenko	1976	27	AC Milan	Ukraine	26

Signing Beckham was a triumph for Real Madrid because it was reported Manchester United had originally agreed to sell Beckham to archrival Barcelona. Beckham's signing by Real Madrid became a prime example of the revenue potential of merchandising, television broadcast licensing, and sponsorships. Beckham's marriage to Victoria "Posh Spice" Beckham of the Spice Girls gave international celebrity status to the man who was already one of the most recognizable soccer stars in the world. Beckham was more than a sports star; he was a global celebrity and icon. He even became a household name to non-soccer fans in America in 2002 when the British film *Bend It Like Beckham* was released, titled after Beckham's ability to make the ball's flight path bend in the air with spin on his free kicks.

The July 2, 2003, press conference held in Madrid to announce Beckham's signing was attended by over 1,000 journalists, 500 of them observing the event from outside the packed venue. The time, 11:00 A.M., was chosen to make the evening news broadcasts in Asia to capitalize on Beckham's popularity there. At the time, UK experts estimated that the only live event related to a single person ever to attract more UK TV viewers than Beckham's signing with Real Madrid was the funeral of Princess Diana.

Beckham took the stage with Placido Domingo's Real Madrid centenary anthem, "*Himno del Centenario*" ("Hymn for the Centenary"), playing in the background. From left to right stood Florentino, Beckham, and Di Stéfano. Flanked by Real Madrid's new superstar, Florentino said:

> He is a great player who is going to become part of the club's great history. He's got a global appeal. He is a man of our times and a symbol of modern-day stardom and what is certain is Real have signed Beckham because he's a great footballer and a very dedicated professional. His team spirit is unsurpassed and he is one of the best English players of all time and if only because of that he is with us. We love Beckham because he makes us the best team on and off the [field].

When Florentino finished, Di Stéfano welcomed Beckham and presented him with a Real Madrid jersey bearing the number 23. Beckham had selected 23 because it was the famous jersey number of star NBA basketball player Michael Jordan. Florentino told the twenty-eight-year-old celebrity, "You have come from the theater of dreams to play for the team of your dreams." Beckham responded with "Joining Real Madrid is a dream come true...Hala Madrid!" The exchange was a reminder that Real Madrid, unlike every other team in the world of soccer, is not a stepping-stone in the professional path of a soccer player or an investment opportunity for a billionaire or investment group. Real Madrid is unique in that it is the pinnacle of any player's career.

As Beckham ran around the field for photos, a small boy crawled under the fence and ran toward his new hero. Security rushed to catch the boy, but Beckham insisted the boy could stay and gave him a hug.

Shortly after the signing, Real Madrid sent the team on a seventeen-day Asian tour, with exhibition games in Beijing, Tokyo, Hong Kong, and Bangkok, leveraging Beckham's popularity in Asia and earning Real Madrid net profits of €10 million. The live experience fueled the Real Madrid community in Asia and attracted more fans. Real Madrid's sustainable economic-sport strategy was working.

The Crisis: Disappointment on the Field, Resignation

The club had started off the 2003–04 season strong, winning the Supercopa de España against Mallorca, and halfway through the season Real Madrid was at the top of the league table and in contention for the Copa del Rey and UEFA Champions League trophies. Then, the team started to lose. In the Champions League quarterfinal stage, Real Madrid was eliminated on April 6, 2004, by Monaco, in one of the biggest upsets of the season. Ironically and embarrassingly, Real Madrid gave up a big lead, and the deciding goal was scored by Fernando Morientes, a player Real Madrid had "loaned" to Monaco because he was not able to get into the Real Madrid starting lineup. They also lost their final five La Liga games and finished in fourth place.

There has been much speculation as to the reasons for Real Madrid's collapse in the second half of the 2003–04 season. In the last twelve games, Real Madrid won three, tied two, and lost seven, including losing the last five in a row. There is no clear explanation for why a team that had been performing so well—dominating the sport—suddenly wasn't.

Any number of factors may have contributed. Some blamed compla-cency or loss of hunger after winning, or lack of leadership on the field. The replacement of coach del Bosque did not sit well with some. Casillas, in the prologue to *Vicente, an Authorized Biography* (Barcelona: Libros Cúpula, 2014), wrote that "his departure from Real Madrid hurt..."[124] Some blamed the new coach's use of players and strategies on the field. Others blamed injuries and the fatigue of the players after a long season starting with the Asia tour. Some pointed to off-field distractions. A few weeks prior to the Champions League Monaco game, Beckham had been fending off media allegations of marital infidelity, and a big story about it appeared in the British tabloids the day before the game.

Even though the team was on an incredible winning streak for the first half of the season, the media seemed to focus in hindsight on the deci-sion to sell Makélélé before the start of the season. The media suggested that Florentino only cared about goals that could be easily celebrated and replayed on TV and cared less about defense. It was Florentino who signed Makélélé for £10m ($15 million) and Conceição for €26 million ($24 mil-lion)—outbidding several teams for both—in 2000, which at the time were high transfer fees for defensive players. Some suggested Florentino and his staff were misreading the data analytics on Makélélé's importance when they sold him.[125] These explanations don't make complete sense because Real Madrid reportedly was trying to sign Frenchman Patrick Vieira, who many believed to the best defensive player at the time; he fit Real Madrid's values and expectations and was three years younger than Makéléle. Makéléle was exceptional positionally, but Vieira ruled the mid-field with his imposing presence, and many believed, at the time, he had a better all-around game. Also, Real Madrid reportedly was willing to pay Vieira more than Makélélé, challenging the claim that Florentino would not pay for defensive talent.[126] For a variety of reasons, at the last minute the deal with Vieira was not completed.

[124] Tom Conn, "Casillas: When del Bosque left, a piece of Real Madrid went with him." *Inside Spanish Football*. http://www.insidespanishfootball.com/103154/casillas-when-del-bosque-left-a-piece-of-real-madrid-went-with-him/.

[125] The book *Soccernomics* points out this part of Florentino's explanation and the fact that Makélélé went on to help Chelsea become successful, his role becoming so recognized that many soccer experts named a positional role after him.

[126] Graham Hunter and Neil Martin, "Vieira close to Real deal." *Guardian*. http://www.theguardian.com/football/2004/jul/28/newsstory.sport8.

Regardless, in the first twenty-six games of the 2003–04 season, before the collapse, Real Madrid's defense allowed twenty-nine goals and was in first place in La Liga, eight points ahead of Valencia in second place.[127] With Makélélé on the team, Real Madrid allowed thirty goals in 2001–02 (finishing third in La Liga) and twenty-seven goals in 2002–03, illustrating not much of a difference in goals allowed with or without Makélélé.

Table 8.2: Real Madrid 2001-2004 Results With and Without Makéléle

| Season | Makéléle on Team | Standing @ 26 Games | First 26 Games of La Liga Season | | | Last 12 Games of La Liga Season | | | End of Season Standing | Champions League Performance |
			Goals Allowed	Goals Scored	Net	Goals Allowed	Goals Scored	Net		
2001-02	Yes	2	30	50	+20	14	20	+6	3	Winner
2002-03	Yes	1	27	59	+32	15	17	+2	1	Semifinals
2003-04	No	1	29	54	+25	25	18	-7	4	Quarterfinals

So the data shows it is difficult to simply point to Makélélé's absence as the single reason for the downward slide. That isn't to say that his loss didn't contribute to the slide; he was a calming defensive presence who was very respected by the players and coach, but to point to his absence as the primary reason is really more convenient sports narrative and opinion than fact. What makes the narrative seductive is that he had a great career at Chelsea, under José Mourinho's approach and with a younger team. One goal difference in the quarterfinal of the Champions League for Real Madrid and people may have a different narrative. Later, I discuss more nuances on the collapse, including leadership, the too-much-talent effect, the too-tired-and-old effect, the impact of age (especially after 2003—04), and other issues, which will challenge the theory that the primary cause was Makélélé.[128]

---

[127] Real Madrid ended in fourth place at seven points below first-place Valencia.

[128] The most intriguing change that I could find in my analysis is that Real Madrid's stars were getting older (from twenty-six when Florentino took over to twenty-nine when he left in 2006). During Florentino's last season (2005–06), the goals scored by their stars decreased dramatically to 58 percent (they had an average 73 percent during the previous three seasons).

Florentino explained Real Madrid's decision to sell thirty-year-old Makélélé publicly. He said, "[Makélélé] wanted half of what Zidane is earning and that was not possible." Even before his departure, Makélélé, who had three years remaining on his contract, staged a weeklong strike to force Real Madrid's hand. In addition, the Frenchman demanded 15 percent of the transfer fee, to which he had no contractual right. For whatever reason, players and others were publicly picking sides, which only enflamed the situation. The management team's experience gave them the confidence to believe that making exceptions beyond their perceptions of the club's values and mission could have disastrous consequences. For example, other players would then start claiming they, too, were exceptions and they needed their contracts renegotiated or deserved a percentage of the transfer fee. It could lead to a slippery slope, especially for a member-owned club. To Florentino and his team, no one individual, regardless of talent, was worth putting the sustainable economic-sport model at risk.[129] It is not possible to fully analyze the decision without understanding how the off-field and on-field decisions impact each other. Makélélé's behavior and demands probably added to Real Madrid's resolve. The club's executives made a choice mandated by steadfast commitment to the values of the Real Madrid community.

When all of the possibilities of the collapse were considered, two organizational reasons related to leadership seemed to stand out to Florentino in hindsight: the importance of certain characteristics of the coach and the importance of a "first among equals" among the stars. Later, Florentino would reflect on the importance of certain attributes of del Bosque. Real Madrid academy graduate del Bosque was a highly regarded midfielder who helped his team win five Spanish league titles in the 1970s, won two Champions League titles as Real Madrid's coach, and had a calm personality—attributes Florentino believes would help a coach be successful in managing stars.[130] The lesson learned seems to have informed Real Madrid's 2013 decision to hire Carlo Ancelotti as coach, and later Zidane.

---

[129] Florentino would be faithful to this mission again in his handling of Di María and signing James in 2014, as discussed in chapter ten in "Learning from Experience."

[130] Del Bosque would later coach a Spanish national soccer team of all-stars to win its first and only World Cup in 2010.

Although there were many superb players on the 2003 team, no one player was a clear leader or "first among equals,"[131] and the five players who were in the running for the World Player of the Year award were similar in stature on the field in varying ways and all within a few years apart. In addition, Fernando Hierro, the captain and the club stalwart whose commanding figure perfectly embodied the club's values and who could have taken a leadership role over the five stars, was gone, and replaced by a captain in his first year in the role. Perhaps there was too much talent on the team, but the negative effects of too much talent can be mitigated with culture and leadership. Later, Cristiano Ronaldo, brought on in 2009, would mature into, and distinguish himself as, a first among equals player and leader; the homegrown, respected, and experienced captain Casillas would become an established leader; and the special attributes of Ancelotti would help him provide leadership.

The team was performing well until the sudden collapse. To blame the loss of Makélélé alone, one would have to explain the similar performance without him in a first two-thirds of the season year-over-year comparison. Perhaps, once the team started to struggle and without the leadership elements discussed earlier in this book, players tried to do too much themselves, which exasperated the situation, and the teamwork suffered. Perhaps they were tired. Regardless, contrary to popular narratives, it is highly likely there wasn't one single reason for the collapse. The ideas and context of leadership and the too-much-talent and too-tired-and-old effects were not widely considered at the time, but my hypothesis is that they had a role in Real Madrid's collapse in the latter half of the 2003—04 season.

Too-Much-Talent Effect

One of the questions I asked in my research was whether having too much talent may have contributed to Real Madrid's underperformance on the field from 2003–06.[132] Coincidentally, one of my colleagues at Columbia Business

---

[131] This is discussed in chapter ten's "Learning from Experience."

[132] It has been suggested that Real Madrid's disastrous 2003–04 season happened because "each

School, Adam Galinsky, who coauthored an academic study with Roderick I. Swaab and Michael Schaerer of INSEAD Business School, Richard Ronay of VU University Amsterdam, and doctoral student Eric Anicich of Columbia Business School, looked into this effect for an academic paper published in *Psychological Science* in June 2014. They used it as the basis for their study of individual and team data from regular season NBA play from 2002 to 2012. They specifically analyzed the Estimated Wins Added, or EWA, which estimates the victories that any given player adds over and above what a replacement player would contribute. They used play-by-play metrics, such as total assists and defensive rebounds, to quantify team coordination. For overall team performance, they simply calculated the percentage of the season's games that were wins. The business school researchers discovered that adding more talent only improved team performance to a certain point, after which it became a liability due to diminished team coordination. Apparently, having too many stars is not a good idea in basketball.

When Galinksy and Swaab conducted a similar study for soccer, based on data from FIFA, their conclusion was the same. Loading a soccer team with star players doesn't guarantee a winning season because at some point, the too-much-talent effect kicks in (pun intended). In soccer, even more than in basketball, scoring requires a team to get the ball to the right person, in the right position, at the right time, which typically involves a number of complex moves performed quickly under time pressure. Remember, Ronaldo typically possesses the ball for a few seconds at a time.

Let's look at baseball as an example where interdependence is not as critical to a game's final outcome, unlike in basketball and soccer. In baseball, while all players must coordinate on the field, a pitcher's or batter's individual performance has more impact on the final score. When Galinsky and Swaab analyzed talent and team performance using MLB data, they got a different result: Accumulating talent did not hurt team performance. There is no such thing as the too-much-talent effect in baseball.

---

star wanted to shine more than the others and played to do precisely this," laying at least some of the blame on the coach for being "unable to guide the players' desire to be creative into a coherent effort." (Tony Davila, *Making Innovation Work: How to Manage It, Measure It, and Profit from It,* Updated Edition. New Jersey: Pearson FT Press, 2012.)

"If you have too many people and they all want to be stars, coordination goes down," Galinsky says.[133] Unfortunately, there is no way to predict when a particular team is nearing the too-much-talent effect threshold. Most teams need people with different skills to accomplish various tasks—a basketball team, for example, needs players who can rebound and excel at defense in addition to star shooters. Galinsky says, "Having a range of skills is critical...When you have interdependence, you need role differentiation."

A warning sign exists when a team is nearing the tipping point: too many team members are competing to perform the same tasks, while other tasks—those that aren't in the spotlight—aren't getting done. Many managers and team members have observed the too-much-talent effect personally. Galinsky asks, "Have you seen a situation where many people on a team are suspicious of each other and they're not integrating their behavior very well?" In general, Galinsky says, it is better not to model your basketball team after the All-Stars—in which every player wants the ball, and no one wants to play defense.[134]

Galinsky and Swaab's research findings support the existence of a too-much-talent effect and explain why it occurs. However, as the professors explained in a final study, people intuitively believe that their favorite team will get better by piling on more and more top talent. This is true in baseball, where teams spending as much money as they can to get as much talent as possible will have positive results more often than in basketball and soccer, which also explains why some lessons of *Moneyball*, which is about a baseball team, may not be applicable to organizations that require interdependence.

When I followed up with Galinsky and Anicich in person to talk about Real Madrid, they told me that a strong culture and shared values can minimize or possibly even eliminate the too-much-talent problem. A shared culture and values may serve to direct attention away from status conflict and toward an overarching group goal. When that group goal is salient and status conflict is minimized, they think coordination becomes easier because stars will be less focused on their own standing within the group (and the need for individual glory that comes with that self focus). They believe that

[133] Adam Galinsky, "Is Your Team Too Talented?" *Columbia Ideas at Work*. http://www8.gsb. columbia.edu/ideas-at-work/publication/1700/is-your-team-too-talented.

[134] Galinsky, "Is Your Team Too Talented?"

an organization's commitment, manifested in mutual values, to channeling focus toward a common purpose and a common vision for the group's future increases the likelihood of stability and success.

My hypothesis is that the additions of Ronaldo and Beckham may have caused the team to be dangerously close to the tipping point of having too much talent. The values and culture kept the team cohesion in place and overcame many of the negative consequences. Actually, I believe the club's culture, including the players with community values, should be given an enormous amount of credit for keeping a remarkable amount of talent working together at Real Madrid. However, as the 2003–04 season went on, other factors such as the star players growing older and more tired also played a role.[135]

It's here that the two organizational factors relating to leadership in maintaining the culture on the field—the importance of the coach with certain attributes and of a "first among equals" among the stars—cannot be underappreciated. When the team started to lose, which can happen just because of bad luck in a sport where scoring opportunities are scarce or because star players are too tired and getting older, there was a vacuum of leadership on the field to get the team back on track, and it snowballed. They lacked a coach who could say he knew Real Madrid values and had won as a player and a coach.[136] And they lacked a player who was clearly first among equals. Also, it was Raúl's first year as a captain to lead a group of megastars.

Yet the analysis depends on a number of almost incalculable factors, including players' injuries and exhaustion levels, which might not be reflected in an official statistical breakdown of likelihoods. The data context matters, too. Because of all these variables and explanations, I don't believe it is reasonable to single out a single factor. In the following season, I believe data demonstrates age had caught up with the stars, and combined with the lack of a leadership on the field and the too-much-talent effect, were most likely key contributors to the club's disappointing last third of the season.

---

[135] See "Too-Tired-and-Old Effect" sidebar on page 195.

[136] The coach that replaced del Bosque was not a star professional player and had never been the head coach of a top European team. He had been the assistant manager of Manchester United, working alongside the highly respected Alex Ferguson.

In October 2004, Emilio Butragueño replaced Jorge Valdano, a former Real Madrid teammate, as the club's Sports Director General and also served as the club's vice president. Butragueño had grown up in Real Madrid's youth academy and eventually would star as a striker and member of the legendary *Quinta del Buitre*. He received the Ballon d'Or Bronze Ball (3rd place) in 1986 and 1987 and the FIFA World Cup Silver Boot in 1986.

During the 2004 presidential campaign, Florentino's opponents tried to explain the club's underperformance on the field as the result of some sort of arrogance on the part of players and/or executives. One opposing candidate promised to sign certain players, while another thought the solution lay in a greater emphasis on the academy and developing homegrown talent. Despite the disappointment on the field, Florentino won the election in a landslide, with over 94 percent of the vote.[137] It was a vote of confidence by the community members, even without the recent trophies.

Expectations for the 2005–06 season, Real Madrid's seventy-fifth season in La Liga, were high, but despite the club's financial success, they were not winning on the field. When the losses on the field continued during the 2005–06 season, Deloitte's Football Money League report of February 2006 stated:

> *Although Florentino Pérez's strategy of recruiting world-class "galáctico" players has not necessarily delivered the anticipated on-field results recently, their presence has facilitated a transformation in the club's financial performance. It is Real's ability to generate revenue from commercial sources such as sponsorships, merchandizing and licensing, that sets it apart from its competitor clubs.[138]*

---

[137] "Landslide win for Real Madrid's Perez." *ESPNFC.* http://www.espnfc.com/story/304876/landslide-win-for-real-madrids-perez.

[138] "Football Money League." *Deloitte.* http://www2.deloitte.com/content/dam/Deloitte/uk/Documents/sports-business-group/deloitte-uk-deloitte-football-money-league-2006.pdf.

As the Deloitte report noted, Real Madrid's incredible financial turn-around stood in contrast to their performance on the field.[139]

Table 8.3: Fiscal Year-End 2000 and 2006 Real Madrid Financial Information

	June 2000	June 2006[140]
Revenues	€118m	€292m
EBITDA (before net gains on disposals)	€10m	€58m
Wages to revenues	66%	47%
Profit (Loss) before taxes	(€23m)	€34m
Net debt	€162m	€84m
Result	Auditor's opinion: unsustainable model	Season Investments: €173m Total 2000–06 Investments: €748m (Players: €502m; Repurchase of Rights: €18m; Sports Facilities [CRM]: €99m; Stadium €129m)

Although the club had won championships, the performance was disappointing relative to the skill level of the players and to the club's financial success.

Table 8.4: Selected Signings and Trophies 2000–2006

	June 2000 – June 2006
New stars signed	6
La Liga championships	2
European league championships	1

---

[139] The club finished second in La Liga to Barcelona and was eliminated at the first knockout stage of the UEFA Champions League by Arsenal.

[140] Information June 2000: Proforma income after adjustment for non-recurring advance options. The extraordinary profit in June 2006 additional to the ordinary profit reported in Table 8.3 was €46 million, due to the sale of transfer rights of players. Therefore total profit reported was €80 million.

In early February, Real Madrid took the top revenues rank in soccer over Manchester United in 2005 in Deloitte's Football Money League revenue ranking. Real Madrid doubled their the revenues from 2000.

Table 8.5: Deloitte Football Money League Rankings, 1999–2000 and 2004–2005

Team	1999–2000		2004–2005		
	Revenues	Rank	Revenues	Rank	Growth Rate
Real Madrid	€138m	#5	276	#1	100%
Manchester United	€217m	#1	246	#2	13%
AC Milan	€165m	#4	234	#3	42%
Juventus	€174m	#2	229	#4	31%
Bayern Munich	€173m	#3	190	#5	10%

As mentioned previously, embracing rivalries is important in helping to define and solidify a loyal and passionate community. In addition, each rival club and its fan community will benchmark itself against the other. Adding to the club's disappointments on the field was a resurgence on the field by Real Madrid's fiercest rival Barcelona. As one Real Madrid executive succinctly put it, "They don't celebrate balance sheets at Cibeles Fountain."[141]

After a meeting of the club's board in late February 2006, with two years left in his term, then-fifty-nine-year-old Florentino tendered his resignation. New presidential elections took place in July 2006, and Carlos Martínez de Albornoz, Pedro López Jiménez, Emilio Butragueño, and Manuel Redondo resigned. The only primary executive to stay was José Ángel Sánchez, head of marketing.

Florentino felt that he had rescued the club financially and put it on the right course, but after careful consideration, he said, "We have constructed a great squad…but perhaps I wasn't able to make them understand the importance of their responsibilities, maybe I have educated them badly."[142] Florentino and his executive team had harnessed

---

[141] F. Asís Martinez-Jerez and Rosario Martínez de Albornoz, "Hala Madrid: Managing Real Madrid Club de Fútbol, the Team of the Century." *Harvard Business School Case.* June 8, 2006.

[142] "Perez resigns as Madrid president." *BBC Sport.* http://news.bbc.co.uk/sport2/hi/football/europe/4757112.stm.

the power of community values, which unleashed extraordinary passion and added world-class players and facilities, but, to him, somehow a breakdown in the responsibilities (e.g., leadership) and education (e.g., culture) existed on the field. The results illustrated how difficult it is to transmit the values from the community through the board of directors and management to the coach and then to the players on the field. He wanted to capture the players' attention with his resignation and send a signal. He thought the action was necessary to help the club.[143]

The 2003–04 LA Lakers:
Too Much Talent or Too Tired and Old?

When I mention the too-much-talent effect to NBA fans, one of the first things that they mention is the 2003–04 Los Angeles Lakers. The season before, the Lakers' attempt to win four straight NBA championships ended in a second-round loss to the eventual champion San Antonio Spurs. Still determined, the Lakers signed future Hall of Famers Gary Payton and Karl Malone—both of whom had yet to win a NBA championship—under free-agent contracts far below their market value. With these players, the Lakers became the first new-era super team, one widely favored to win the NBA championship. While the Lakers did reach the finals, their run to the championship ended in a five-game loss to the Detroit Pistons. For many teams, making the NBA finals is success. But for a team stacked with so many future Hall of Famers, not winning the championship meant failure for the team and their fans. To many, they exemplified the problem of too much talent. Therefore, I analyzed the data and considered context to determine if too much talent was the problem.

As a backdrop to the season, two weeks before the Lakers signed Payton and Malone, their superstar Kobe Bryant was charged with sexual assault in Colorado. As a result, Bryant spent much of the season flying back and forth to Colorado for court appearances. Meanwhile, Bryant's feud with fellow superstar Shaquille O'Neal continued as they made critical public remarks

---

[143] One thing worth noting, and not often mentioned, is that in 2006, Roberto Carlos was thirty-three years old and Zidane and Figo were thirty-four. Real Madrid's players were past peak performance age, which is discussed in the "Too-Tired-and-Old Effect" sidebar (page 195). Florentino and his executives would later reflect on this.

about each other. Bryant wanted to test free agency the following summer when his contract ended. O'Neal wanted a large contract extension before the season, which was rejected. The team's discussions with coach Phil Jackson on his contract extension had been put off until after the season.

The Lakers had an incredible 19–5 start to the season. They were playing beautiful team basketball in Jackson's triangle system of offense. But then Malone injured his knee (torn MCL) in December and was out for most of the season, and the team didn't have a reliable backup player. Also, O'Neal, who was now thirty-one years old and as big as ever, and Kobe Bryant, who was flying back and forth so much to Colorado, were both becoming visibly physically exhausted. Bryant was quoted as saying he didn't touch a ball the entire off-season because he was too distracted, and the data shows his shooting percentages dropped. Before the play-offs, the actual "Big Four" of O'Neal, Bryant, Malone, and Payton played in only twenty games together. Gary Payton was thirty-five years old and Karl Malone was forty years old. Many people forget neither Malone nor Payton were in their primes. At the end of the season, the injuries were mounting as Malone had a sprained right ankle, Devean George had a strained calf, Derek Fisher had a pulled groin muscle, and Rick Fox had a dislocated right thumb.

Despite all of this, the injury-depleted, older, and tired Lakers still managed a respectable 56–26 record and entered as the number-two seed in the Western Conference play-offs. My hypothesis is that a team with too much talent can be successful but only with necessary cultural and organizational elements. With all of the injuries and distractions, even getting to the finals was due in part to Phil Jackson's presence and adjustments, as well as having a system of offense. The one thing Jackson and the Lakers could not overcome was the too-tired-and-old-effect. In the play-offs, the Lakers easily beat the Houston Rockets featuring Steve Francis and Yao Ming. In the second round, the San Antonio Spurs took the first two games, and the Lakers won the next four. The Lakers managed to beat a tough and physical Kevin Garnett–led Minnesota Timberwolves team. However, Malone reinjured his knee and was relatively ineffective in the finals. In addition, the too-tired-and-old-effect started to impact Gary Payton. Payton, who was good during the regular season, started to show fatigue in the play-offs. The toll of the long regular season and more intense competition and defense in the play-offs caught up to Payton. He had a player efficiency rating (PER) of 17.3 in the regular season which fell to 11.1 in the play-offs, his shooting percentage went from 52.8 percent to 47 percent, and his three-point shooting went from 33 percent to 25 percent. He couldn't keep up with the stronger and faster Chauncey Billups, who tired him out. The Lakers were heavily favored to win the title, but the young, cohesive Pistons that were peaking at the right time won easily. Detroit outscored the Lakers in the fourth quarter of every game, except game five, in which they were winning by a large margin and won their championship. The Pistons' execution, defensive pressure, and hustle wore the Lakers down. In game four of the NBA finals, Malone was limited to just two points. After giving it his all, in game five, Malone could not even play. The Lakers were aging veterans with tired legs.

To make matters worse, when things started to break down, there was uncertainty of who was the leader of the team—O'Neal or Bryant. This is another example of a leadership issue exposed in difficult times as players' bodies are starting to break down. Derek Fisher rhetorically asked, "Was it Shaq's team or Kobe's team?"[144] To me, the 2003–04 Lakers demonstrate how a coach with credentials and a system can help overcome the consequences of too much talent and even address the leadership issues when there isn't a clear first among equals, but he can't necessarily overcome the too-tired-and-old effect, age, and injuries.[145]

---

[144] Phil Jackson and Hugh Delehanty. *Eleven Rings: The Soul of Success* (New York: Penguin Group, 2014).

[145] Aaron contributed an article to *Forum Blue & Gold* that addressed much of this. The responses also were helpful. See more at http://www.forumblueandgold.com/2009/09/11/misunderstood-lakers-teams-2003-04/.

PART FOUR

Galácticos 3.0
(2009–14)

Chapter 9

CALDERÓN PERIOD (2006–09)

FLORENTINO PÉREZ resigned in February 2006 and Ramón Calderón, a lawyer and former board member, was elected president of Real Madrid in July 2006. The Real Madrid election generated a great deal of controversy with large question marks regarding the way it was administered. Many Real Madrid members complained that their names appeared on the list of those who voted by mail even though they had actually voted in person. The final decision was left with the courts. It is incredible that a club of Real Madrid's stature should have conducted elections with no guarantees as to the legitimacy of the election process. Because of evidence of vote rigging, a court annulled the vote, but, in the end, Calderón became president. It didn't matter that the men who stood accused of rigging the vote were Calderón's opponents; the inescapable conclusion for the community was that Real Madrid's institutional situation did not reflect their values and international prestige.

Calderón's presidency was marred with controversy since its beginning. Early on, Calderón had been accused of "selling" season tickets in exchange for votes in the presidential election (nothing was proven). In March 2008, Calderón was accused of manipulating the selection of the General Assembly.[146] Real Madrid club members are empowered to vote

---

[146] He was accused of introducing in the General Assembly meeting some people who were not even members of the club, thus altering the result of the voting. This case is still in court. The General Assembly currently is composed of 2,046 member representatives, which, besides the members elected, includes the members of the board, honorary members, and the first 100 club members.

at annual general meetings (AGMs) on behalf of the entire membership regarding the budget.[147] In the summer of that same year, Calderón failed to sign Cristiano Ronaldo from Manchester United. In December 2008, Real Madrid signed two players in the winter transfer market, only to discover via the press that UEFA rules dictated that only one of them could be registered to play in the knockout stages of the Champions League.[148] To some community members, this appeared to be at a minimum incompetence, if not gross negligence.

In January 2009, the Spanish sports daily newspaper *Marca* published allegations of manipulation in the confirmation vote on the financial budget at the December 2008 AGM meeting. *Marca* reported that, in what was effectively a vote of confidence, Calderón's budget was passed only because his directors admitted nonmembers into the General Assembly and denied entry to about 200 bona fide members. The newspaper printed pictures of at least ten of those who were fraudulently admitted. Calderón denied any wrongdoing, but clearly the embattled president was losing the community's trust.

According to an ESPN.com article, questionable signings caused fan unrest.[149] In several instances, the team was accused of significantly overpaying for relatively average players or players who had allegedly been offered to other clubs at a fraction of the cost paid by Real Madrid. Transfer fees for some players seemed suspiciously high to journalists. There were allegations about fraudulent commissions in the signing of players. None of the allegations mentioned were ever proven, but there always seemed to be a cloud of suspicion.

All of this was shocking to the Real Madrid community. The retooling that Florentino and his management team had done to improve accountability, financial responsibility, transparency, good corporate governance, and trust had largely evaporated, in just a few years.

---

[147] In the 2014–15 Corporate Responsibility Report, functions and responsibilities of member representatives are described.

[148] UEFA rules state that a maximum of three new players can be registered for the knockout stages by February 1, and only one can have played in another European competition, such as the UEFA Cup.

[149] Eduardo Alvarez, "The metamorphosis of Calderón." *ESPNFC*. http://www.espnfc.us/story/611017/the-metamorphosis-of-calder%C3%A3%C2%B3n.

On the field, the club was winning, doing well in La Liga compared to the beginning of Galácticos 2.0. Real Madrid won two La Liga championships. The trouble was, the Real Madrid community didn't like watching. The coaches instilled what were perceived as "boring" defensive tactics. The community appreciated the sporting values of the players working hard and never giving up as the club won a closely contested La Liga championship over Barcelona in 2006–07 and another championship in 2007–08. However, Real Madrid did not advance past the Round of 16 in the UEFA Champions League, which is the top priority for the community. The Champions League results were in stark contrast to 2001–03.

Table 9.1: Comparing 2006–08 to 2001–03 (Galácticos 2.0)

La Liga Champions								
	W	D	L	GF	GA	GD	Position	League Result
2006–07	23	7	8	66	40	26	1	Round 8
2007–08	27	4	7	84	36	48	1	Round 8
2001–02	19	9	10	69	44	25	3	Winner
2002–03	22	12	4	86	42	44	1	Semifinals

In addition, executives did not sign Ronaldo, from Manchester, and Kaká, from AC Milan, two attacking and exciting players the community highly valued. The sustainable economic-sport model was broken.

Once again the Real Madrid community proved that, even though the team won two successive Spanish league titles during Calderón's presidency, winning without living up to the values and expectations of the community was not good enough for them. Calderón resigned under pressure from community members who expressed their anger during the games and through the media. The Real Madrid community let their feelings be known and did not have to wait a few years for the next election to remove Calderón.

Even with the drift of strategy, the revenues continued to increase from 2006 to 2009, in part because of the momentum of broadcasting, marketing and sponsorship initiatives, and contracts previously implemented.

However, signs were starting to emerge that issues were developing. For example, *Sports Illustrated* reported that as many as 600 of the 4,500 VIP seats were empty during games.[150]

Table 9.2: Fiscal Year-End 2006–09 Real Madrid Financial Information

	June 2006	June 2009
Revenues	€292m	€407m
EBITDA (before net gains on disposals)	€58m	€93m
Wages to revenues	47%	46%
Profit (Loss) before taxes	€34m	€25m
Net debt	€84m	€327m[151]

Table 9.3: Selected Trophies 2006–2009

	June 2006 – June 2009
La Liga championships	2
European league championships	0

---

[150] "Real Madrid's $400 million gamble." *Sports Illustrated.* http://www.si.com/soccer/2009/07/09/real-madrid.

[151] Florentino was declared president of Real Madrid on June 1, 2009. During the month of June, his presidency incorporated superstars like Cristiano Ronaldo, Kaká, Benzema, and others. Florentino had to heavily invest in superstar players to cover the lack of Calderón's incorporation of new superstar players. This is the reason for the increase in debt.

Chapter 10

FLORENTINO PÉREZ'S COMEBACK (2009–14)

F LORENTINO PÉREZ maintained a discreet silence during Calderón's mishaps. After Calderón's resignation, Florentino's supporters urged him to return. At the time, Spain was at the beginning of a major financial crisis that included a bursting property bubble, a collapsing banking system, and a ballooning unemployment crisis (especially among young people). Although the bottom wouldn't be reached until 2012, in 2009 the Spanish economy was in crisis mode. By March of that year, the Spanish stock index (IBEX 35) was down more than 50 percent from its peak in 2007.

Many community members believed that while they may have been disappointed on the field during some of Florentino's years as president, at least he delivered the best players to Real Madrid (which Calderón couldn't) and still maintained the accountability, transparency, trust, and good corporate governance that was important to the club's identity (which Calderón didn't). Going deeper into a crisis, the community also wanted someone who could manage the club properly.

Even though Florentino was extremely busy at Grupo ACS, he believed it was his duty to run again. Having had the time to reflect and develop ideas and strategies on how to improve, on May 14, 2009, he announced his candidacy for president of Real Madrid during a press conference at the Hotel Ritz Madrid. He quickly made Real Madrid's pursuit of Cristiano Ronaldo a high priority, calling it essential for the club's image and financial interests. He said Real Madrid should have bought Ronaldo in 2007 and that the signing of Manchester United's world player of the year was as essential then as was the purchase of David Beckham in 2003. He explained the link between recruitment of the best players and the club's financial performance: "When Beckham arrived, our sponsors significantly raised their payments to us and we rescued the finances of the club. In the last few years the club did not reinvest in the type of players to continue with that model."[152] In the back of his mind, he was also thinking Ronaldo could be the next Di Stéfano.

All members in the community were aware that Florentino was the only one capable of correcting the drift of the club, and no other club member presented his own candidacy, so, on June 1, 2009, Florentino was declared the new president of Real Madrid. To reassemble his management team, Florentino immediately reinstated Carlos Martínez de Albornoz, Pedro López Jiménez, Emilio Butragueño, and Manuel Redondo to join José Ángel Sánchez, who had stayed on at the club as Executive Director after Florentino resigned in 2006.

The present executive management structure is that only four persons report directly to the president: José Ángel as Director General of the Club; Manuel as Director of the Presidential Office; Carlos as Director of Control and Internal Auditing and member of all management committees; and Emilio Butragueño as Institutional Relations Director. Pedro López Jiménez rejoined the board. The head of marketing is Begoña Sanz, who was José Ángel's right hand when he was Marketing Director, and she reports to José Ángel. These professionals have an extremely close partnership based on trust and respect. They believe it is important to challenge each other and ask questions. Florentino gets a lot of the media attention, but it is really an entire close-knit group of executives making decisions.

In his second term, Florentino and his team immediately went to work on reestablishing governance of the club, operating procedures, management committees (management board, economic committee, and purchasing committee), ethical code, corporate responsibility functions, transparency of all functions and overall report, and risk metrics and analysis.

Real Madrid's first player move was to sign Brazilian superstar Kaká from AC Milan in June 2009 for an undisclosed fee, believed to be £56

---

[152] Grahame L. Jones, "Mad money dominates the world soccer scene." *Los Angeles Times*. http://articles.latimes.com/2009/jun/17/sports/sp-soccer-commentary17.

million ($87 million). Weeks later, Real Madrid officially announced on its website that an £80 million (€94 million, $125 million) offer for Portuguese Ballon d'Or winner Cristiano Ronaldo had been accepted by his team, Manchester United. The transfer fee broke the world record, making Ronaldo the most expensive player in history. Florentino's new superstar signings eventually included Spanish Xabi Alonso (2009), French Karim Benzema (2009), German Mesut Özil and Argentine Ángel Di María (2010), Croation Luka Modrić (2012), Welsh Gareth Bale and Spanish Isco (2013), and German Toni Kroos and Colombian James Rodríguez (2014). There has been a mix of fantastic offensive and defensive players, as well as a focus on youth.

With Florentino and his management team back in charge, the economic model was working well again and operational procedures regarding transparency and accountability were reestablished and improved. Real Madrid was becoming one of the top community brands in the world. However, there was still inconsistency on the field, although this can be expected as it typically takes time for a bunch of new players to gel together. With experience and reflection, the management team would instinctively adjust and make more directed investments for the future.

The good news was that unlike the start of Galácticos 2.0, the club did not have to deal with a desperate financial emergency. There had been significant underinvestment and the club was losing economic steam, so it had to borrow money again to kick off the signing of the players, but the debt would be quickly paid down.

Learning from Experience

Getting the organization back on strategy after the Calderón years and transforming Real Madrid into the most valuable sports team in the world required Florentino and the management team to focus more intently on what it means to win with values. At that time, the academic article on the too-much-talent effect hadn't yet been published, but the management team instinctively had some sense that there were challenges in having the best players at every position. In addition, they had learned how difficult it was to get the values from the community to the coach and to the players. However, they were convinced there were ways to address those challenges and only needed to look more closely at their history (Galácticos 1.0) for inspiration. Though it would take time to act on all of them, the lessons learned were:

- The importance of certain attributes of the coach
- The importance of having a player who is "first among equals"
- The importance of the president consistently driving the values

Drawing on what they had learned from experience, Real Madrid's management team also added new emphasis to the role of leaders and role models and began investing in and grooming the next generation.

Aside from leadership, I analyzed the transfer signings between Galácticos 2.0 and 3.0 to see if Florentino had a bias in favor of offensive players. I found that the amount of money spent for offensive players was certainly higher, but that was in line with market conditions. I examined the actual number of signings that were the highest transfers paid by position as well as offensive and defensive orientation, and the analysis was murky at best. Depending how one wants to characterize certain players' roles, one could argue that there were essentially the same number of offensive and defensive players signed in both eras. Having said that, in Galácticos 3.0, many more of the "defensive" signings have worked out (e.g., Casemiro, Raphaël Varane, Fábio Coentrão, Sami Khedira) than in 2.0 (e.g., Sergio Ramos).

The one clear difference between Galácticos 2.0 and 3.0 is that the age of the players signed is younger in 3.0. Real Madrid had a major transition when Florentino was reelected in 2009. The club signed a bunch of the best players in the world all at the same time instead of bringing them in one at a time as in 2.0. The average age of Cristiano Ronaldo, Kaká, and Benzema when they joined Real Madrid was 24.3. In contrast, the average age of Figo, Zidane, Ronaldo, and Beckham was 27.8. Not only did the average age of star players go down in 3.0, the average age of the team also went down. It seems one of the lessons learned is that the club cannot rely on too many older, established stars, and that there are benefits to developing younger players in the Real Madrid culture as they reach their peak ages and performance. For example, Casemiro was twenty-one in 2013 when he signed with Real Madrid. He started his development in the Real Madrid Academy before being promoted to the first team. Bale was twenty-four when he was signed in 2013 and James twenty-three in 2014.

Importance of Certain Attributes of the Coach

The head coach plays a fundamental role, not just from a technical or tactical view but from other equally important aspects. It must be taken into consideration that he has several press conferences each week and they will be watched all over the world. Since he is constantly in the spotlight, his figure represents the good name of the club worldwide. In other words, he is one of the club's main ambassadors. In addition, he has to lead the players and convey the right messages and suggestions to let the players know how the club has to be represented.

At the peak of Galácticos 1.0 in the 1950s, the club was coached by Miguel Muñoz. As previously mentioned, Muñoz scored Real Madrid's first-ever goal in the European Cup tournament in 1955. He subsequently captained Real Madrid in two consecutive competition wins in 1956 and 1957 and retired from playing the following year at nearly thirty-six. Muñoz served a brief apprenticeship as coach of Real Madrid's reserve club before being appointed coach of the first team in 1959. Muñoz was ideal because he could relate to the players and had their respect as a winner. He also knew what Real Madrid stood for.

The most difficult thing in implementing the Real Madrid strategy and fighting the too-much-talent effect is transmitting the values and expectations of the community from the management team to the coach and then to the players. The coach is essentially the fulcrum, balancing, sometimes precariously, influential players on the one side with a president who represents the club members and community on the other. It is not always the most comfortable spot to occupy, as history bears out (as discussed in chapter three's "Nostalgia for Galácticos 1.0").[153]

---

[153] Since Bernabéu ascended to president in 1943 and effectively created the modern Real Madrid, there have been forty-eight different managerial appointments. Only twenty-three of them have lasted a full year, and only eight of them more than two. Ten coaches have managed the club twice and one of them, Luis Molowny, four times. Miguel Muñoz holds the record for the longest-serving manager but also the second shortest, while the only individual to have spent less time in charge—Jose Camacho—did not actually oversee a competitive game. Most notoriously, Real Madrid has fired a coach the month before a victorious European Cup final and also straight after one.

Managing young, rich, famous, and talented stars is a challenge. The coach must contend with different player personalities, preferences, and egos, and that task is made more difficult by the cultural and language differences that exist in such an international team. Florentino has learned to seek coaches who possess certain characteristics that contribute to effectively conquering such challenges. First, the coach has to respect, model, and communicate the values of the community. This includes, importantly, the style of play as well as respecting the community value of economic responsibility. Second, when coaching Real Madrid, a calm presence helps maintain the team's focus despite the constant distractions of media exposure, rumors, and scrutiny. Lastly, for Real Madrid, a coach that has won a championship and is recognized as an elite player has credibility with players and staff and an understanding of what the players are going through.[154]

In 2013, Real Madrid hired the Italian Carlo Ancelotti. Nicknamed *Carletto*, Ancelotti played as a midfielder and had a successful career with Roma, captaining the team. He won four Coppa Italia honors with Roma and was part of the legendary late-1980s Milan team, with which he won two European titles in 1989 and 1990. Ancelotti was a cautious, composed, hardworking, and creative player, who was regarded as one of the best Italian midfielders of his generation. As a coach, he led Milan to two European championships in 2003 and 2007.

Ancelotti is calm and has the credibility to get stars to buy into a system.[155] Hiring a coach who is respected for winning as a player is a nuance that some people overlook. It is important to star players that they are getting a message from a former winning elite player. Something that Florentino also learned is that he needs to consider the right coach at the right time. For example, he believes that Ancelotti may not have been the perfect coach in 2010 when Florentino felt the team needed

---

[154] Real Madrid executives know that studies examining a coach's playing history provide almost no guide to success as a coach. However, most studies look at all coaches and teams and not former star players with calm temperaments coaching teams with star players. Regardless, even in those cases, which I analyzed, the analysis is inconclusive at best. The Real Madrid executives look to what has worked at the club and what the community values and expects.

[155] Ancelotti said that he played his Milan squad a video of the Al Pacino speech in *Any Given Sunday* (1999) before the Champions League final against Juventus in 2003, which Milan won. The movie has a rousing team talk given by Miami Sharks coach Tony D'Amato and its lesson is about winning "one inch at a time."

more formalized and disciplined practices, and maybe Real Madrid would not have been set up for its run now without then-coach José Mourinho—we can only speculate.

Although a winner of the UEFA Champions League as a coach for Porto in 2004 and Inter Milan in 2010, Mourinho was never an elite player and never played on an elite team or in a major European soccer tournament. However, he did win the first-ever FIFA Ballon d'Or Best Coach Award in 2010 before joining Real Madrid. Mourinho is known for his tactical knowledge, for his charismatic (but very controversial) personality, for getting results, and for drawing attention to himself. In a press conference upon joining Chelsea in 2004, Mourinho said, "Please don't call me arrogant, but I'm European champion and I think I'm a special one," which resulted in the media dubbing him "The Special One."[156] Mourinho's win percentage at Real Madrid was the highest he ever had (72 percent versus 66 percent at Chelsea and 62 percent at Inter Milan). Although a very respected and successful coach, he did not reach the level of success expected at Real Madrid (which is to win the Champions League), and it may be that his charismatic personality, lack of elite player credentials, or tendency to attract attention to himself were disadvantages in the unique Real Madrid environment. On the other hand, it could have been bad luck, and once again, one goal could have dramatically changed the narrative. Without question, the players who share the values of the community are at the top of the sustainable economic-sport model (see figure on page 20), rather than the coach. Florentino and others at Real Madrid are quick to point out Mourinho instilled a lot of discipline and professionalism to training, and although it didn't go as planned for either party, he may have been the right person at the right time to get things set up for La Décima.

At the start of 2014–15 season, after winning La Décima, Real Madrid went on to win twenty-two games in a row with Ancelotti as coach, and at the end of 2014 held four trophies (Champions League Cup, Club World Cup, European Super Cup, and Copa del Rey). But then several key players—including James, Modrić, Bale, Benzema, and

---

[156] "The world according to Mourinho." *BBC Sport.* http://news.bbc.co.uk/sport2/hi/football/teams/c/chelsea/4392444.stm.

Ramos—missed games due to injuries, and the team was out of sync as the usual starters adjusted to new players and tactics. Ancelotti was criticized for his players seeming tired or overused. Real Madrid finished second in La Liga, after being the leader for most of the season, and lost in the semifinals of the Champions League at the end of the season. The club started to look into whether the players were getting injured or too tired because they were fatigued from playing too much or if they were not training properly (too much or too little). In the end, the club felt that the drop-off at the end of the season was enough of a serious issue going forward that they needed the coach to be more sensitive to it. It was one of the considerations when Real Madrid fired Ancelotti and replaced him with Rafael Benítez.

Benítez came to Real Madrid with ample international experience and a long list of titles that includes Champions League, Club World Cup, European Super Cup, and La Liga trophies. He is known to be a methodical tactician, tireless worker, and soccer scholar. But he had two important qualities beyond his achievements. First, he has knowledge of the club and its values. Benítez is a homegrown talent. He made his way through the Real Madrid youth ranks from age thirteen to twenty and even coached at the academy. Although he was not an elite player, he took charge of Liverpool in 2004 and won the Champions League during his first year. Depending on the time, circumstance, character, and makeup of the team, Real Madrid believes that knowledge of their values can be more beneficial than elite status. Real Madrid also wanted a coach who would be more familiar with the academy in terms of giving the academy players on the team more opportunities, which is what the community wants. The other thing that attracted Real Madrid to Benítez was his sensitivity to what I refer to as the too-tired-and-old effect, which is discussed in more detail later. Essentially, Real Madrid's star players need the right balance between too much and too little training and playing. The coach can't be too easy on the players to be liked and can't be too tough on the players to be resented. This is why credentials as being a winner as a great player and coach allow the coach some more leeway with star players.

The principal criticism leveled at great players going into coaching is that they can't understand why their players can't repeat what they themselves were capable of. Meanwhile, more limited players-turned-coach such as Mourinho, Arsene Wenger, or Rafa Benítez can identify more easily with those lacking elite talent, and understand how to motivate them to maximize their talent individually and as a unit. This is a different skill than managing and motivating elite players. Most management books, and even most sports management books, implicitly assume the management and motivation of average or good personnel; very few books (and analysis) focus on managing and motivating elite talent, let alone famous, rich, and young stars.

Benítez had the Real Madrid connection and the training discipline. However, he did not have the star player credentials, nor did he have an attacking game plan, the lack of which really upsets the community. In addition, when he rotated or substituted players to prevent them from getting too tired at the end of the season and to reduce injuries, the press heavily criticized him and implied that players questioned the decisions. My hypothesis on the hiring of Benítez is that certain pressures may force teams into deviating from doing what they may have learned, including competitive comparisons with a rival's success. For Real Madrid, if the coach can't motivate the star players for whatever reasons and/or deviates from what the community expects to see on the field, then I would expect problems. I believe that the Real Madrid executives really understand all of this, which is why they were carefully investing in preparing former Real Madrid legend Zinedine Zidane to be the first team coach. During interviews with Real Madrid, there seemed to be an acknowledgement and excitement that Zidane was the perfect candidate and heir and link to Muñoz and del Bosque, but there was also caution to try to ensure his success because he is so beloved. Also, the club executives believed that many star players have not been successful coaches because they may have lacked preparation.[157]

Changing coaches can create some difficulties because the coach inherits players suited and trained for the system/formation of the previous coach. It can take the players time to adjust and then the coach time to get the right players. In the meantime, the coach is left with the difficult decisions of putting the players in positions to succeed, rather than implementing a system. The complication is that changes not only

---

[157] Zidane is discussed in more detail in chapter twelve in "Investing in the Coach."

happen as players are signed, sold, and released, they happen as the players on the team mature or get older and their performance, expectations,
and roles change. A soccer team is a complex, dynamic, living organization that really has to be nurtured on a daily basis. It takes a special
coach to be flexible enough to adapt to an ever-changing group. If the
coach can't adapt, it is easier to replace the coach than to replace the
team, so a team often chooses a leader who will be useful at the certain time, given the circumstances of the team and its players, and then
replaces the coach as the team and circumstances change. This helps to
explain why Real Madrid has had so many coaching changes.

Phil Jackson ("Zen Master") and Steve Kerr ("Ice")

Phil Jackson is an American example of a coach who has several attributes
to manage a team full of star players. Jackson won two NBA championships
as a player with the New York Knicks and successfully coached the Chicago
Bulls with Michael Jordan and Scottie Pippen and the Los Angeles Lakers with
Kobe Bryant and Shaquille O'Neal to a total of eleven NBA championships.
Though he was not a star, he was respected as an intelligent and hardworking
player and winner. As players have acknowledged in interviews, they listened
to Jackson and gave him a lot of leeway because he was a winner.[158] When
Jackson told star players they needed to trust and cooperate with others to
work toward one goal, he had credibility.

In addition, Jackson's nickname is the "Zen Master" because of his calm
demeanor and adherence to Eastern philosophy.[159] He introduced his teams
to yoga and meditation and regularly assigned his players books to read.[160]

---

[158] "Courtside Chemistry: How NBA's Phil Jackson Won 'Eleven Rings.'" *NPR*. http://www.npr.
org/2013/05/21/183974460/courtside-chemistry-how-nbas-phil-jackson-won-eleven-rings.

[159] Jackson admits to consulting a therapist to figure out how best to deal with a superstar like
Kobe Bryant and says, "Managing anger is every coach's most difficult task. It requires a great deal
of patience and finesse because the line between the aggressive intensity needed to win games
and destructive anger is often razor thin." http://www.dailymail.co.uk/news/article-2326110/
Phil-Jackson-compares-Michael-Jordan-Kobe-Bryant-talks-Kobes-temper-blames-prostate-cancer-
diagnosis-playoff-loss-leaked-memoir.html.

[160] It is unclear whether Jackson would have had the same success if he were not coaching stars.
Each club, time, style, and culture is unique, so what works for one may not transfer elsewhere,
but Jackson's ideas about coaching basketball stars are very much in line with Real Madrid's club

When I was at Michael Jordan's adult fantasy basketball camp in 2006, I asked Jordan about Jackson. According to Jordan, Jackson's calm personality seemed to make it easier to manage different players' egos and to deal with each player individually.[161] He pointed to himself, Scottie Pippen, and Dennis Rodman, three very different personalities, as examples. According to Jordan, Jackson's calmness enabled him to diplomatically help each of them, in difficult situations, to "push the pause button," reflect, and try to stay in the moment, and focus on the team's goals and their role and responsibilities in achieving them. He added that Jackson also had the credibility to hold the players accountable.

Two things often overlooked about Jackson are that he had a "system of offense" on the court called the triangle offense, and he had a strategy to manage a long season. The triangle system of offense not only required a high level of selflessness but also gave players a pivotal and defined role, which is important for teams with interdependence. Interestingly, the triangle system wasn't designed for the stars who could always find a way to score but for all of the other players to have a role in moving together in response to the way the defense positions itself. The system was reliable in that it gave players something to fall back on in pressure situations—the players only had to worry about playing their part in the system, and inevitably good scoring opportunities would be created. The system gave a clear purpose to the group and established defined roles that were critical for performance. The system worked with the star players that he coached, but may not work as well with teams with less talent. Jackson believed his teams needed to pace themselves through the grueling eighty-two-game season as if they were running a marathon, not a series of sprints. He used a large rotation of players at the beginning of seasons, utilizing backup players regularly to make sure they could merge seamlessly with their teammates on the court and understood

---

philosophy: "You have to have a superstar on your club to win a championship in this day and age. You may have to have two terrific players to do so. But the reality is that they have to incorporate all of their other teammates. We get very focused on that...trying to make everyone on the team—even nine, ten, eleven, twelve[th-best players]—just as important, and have a real role that's meaningful...[Those players] are what make the atmosphere, and they are what make the *esprit de corps* what it has to be to be a genuine team effort. Because if they're pulling the wrong direction, if there's jealousy or there's just not the right attitude, it will eventually work its way into the group. And it's a cancer."

[161] Michael Jordan invited many basketball greats to coach and teach. My coaches over the years included Chuck Daly and Flip Saunders, both of whom taught me a lot about life and sports. However, the person I learned the most from about life was Bill Walton. He had so many stories about and lessons learned from John Wooden, Larry Bird, and Jerry Garcia.

the triangle system. Late in the season, he would slowly trim down the rotation of starting players to get the regular players more time together to get ready for the play-offs.

It is fair to wonder whether Jackson, and the triangle offense, would have been as successful if he had different teams, different level of players, and different environments. But all he could do is coach what he was given, and perhaps he knew his strengths in selecting which teams, players, and environments to coach instead of just taking any coaching job.

Meanwhile, Steve Kerr had a fifteen-year NBA career, won five NBA Championship rings (three championships with the Chicago Bulls under Phil Jackson and two championships with San Antonio Spurs under Gregg Popovich), hit the winning shot with an assist from Michael Jordan in the decisive game six of the 1997 finals, and shot 45.4 percent from three-point range in his career, still the best in NBA history. In college, Kerr's nickname was "Ice" because he made critical shots. Kerr was hired to replace Mark Jackson as coach of the Golden State Warriors in the 2014–15 season. Jackson had just taken the Warriors to consecutive playoff appearances for the first time in over twenty years. Mark Jackson is a highly respected and successful player and coach who had a reputation of being a "tough" and "old school" player, a vocal leader on the court, and showing his emotions. When Jackson played, he was known for backing down opposing point guards in the post for fifteen or more seconds at a time. As a coach, he instilled a controlled offense. Jackson never won an NBA championship as a player or a coach. The Warriors stated the team was better than when Jackson first arrived but felt a different coach was needed to lead its two star young players to win a NBA championship. Replacing Mark Jackson with Kerr was considered a controversial and risky decision because Kerr had no coaching experience.

The Warriors' two star young players, Stephen "Steph" Curry and Klay Thompson, loved, and excelled at, taking three-point shots. The sons of former NBA players, Curry and Thompson are nicknamed the "Splash Brothers" due to their ability to "splash" the net with the ball. Kerr had credentials as a player and a calm demeanor. Also, he played for two of the best NBA coaches of all time (Jackson and Popovich), and with some of the best players of all time (Jordan, Pippen, Robinson, and Duncan). Kerr created an open, quick-attacking, unselfish, sharing, three-point shooting style offense that was much different than the way NBA teams traditionally played. Conventional wisdom was that three-point shooting teams couldn't win NBA championships. The Warrior's new offense was beautiful and exciting to witness and became must-watch TV. NBA fans would talk about how real-life Steph Curry was better than video-game Steph Curry, and would want to see his statistics after the game. Largely unnoticed is that through unselfish teamwork, speed, and hustle, the Warriors had fluidity on defense and were also one of the best defensive teams. Mark Jackson deserves some of the credit for this as he had instilled a lot of defensive discipline as coach. Under Kerr, the Warriors developed an authentic identity and culture. Its star players and coach all had reputations for being "values and teamwork-oriented, up-tempo, three-point-shooting and scoring machines." Also, Curry was not a relative physical giant in the NBA at six feet and three inches (1.91 meters) tall and played a style that many people (especially kids) could relate to and mimic as opposed to a high-flying, gravity-defying monster dunk style that most mortals can't even try to replicate. Steve Kerr and his Warriors won the NBA championship in his first year. One of the most amazing things about the championship is that the MVP of the finals wasn't Curry or Thompson, but a season-long reserve player, Andre Iguodala. Kerr was able to get Iguodala to embrace coming off the bench, after starting every game in his previous ten seasons. Iguodala was the Warriors' poster boy for the unselfish values of the team. Kerr had important attributes as coach to get the team to maximize its performance.

Importance of the First Among Equals

Another way Real Madrid promotes its values is by giving the club someone that they all look up to and respect—a role model. The "first among equals" star in the 1950s was Di Stéfano, who is considered one of the greatest soccer players of all time. There were plenty of other stars, such as Puskás, but it was clear that Di Stéfano was the "sun in the galaxy." Di Stéfano joined Real Madrid when he was in his late twenties, so he already had some maturity as a person and player.

When Cristiano Ronaldo joined Real Madrid, he was twenty-four years old, several years younger than Di Stéfano. By the age of twenty-two, in 2007, Ronaldo had received Ballon d'Or and FIFA World Player of the Year nominations. The following year he won his first Ballon d'Or and FIFA World Player of the Year awards.

Typically it takes some time for a new young player to absorb and appreciate the expectations of the Real Madrid community. According to the coaches, from the beginning, Ronaldo has always been an incredibly hard worker and practices and trains with as much intensity as he plays in a game. All the coaches talk about how he sets a marvelous example and has an incredible winning mentality. His sculpted body is a visible reminder to his teammates and community members of his dedication and commitment.

Cristiano Ronaldo practices in three key areas: tactical (awareness, understanding, decision making, and goal-scoring scenarios), physical (speed, strength, stamina, and agility), and technical (the basics, passing, shooting, moves, turns, and other skills to dominate one to one). He is constantly working on one-touch and two-touch plays (with many repetitions at a time), plus the moves to become unpredictable and therefore very hard to defend against. He spends time in the video room studying the tendencies of other players. The coaches add that Ronaldo has the "personality," winning mentality, and attitude.

The coaches pointed out that what goes unnoticed on the field is how he has adjusted his game to increase the effectiveness of the team as a whole. He has learned to create space and use the physicality he has added to his body and game to give his teammates more opportunities. The coaches described how he made slight adjustments to help the overall team when Bale joined. All the players said he was a great teammate and knew when and how to diffuse the pressure with a good sense of humor or unite the team with playful rituals (for example, Ronaldo's and the team's war cry is "*Siiiiiii*"). He grew into a respected teammate and leader by example and consequently won the Ballon d'Or in 2013 and 2014. Although he is known for scoring goals, he also quietly assists and sets up his teammates, enabling them to score. In 2014–15, he was Real Madrid's top assist provider with twenty-two in fifty-four appearances. Even without the ball, Ronaldo helps the team. The coaches pointed to the extra possessions Ronaldo creates for his team with his speed and intensity by pressuring goalies or defensive players to make quick, long passes that are often unsuccessful. His dominant presence as a scoring and assist threat causes defensive players to have to stay close to him (a pull like grav-ity) that creates space and opportunities for his teammates. The coaches praised him for how he helped James fit into the team, and James was one of the biggest beneficiaries of Ronaldo's assists. The coaches describe Ronaldo as feeling a deep personal responsibility to everyone if he doesn't perform at the highest standards that he expects from himself, like he is letting down the people he loves. They say this passion is very rare for a player with his extraordinary talent and success.

Beyond the incredible skills, what Ronaldo contributes to the team is an extraordinary work ethic. It is difficult for a coach to constantly tell star players what to do and to push them. Ronaldo sets the example for the hard work so the coach doesn't have to motivate stars to work hard in practice. Similar to the extremely competitive champions, like Michael Jordan and Walter Payton, he doesn't need a coach to tell him to work hard. He shows up for practice and training ready to compete with the same intensity as he would for a game. He is self-motivated and driven, and he doesn't want to be outworked or beaten in anything. This intensity and work ethic drives the other star players in a way the coach can't. The younger players mimic his good habits. The coach has to have an excellent relationship with the first among equals because it is symbiotic. Complementing Ronaldo are the captains. Like Ronaldo, the captains, because of their seniority, set the tone and have a trusting relationship with him to let him take the lead on certain things.

In the 2013–14 season, Ronaldo was twenty-seven to twenty-eight years old, like Di Stéfano when he joined Real Madrid, and like Di Stéfano, he earned the right to be the first among equals. His leadership and contributions were invaluable in winning La Décima. Just like Di Stéfano, Ronaldo is surrounded by some of the best players in the world in their positions such as Bale, Benzema, James, Kroos, and Ramos, as well as very promising players emerging from the academy like Jesé, Carvajal, Nacho, and Lucas Vázquez.

Back in 2003, Real Madrid could boast of having one of the best teams in soccer history. In fact, five of the top ten players in consideration for the 2003 FIFA player of the year award played for Real Madrid. But there wasn't one first among equals. Today, there are many talented players but only one clear first among equals: Cristiano Ronaldo. In Galácticos

Cristiano Ronaldo, Real Madrid's all-time leading goal scorer and the all-time leading goal scorer in the UEFA Champions League.

1.0 there were Bernabéu and Di Stéfano, and in Galácticos 3.0 there are Pérez and Ronaldo.

The Importance of the President Consistently Driving the Values

When Florentino took over in 2000, he was an outsider. He knew that, when evaluating talent, he wanted the players to have the same core values as the community. He could assess the data analytics provided by the technical team, but because of soccer's complexity, the interpretation of the data can be highly subjective depending on competition level, system used, and even the definitions used in describing actions. Also, data needs context. Admittedly, he was not an expert in soccer-skill appraisal, evaluating how players would work together, or how they should be coached. Florentino provides the mission and values and then relies heavily on the expertise and execution of the people he hires.

Probably the biggest misperception in the media is that Florentino makes the decisions himself. He is very much about consensus and having people come to decisions together, around a set of values and expectations. Over time, Florentino has learned what works and what doesn't work and whose opinions should mean more than others. Also, he has learned that day-to-day factors (e.g., moods, opinions, favorites, etc.) quickly change in sports. He now takes things more in stride and has learned to block out the overwhelming intensity of the opinions, second-guessing, and criticism of media, current and former players and coaches, agents, and so on. He has realized that at the beginning of the season it can take some time for players to click, and therefore patience is needed and one cannot quickly jump to judgments; and the same is true when the team is doing well in the middle of the season, because injuries and other unforeseen occurrences can happen. That is why typically it is best to wait until the end of the season to review the data and information carefully and thoughtfully together as a team and come to a consensus in making judgments.

Another misperception in the media is that Florentino micromanages the coaches. We've learned from numerous interviews with coaches that Florentino never tells them who to play or how to play the team members. Perez has addressed this publicly: "Since I arrived in 2000 none of the coaches have ever said that I have suggested anything to them. They have always had full autonomy." Former Real Madrid coach Ancelotti has also spoken about this point in an interview: "Even in Madrid I was accused of picking the team according to the president's desires. Benítez has his own ideas and he puts these into action on the field." Typically, Florentino and the board review the coaches' performance at the end of seasons. He doesn't make material decisions without consulting with board members. Florentino and his team invest in the best training facilities and infrastructure, and then it is left to the coach and players to be led by the community's objectives. The coaches may feel pressure by the community to play certain players or choose not to rotate players to appease the community.

Florentino and his management team are as convinced as ever that the sustainable economic-sport model is the right model. Over time, Florentino has gained experience and has greater confidence to make the decisions that are best for the entire community in the long-term even if by doing so he risks criticism. This was evident in the management team's decisions regarding the transfers of Ángel Di María and Xabi Alonso, who played integral roles in helping Real Madrid win La Décima. In the summer after the Décima win, Real Madrid sold Di María to Manchester United for £60 million ($98 million), and Alonso to Bayern Munich for £5 million ($8 million). Florentino defended his club's move after Ronaldo openly criticized the sale of Di María. The Real Madrid president insisted there was no feud, saying, "I know Cristiano Ronaldo very well. Cristiano is the best player in the world and his loyalty to Madrid is unquestionable."[162] Florentino revealed that Di María left Real Madrid no option but to sell him after the Argentine midfielder turned down an improved contract that would have made him the club's second-best-paid player behind Ronaldo. In an interview, Florentino said:

> I've been here since 2000. Since then a lot of players have come and gone, and my experience tells me that the ones that leave are always the best and those that arrive are always questioned. My first [signing] was [Zinedine] Zidane and the last [before this summer's transfer window] was [Gareth] Bale. We made the best offer that we could to Di María, and he didn't accept it. Hence, we brought in James, one of the best players at the [2014] World Cup and the FIFA World Cup Golden Boot award winner.

---

[162] "Real Madrid president denies row with Cristiano Ronaldo over transfers." *Guardian*. http://www.theguardian.com/football/2014/sep/05/real-madrid-row-cristiano-ronaldo-florentino-perez-transfers.

> Di María and all of those that have left have our grati-
> tude and respect. A player that is under contract and leaves
> is doing so because he wants to. Real Madrid has always
> respected contracts. Di María had financial requests that I
> considered legitimate, but we couldn't satisfy them. I reiter-
> ate that we made him the best possible offer. With the excep-
> tion of Cristiano, Di María would have been the highest paid
> at Real Madrid. Had we accepted his financial demands, it
> would have created an unbalanced treatment that would have
> put the club's stability in danger. Di María left to Manchester
> for a fee that we considered fair and that is why the transfer
> was completed. We wish Di María the best professionally
> and personally.

It wasn't that Real Madrid couldn't afford the money to pay what Di
María wanted, but rather that it couldn't afford the resulting damage
to team unity and fairness as well as match the club's values.[163] In the
same interview, Florentino noted, "In this club, we follow a sporting-
economic equation which (former club president Santiago) Bernabéu
taught us…"[164]

Florentino also spoke of Alonso's unexpected move to Bayern on a
two-year deal. "Xabi came to us and told us that he wanted to leave," he
said. "He thought it was the best for him and for the club. Our relationship with Xabi is excellent and we accepted his proposal. Xabi is in the
final stages of his sporting career and wants to manage it in this way. We
understand it and we respect it."

Clearly, Florentino has the confidence and stature to stand up for what
he believes is right, even if it seems unpopular in the press. Over time he
has implemented some other adjustments to make such decisions easier.
For example, he travels less with the team to limit his personal relationships with players and prevent conflicts. He does not regularly speak to

---

[163] This is the same reasoning behind Florentino's earlier decision to sell Makélélé to Chelsea.

[164] "Real Madrid president Florentino Pérez defends sale of Ángel Di María to Manchester United
after Cristiano Ronaldo's criticism of La Liga club's summer transfers." Daily Mail. http://www.
dailymail.co.uk/sport/football/article-2745061/Real-Madrid-president-Florentino-Perez-defends-
sale-Angel-di-Maria-Manchester-United.html.

players and coaches as a group. He does it only once or twice a season, and, from time to time, before an important game. After games, if he goes to the locker room, he may say something short to some of the players on their departure. He doesn't speak by phone to the players. From time to time players contact him directly, often affectionately referring to him as "Presi," but the contact usually relates to a personal matter and not what is going on on the field or in the locker room. Florentino is not involved with the internal discipline of the players; it is handled by José Ángel, although Florentino is informed of a particular sanction before it is applied to the player. These sanctions are never made public.

As Florentino mentioned, Real Madrid brought in James, one of the best players at the 2014 World Cup and the FIFA World Cup Golden Boot award winner. One thing that is often overlooked by the press, but not Real Madrid, is that James plays for the Colombia national team, which earned the award for sportsmanship at the 2014 World Cup tournament, lending support to the idea that James would fit into Real Madrid's values and culture.

Interestingly, although there were rumors that Real Madrid had some interest in the talented striker Luis Suárez, Real Madrid did not sign him. When I asked Florentino about this, he simply said Suárez was a fantastically talented player. He knows that Suárez has incredible statistics. However, anyone who watched the 2014 World Cup would know that Suárez had bitten three opponents, including one at the tournament in Brazil. Also, previously he was found guilty of racially abusing a player (a decision Suárez disputes). Still, Suárez was signed by Barcelona in a deal that made him the third most expensive player in soccer history. I had to wonder if Real Madrid decided not to pursue him because such behavior was inconsistent with the values and expectations of the club's fans and members, which could mean that Suárez, even with his immense talent, might never have been fully embraced by the Real Madrid community at the time and could have impacted the economic-sport model. As a matter of policy, no one at Real Madrid would answer the question.

While Madrid spent €80 million ($99 million) on James, who arrived from Monaco, Barcelona bought Suárez from Liverpool for £65 million ($99 million). In 2014–15, the top three players in terms of jersey sales were number one, Cristiano Ronaldo, number two, Lionel Messi, and number three, James Rodríguez. The jersey sales demonstrate the idea that fans idolize and identify with these players.

Early on, James was scorned by many Real Madrid fans who mourned the loss of Di María. They compared it to Makélélé being replaced by Beckham. They asked: What was the Colombian going to bring that the Argentine superstar didn't already have? The answers, according to critics, were superficial qualities—his good looks, a clean-cut image, and marketability. However, there was something that the fans and media missed (and may find shocking): defense. In fact, James added a new dimension to the club's defensive midfield. Until he got hurt in February 2015, James was eighth on the team in average tackles per game with 1.6. Of the seven players ahead of him in this category, five were defenders. The other two were Kroos, who played a deeper position, and Isco, who also tended to play deeper in then-coach Ancelotti's system. James was also seventh in interceptions per game with 0.9. With the exception of Modrić, the remaining six players ahead of him were defenders. James was also only dispossessed of the ball 0.5 times per game, his career best statistic so far.[165]

But everyone wanted to see how James would deliver offensively, especially after the World Cup, and he has not disappointed. Until he got hurt, he had five goals and five assists in La Liga. He had one goal and one assist in the Champions League and added one assist in the Copa del Rey. He was second in the team in key passes per game with 2.5 (his career average is 1.9), and he was also averaging more crosses and long balls in the season than he ever had before. His passing success rate was also at an all-time high. When he was on the field, Real Madrid scored every thirty minutes—without him, every forty-two minutes. In essence, James was exceeding expectations in every way, before getting injured.

For those wondering, Di María averaged 0.7 tackles per game for Manchester United and 0.8 interceptions during the same time (he averaged 1.3 tackles per game in his last season for Real Madrid and 0.6 interceptions; he is dispossessed 1.5 times per game, which was around the same figure for Real Madrid last year). After a bright beginning, he

[165] David Salazar, "Real Madrid vs. Barcelona 2014–15: James Rodríguez vs. Luis Suárez – Which Side Is Getting the Most Out of Its Summer Transfer Acquisitions?" *Latin Post*. http://www. latinpost.com/articles/27207/20141205/real-madrid-vs-barcelona-2014-15-james-rodriguez-vs-luis-suarez-which-side-is-getting-the-most-out-of-its-summer-transfer-acquisitions.htm.

started only one of the last ten games of the 2014–15 season. In 2015, Manchester United sold Di María to Paris Saint-Germain for £44.3 million ($72 million)—as mentioned, Manchester United had paid £60 million for him to Real Madrid the previous summer. In the 2013–14 La Liga season with Di María, Real Madrid scored 103 goals and allowed 37 for a net +66; without him (and even with the injuries) in 2014–15, Real Madrid scored 118 goals and allowed 38 for a net +80.

As it turned out, Real Madrid's investment in James was making good economic and statistical performance sense, while contributing positively to the team dynamics. Di María, on the other hand, was asking for more money than Real Madrid would pay, and Real Madrid replaced him because meeting his demands would not have been in keeping with the community's values of being economically responsible or with the tradition and policy of relative fairness, among other things.

Bold and Brave Actions

The importance of the president consistently driving the values can require a united executive group's bold and brave actions. For decades, the most extreme and boisterous socios who sat behind the south goal of the stadium were called the Ultra Sur, and they generated a lot of noise and atmosphere at home games, while sometimes also being involved in offensive chanting, acts of violence, and spreading extreme political and xenophobic ideology. Most presidents struggled with what to do with them when their passion went too far or their values deviated from the club's because they represented an estimated nine hundred members. For decades, they have led the support and cheering at the stadium, and the club tries to embrace differences.

When Florentino first became President in 2000, he sent a message to the Ultra Sur stating that no violence, xenophobic attitudes, or extreme political signs of any kind, would be allowed in the stadium. Consequently, Real Madrid removed all the separating fences between the stands and the field. During Forentino's presidency, there were no negative experiences with Ultra Sur in the stadium. However, in 2012, outside the stadium and before a game, tensions between two factions of the Ultra Sur escalated to the point that the police had to intervene.

Then, Florentino with the support of the executive team and the board of directors took the very bold and brave action of reassigning the Ultra's seats to younger members to lead the stadium in cheering, and they banned some of the most radical Ultra from the stadium. A new group called Grada de Animación (animation stands/terrace) has taken over. The group is required to cheer the team throughout the whole game and sing along with songs started by the leader. All group members sign a contract with their ID cards, meaning the club is aware of every member of Grada de Animación. The crucial part of the contract between Grada de Animación members and Real Madrid is to ensure that the group is full of young men and women supporting Madrid throughout the whole game without racism, violence, or politics. Whoever breaks the contract gets expelled, which is what happened when a fan called an opposing player unflattering words. The Bernabéu has always been a very demanding crowd and Real Madrid does not want to change that tradition; it just wants to ensure that its values are upheld.

Señorío

In 2009, Real Sociedad, a soccer team based in San Sebastián of the Basque region in Northern Spain, was celebrating their 100-year anniversary while teetering on the brink of bankruptcy. They were under administration and relegated to the second division, after having been in the first division for forty consecutive years. They called some other Spanish teams to play them in a friendly exhibition to celebrate the centennial year and raise money. Many turned them down or asked for money. Real Madrid accepted the invitation and agreed to play for free and put its stars in the starting lineup.[166] This classy behavior is what Real Madrid community members call Señorío. Señorío is an attitude, an approach for doing things—roughly translated as "gentlemanliness," "chivalry," or more loosely, "class." It was first introduced into the lexicon of Real Madrid during the first term of Florentino's presidency. Alex Ferguson, the longtime coach of Manchester United, recalls in

---

[166] Oier Fano Dadebat, "La Liga: Shabby Barcelona are miles away from Real Madrid in class and dignity." *International Business Times*. http://www.ibtimes.co.uk/la-liga-shabby-barcelona-are-miles-away-real-madrid-class-dignity-1496194.

his autobiography: "I was surprised when, after my last match...I received a beautiful gift, a silver replica of Cibeles, the fountain where Real Madrid celebrate title wins, and a lovely letter from president Florentino Pérez."[167]

The community also displayed Señorío when many Madridistas gave a standing ovation for legendary playmaker Francesco Totti of A. S. Roma when he came onto the field as a substitute in a Champions League game at Bernabéu Stadium in 2016. The thirty-nine year old was born in Rome, played three years on the Roma youth team, and then played his entire professional career for Roma. After the game, Totti said his only regret is that he never played for Real Madrid. The Roma captain described his feelings about the standing ovation after the game: "It's a unique emotion...I really didn't expect it to be so strong. It means I've given a lot to the game of football, and this is my thanks from an amazing stadium." Real Madrid fans have given similar standing ovations to Italian star players Alessandro Del Piero and Andrea Pirlo.[168]

Real Madrid's Player Selection Process

Real Madrid obsesses over player selection; however, not in a way many people may think. Most of the players on the team are considered among the best in the world and they are followed by millions of fans all over the planet. Therefore, Real Madrid feels that the players must be the club's best representatives. Thus, they have to behave according to the essence of the club: its values and culture.[169] The players have to make the community proud of belonging to the club, regardless of the results.

---

[167] Sir Alex Ferguson, *Alex Ferguson: My Autobiography* (London: Hodder & Stoughton 2013).

[168] Ben Gladwell, "Roma stiker Francesco Totti overwhelmed by Bernabeu ovation." *ESPNFC*. http://www.espnfc.com/as-roma/story/2825492/roma-striker-francesco-totti-overwhelmed-by-bernabeu-ovation.

[169] They recognize many of the players are relatively young and have a lot of money, fame, and various influences and, from time to time, may make irresponsible decisions that in hindsight they may regret. Depending on the severity, actions can range from impacting the club's attitude about whether to sell or release the player or handling the matter privately with a discussion and a fine that is not reported. Real Madrid is obsessive about trying to handle these matters privately and confidentially in order not to negatively impact the club or the player. Just about every team has players with some problems; the important aspect is how the club deals with them.

The players have inherited a very rich legacy and they have the obligation to preserve it because it is a key part of the treasure. Together with the community, the players in essence hand the legacy to future generations. This is the Real Madrid trademark.

Real Madrid's emphasis on teamwork extends to the process through which player and other personnel changes are made, and the decision-making roles and responsibilities are clearly delineated and fit into a values framework of the community. When the season ends, the Real Madrid management team asks the coaches and the technical team which positions they would like to improve, in terms of both technical skills and club chemistry. The technical aspect of evaluation is essential, and the head coach's opinion is vital. Strengthening the team is always the main objective. A group of people make the final decision, taking into consideration many different factors.

If management believes that a player is not behaving in a way consistent with community values, either on or off the field, then they will most likely replace the player. A player's negative behavior can range from poor work ethic to poor representation of the club, to creating locker room conflicts, or making threats and demands. With regards to on-the-field performance, Real Madrid coaches and technical staff manage players from the beginning levels, and work with them as they advance through the ranks. They consciously seek to replace players who do not have the level of skill or the potential to compete for a first team position. In addition, they need to make an assessment if a player's skill level or contribution is commensurate with his salary expectations. Real Madrid believes they have to do this to meet the community's values and expectations, and it also ensures that the players feel the club is a meritocracy and fair. Obviously this can create problems with popular players whose age or other factors start to impact skill level and performance. Beyond values, professionalism, and personality, the club analyzes other aspects such as tendency for injury.

The club views that they are not just signing a player but a future ambassador. The ideal would be, of course, to hire the best player in the world for a position, someone who has the strongest commitment to Real Madrid's values and professionalism, who fits into the coach's system, and puts the team first at all times.[170] This may not be possible, given that one of the club's values is economic responsibility, and paying a sky-high salary and transfer fee may not be the fiscally responsible thing to do.[171]

While the book *Soccernomics* argued that teams overpay for Golden Boot award players in FIFA World Cups, when looking at their overall statistics, Real Madrid would argue that those elite, proven players score when the pressure and level of competition is the greatest. This is critically important when scoring opportunities are at a premium and Real Madrid is focusing on winning championships against the best competition in pressure situations, not just getting to the final stages. A statistical average over long seasons, which includes playing weaker teams in less-important games, may lead to certain beliefs about a player. However, upon closer examination of only high-profile, pressure games, where trophies are on the line or the competition is very high quality, the statistics may lead to another belief and the willingness, deservedly, to pay more. Real Madrid knows that luck and randomness play a major part in soccer, especially in play-off formats with one or two games (discussed further in chapter thirteen, "Challenges"), but the club tries to identify any statistical competitive advantage going into the Champions League. The value of that advantage may be more to Real Madrid and its economic-sport model than it may be for other teams; therefore, it is difficult to compare a player's value to Real Madrid versus another team, especially considering the value both on and off the field. In addition, it is difficult to argue that Real Madrid overpaid for a player when the club has an economic-sport model based on community values to maximize the economics of the player relative to his absolute cost, as well as the cost as a percentage of revenues.

---

[170] When describing the NBA's San Antonio Spurs' General Manager, R.C. Buford, in 2014, Aaron Bollwinkel of nbadraft.net pointed out: "The Spurs focus is clearly on maintaining a winning culture and having a cohesive direction, and within that Buford rarely makes decisions that would compromise the overall plan of the Spurs machine. Buford signs guys that fit Pop's game plan, Buford drafts players that fit the Spurs culture, and Buford keeps his decisions in line with organizational goals."

[171] According to Howard Beck's 2007 *New York Times* article titled "Spurs' Winning Culture Has Other Teams Wanting the Secret": "However one defines that [San Antonio Spurs'] culture... Those who have lived the Spurs' way say it is about high character and low risk, humility and honesty, and payroll prudence."

Examining selected Real Madrid player performances during their time in La Liga and the Champions League illuminates the types of players the team values on the field. I selected players that played at least fifty games for Real Madrid. I did not examine players' statistics before or after they played at Real Madrid because they could have played in a different system with a different caliber of players. The Champions League games should have higher quality opponents than a typical La Liga game since teams must qualify. (For MLB enthusiasts, see Appendix B: "Season Averages vs. Postseason in Baseball" for a similar analysis to the one below.) The analysis shows that Di Stéfano and Gento (Galácticos 1.0), Figo and Raúl (Galácticos 2.0), and Benzema (Galácticos 3.0) averaged higher goals per game in the Champions League than in La Liga.

Table 10.1: Goals per Game in La Liga and Champions League

Goals per Game*			
	La Liga	Champions League	% Change
Galácticos 1.0			
Di Stéfano	0.77	0.84	+10%
Gento	0.30	0.35	+19%
Galácticos 2.0			
Figo	0.23	0.27	+15%
Raúl	0.41	0.50	+21%
Galácticos 3.0			
Benzema	0.46	0.56	+20%

* Puskás and Zidane didn't have more than fifty games in the European Cup/Champions League for Real Madrid.

Examining Cristiano Ronaldo and Messi, since Ronaldo has been at Real Madrid, illustrates how dominant both players really are, averaging around a goal per game, which is absolutely remarkable. Comparing their goal-per-game numbers with the Real Madrid legends in Table 10.1 highlights how amazing they both are to average that rate. This is especially true if one considers that the average goals per game have gone from around 3.5 overall during the time of Galácticos 1.0 to just above 2.5 over the last several decades. Both of their Champions League goals per game are lower than in La Liga, but that can be attributed somewhat to moving from simply ridiculous to merely obscene (and moving closer to the mean).

Table 10.2: Goals per Game in La Liga and Champions League

Goals per Game*			
	La Liga	Champions League	% Change
Ronaldo	1.13	0.98	-13%
Messi	1.13	0.91	-19%

* Since Ronaldo joined Real Madrid. Data from Opta Sports Data.

I also examined the goals per game in the Champions League knockout rounds because these goals are typically against even greater competition (final-sixteen teams) versus the larger group stages. Obviously, there are fewer data points, less than the fifty games used above as a cut-off, but we see Ronaldo is still close to one goal per game.

Table 10.3: Goals per Game in Champions League Knockout Rounds

Goals per Game*			
	Appearances	Champions League KO Round Goals	Goals Per Game
Ronaldo	32	29	0.91
Messi	35	27	0.77

* Since Ronaldo joined Real Madrid. Data from Opta Sports Data.

Examining the median for the top fifty scorers in Champions League history in the tournament, we find what we expected: on average most players, even the best ones, have slightly lower performance in the Champions League, probably due to more competitive teams and/or teams playing more conservatively. Ronaldo's and Messi's goals per game in the Champions League are two times the average of the top fifty players, demonstrating how truly incredible they are. The percentage change in goals per game is -5 percent for the best players in the Champions League, while Real Madrid's players over history are 10 to 20 percent higher.

**Table 10.4: Median Goals per Game for Top Fifty Scorers
in Champions League History**

Reg. Season	Champions	% Change
0.48	0.46	-5%

Getting back to Real Madrid's player selection process, how a certain player will fit into the club's system is a big consideration. I was given behind-the-scenes access to the sophisticated data and analysis used by the coaching staff. The data and color charts and heat maps look like they were from the NASA space program. The use of words such as "gravity score,"[172] an actual sports-analytics term, indicated that this is hardcore stuff. It would seem that every aspect is tracked. During games, Real Madrid has two different filming systems: Mediacoach, with two bundles of four HD cameras, which tracks players for technical and fitness data, and Prozone, with one bundle of four HD cameras, doing similar tracking to Mediacoach. The reason for two systems is that often definitions describing actions, and proprietary data, analysis, and emphases are different among data firms.

Real Madrid believes it doesn't take a large data analytics staff to figure out that Ronaldo and Messi are great players. The club does not believe that statistics are the final word on the value of players in the market, but statistical analysis, when used properly and combined with other elements like assessing personal values, can sometimes avoid costly mistakes in transfer fees. Also, one needs to take into account playing styles, roles, and preferences when looking at the numbers. You need context. Regardless, Real Madrid believes it is the analysis of values that helps the team avoid big mistakes on the field, or threaten the economic-sport model necessary to afford players like Ronaldo.

Once the managers and technical experts (including statistical data experts) know which positions they want to improve, they typically identify two or three candidates that they believe would be better "fits" than the incumbents in those positions. Before making recommendations,

---

[172] In sports analytics, a gravity score is the tendency of defenders to be pulled to certain parts. It illuminates where defenders position themselves and helps determine the success and failure of offenses.

they will make repeated calls to people who know the player and his character. They really dive deeply into a player's personality and values to see if he's a match with Real Madrid. This is done by coaching and technical staff first. However, there may be the temptation to rationalize and make accommodations for a player with more wins who doesn't conform to the sought-after values. To compensate for or avoid that, the president needs to be established and experienced in these matters. The executives will sometimes utilize outside consultants and advisors to develop a better picture around values and fit. Others in the organization also do character and background checks. Real Madrid may lose out on talent when prioritizing character to that degree, but Florentino believes the club finds A-level talent with A-level character. Obviously, these checks don't need to be made for Real Madrid academy players when they are graduating.[173]

The decision to sign a particular player rests exclusively with the managers and technical experts, provided that the player fits with the values of Real Madrid. The departments mentioned below develop a post-contract strategy to maximize the image and revenues for the club, as well as to assimilate the player.

Finance and marketing managers then work together to evaluate the two to three candidates in terms of costs and marketing considerations, as well as their conformance to the club's culture. Marketing then works with the finance staff to quantify each player's potential marketing impact (image rights, sponsorships, etc.). There are many hypothetical models that try to estimate a player's value and revenue impact. Some models even try to quantify the relative return both on and off the field. Real Madrid does not assign a numeric value to any one player. Management thinks valuation is more of an art than a science. Part of the science is in analyzing actual market dynamics or competing proposals. When

---

[173] In the press, Real Madrid's interest in a player may be overstated or understated and manipulated by a variety of interests (e.g., player, agent, the teams interested or not even really interested). For example, Real Madrid was very interested in signing David Beckham but in order not to tip their hand, Real Madrid tried to seem less interested. The opposite is true also, which can cause the price of a player to increase. In the end, because of Real Madrid's financial position, history, tradition, values, ability to compete for championships, training facilities, and community it feels that it is in a unique position to attract and retain the best players it seeks.

dealing with a team sport, valuing a player's contribution on the field and in marketing opportunities is an art. For example, art comes into play when the executive team compares the cost to acquire each candidate relative to other club members, in order not to make offers that could be perceived as disproportionate, because fair and equal treatment is a key element of the Real Madrid culture. That means that Real Madrid may pass on signing an otherwise promising candidate even if the club can afford him financially. The more experience Real Madrid management has, the more they focus on maintaining the perception of fairness as well as economic responsibility, even if it leads to unpopular decisions or popular players choosing to go elsewhere. In the end, acquiring new players is a collaborative effort based on shared decision making that cuts across functional silos and is driven by four imperatives: transparency, club philosophy, social responsibility, and economic responsibility. Real Madrid seeks to support the acquisition of the right talent with both a visible structure (e.g., codified values, organizational hierarchy, etc.) and an invisible one (e.g., history, tradition, captains, academy players, etc.) to try to assemble the best team members to play together, resulting in the best overall performance in accordance with the community's values and expectations.

Too-Tired-and-Old Effect

Many factors (e.g., genetics, diet, conditioning, previous injuries, etc.) determine a player's peak age, and it can vary significantly from athlete to athlete. The timing may vary but unfortunately the results are unavoidable: athletic performance declines for a player after a peak age. Also, the older a player is, the longer it takes to recover to be able to compete at peak performance. When analyzing data, it is important to understand context. Age is often neglected when reviewing statistics. Sian Allen and Will Hopkins, at the Sports Performance Research Institute in New Zealand, examined scientific literature to determine the age at which athletes competing in various sports hit peak competitive performance:

Table 10.5: Peak Ages for Male Athletes by the Sports Performance Research Institute in New Zealand

Sport	Peak Age
Sprinter	25
Olympic Distance Triathlete	27
Marathoners	30
Ironman Distance Triathlete	32

Generally, the authors noticed that athletes competing in "sprint" events requiring explosive power peak much sooner than athletes competing in endurance or game-oriented events, perhaps because older athletes are able to use experience and savvy to their advantage. Glaringly missing from the review was soccer, but soccer peak age is probably in the middle of sprinting (twenty-five) and endurance (thirty-two), although sprinting and speed is becoming increasingly important in soccer, discussed in more detail in the sidebar "More Speed—It Is a Young Man's Game." Also, in the sidebar "Analyzing Stars, Workhorses, and Juniors," I discuss the ages of Real Madrid's stars.

No one works harder at slowing the impact of the aging process than Cristiano Ronaldo. Some of the data indicates the effects are there, but he is changing his physique and game to adapt. Adam Bate of Sky Sports reported that in Ronaldo's first season at Real Madrid in 2009–2010, he averaged 3.3 dribbles per ninety minutes; in the 2013–2014 season it declined to 2.4; and in 2014–2015 it declined even further to 1.6.[174] However, Ronaldo's goal-per-game ratio has not suffered because, like other world-class athletes, he has adapted his game to becoming a pure finisher with help from his teammates, and he utilizes his experience and savvy to his advantage.[175] Zidane retired in 2006 at thirty-four years old, after he had finished second in FIFA World player of the year, behind Fabio Cannavaro, who was thirty-three at the time. Ronaldo was born in 1985, and as of this writing is thirty-one years old. Craig Alexander won his third IRONMAN World Championship when he was

---

[174] Adam Bate, "Cristiano Ronaldo controlling his Real Madrid decline." *SkySports*. http://www.skysports.com/football/news/11096/10155108/cristiano-ronaldo-controlling-his-real-madrid-decline. More aggressive fouling (or attempted fouls) of Ronaldo when he dribbles may also impact this.

[175] Some have suggested that although the goals-per-game average is consistent, recently Ronaldo scores more goals in games and has more games with no goals. I examined this. It is not accurate.

thirty-eight years old, six years after the typical peak age in the sport. In fact, Alexander won all three of his world championships after the average peak age for the sport. Alexander's performance demonstrates that an athlete can still achieve incredible success many years after the average peak age.[176]

Statistics are kept on injuries. Soccer has a relatively high injury incidence (seventeen to twenty-four injuries per 1,000 playing hours) compared with many other sports.[177] According to the UEFA Elite Club Injury Study 2013–14 season report examining twenty-nine teams: on average, teams had 213 training sessions (19.7 per month) and fifty-nine games (5.5 per month) over an almost eleven-month season, and "on average, across all clubs, each player missed 2.2 training sessions and 0.6 matches each month because of injury."[178] Professors Nader Rahnama, Thomas Reilly, and Adrian Lees published a paper in February 2002 in the *British Journal of Sports Medicine* that analyzed the injury risk associated with soccer games from the English Premier League from 1999–2000. They concluded that "playing actions with high injury risk were linked to contesting possession. Injury risk was highest in the first and last fifteen minutes of the game, reflecting the intense engagements in the opening period and the possible effect of fatigue in the closing period. Injury risk was concentrated in the areas of the pitch where possession of the ball is most vigorously contested, which were specific attacking and defending zones close to the goal."[179] The highest risk of injury is in the second half and in the last fifteen minutes of the game. This is most likely why some coaches prefer to substitute players at the end of games when leading. However, the Real Madrid community typically doesn't like to see substitutions of star players.

Despite widespread belief that Real Madrid has more than its share of injuries, according to official reports, over the last few seasons the club is generally average with top contenders for the Champions League trophy in the

---

[176] In Ironman, an athlete has time to taper and rest for one big event. In soccer, players have many games over a season and sometimes games are twice a week, depending on tournaments.

[177] J. Ekstrand, "Soccer injuries and their prevention." Linkoping University Medical Dissertions, No 130, Linkoping, Sweden, 1982.
    RD Hawkins, CW Fuller. "An examination of the frequency and severity of injuries and incidents at three levels of professional." *British Journal of Sports Medicine*. 1998; 32: 326–32.

[178] "2013/14 season report Team X." UEFA Elite Club Injury Study. http://www.uefa.org/ MultimediaFiles/Download/uefaorg/Medical/02/19/04/32/2190432_DOWNLOAD.pdf.

[179] N. Rahnama, T. Reilley, and A. Lees, "Injury risk associated with playing actions during competitive soccer." *British Journal of Sports Medicine*. http://bjsm.bmj.com/content/36/5/354.full.

main injury parameters, namely incidence, burden, and players' availability.[180] Obviously, it is not just the number of injuries that matters but which player(s) and the quality and availability of the replacement(s) that also matter. This is particularly true if a team doesn't rely on a consistent system that players are familiar with and instead relies more on improvisation required with familiarity of the other players, which is mostly true for Real Madrid.

While statistics are kept on reported injuries, there is no real data on when the athlete is playing through injuries, aches and pains, and physical and mental exhaustion and stress. As discussed previously, Real Madrid and other major teams that can afford the best players are competing for several trophies during the year, and then their players also play for their respective national teams. The soccer stars' national teams rely upon them to perform at the highest level in international competitions, as well as in the qualification rounds. The pressure to perform and the physical conditioning, playing, travel, and public relations commitments entailed by a demanding schedule slowly take a physical and mental toll over a long season. If not properly rested, these star players face an increased risk of suboptimal performance or injury. The older a star player is, the higher the risk. Professors Jan Ekstrand, Mike Walden, and Martin Hägglund wrote a paper in the *British Journal of Sports Medicine* in August 2004 that investigated the injuries and performances of soccer players from European teams in the 2002 World Cup. They concluded: "The players who underperformed had played more matches during the ten weeks before the World Cup than those who performed better than expected…(60 percent) [of the players] who had played more than one match a week before the World Cup incurred injuries or underperformed during the World Cup." Players deemed to have underperformed in international tournaments held in the midsummer were found to have played more games in the later part of their domestic and continental competitions than others judged to have done well.[181] This analysis tells us what we would suspect, that players are impacted by being too tired. It happens at the end of the games, when they are susceptible to injury. It happens in competitions when they have played too much.

---

[180] Santiago Siguero, "Real Madrid score top marks in UEFA report." *Marca.* http://www.marca.com/en/football/real-madrid/2016/02/20/56c7a27f268e3efc2a8b466e.html.

[181] J. Ekstrand, M. Walden, M. Hagglund, "A congested football calendar and the well being of players: correlation between match exposure of European footballers before the World Cup 2002 and their injuries and performances during that World Cup." *British Journal of Sports Medicine.* 2004; 38: 493-7.

Playing too often can happen for the best athletes playing for the best teams, especially when considering their national team commitments, which are during the season and off-season. An example of the potential conflict between national teams and European professional soccer team priorities is when, in November 2014, Real Madrid was without the services of then-twenty-nine-year-old star midfielder Luka Modrić for months after he suffered a thigh injury in Croatia's 1–1 draw in an international game against Italy. Modrić's versatility and work ethic are important to Real Madrid's performance as well as the team chemistry. After Modrić came back from injury, he was injured again a few weeks later. The Croatian national team doctor said, "Ancelotti [Real Madrid's then-coach] did not spare Luka at all after he returned from a long-term injury...He played ninety minutes in every game. Ancelotti put Modrić under a lot of pressure, instead of giving him minutes bit by bit...Modrić was not injured because of the knocks he received but because he was not 100 percent fit. If he hadn't been overworked, his lower leg would not have moved to the side under that tackle."[182] The national team doctor is unquestionably putting the national team's priorities over Real Madrid's, but he is also identifying that the player is too tired as a result of playing for both teams, which led to another injury.

Injuries during international soccer games caused many Real Madrid players to miss multiple games in 2014–15 and 2015–16. Interestingly, there appears to be a specific time period where this happens more, from August to November, the first months of league competition and when national team commitments are the busiest during the season.[183]

After winning the World Cup in the summer of 2014, Toni Kroos, the German midfielder, started thirty-six of thirty-eight of the La Liga games for Real Madrid in the 2014–15 season, and was an unused substitute in the other two. Some argued that Kroos was not the only player who's been overused at Real Madrid—he's just the one to have remained fit enough to keep accruing minutes. If everyone was available, critics argued, then-coach Ancelotti

---

[182] "Luka Modrić injury caused by Real Madrid boss Ancelotti - Croatia doctor." *ESPNFC*. http://www.espnfc.us/spanish-primera-division/story/2409087/luka-modric-injury-caused-by-real-madrid-boss-carlo-ancelotti-croatia-doctor-boris-nemec. (The Croatian national team doctor's claim that Modrić played the full ninety minutes in every game is not correct.)

[183] Dermot Corrigan, "Rafa Benitez defends Real Madrid club doctor." *ESPNFC*. http://www.espnfc.us/real-madrid/story/2678780/rafa-benitez-defends-real-madrid-club-doctor.
Gerry Delahunt, "How can Real Madrid prevent injuries?" *Managing Madrid*. http://www.managingmadrid.com/2015/8/8/9120567/real-madrid-injuries-2015.

invariably tended to pick his favored starting lineup week in and week out.[184] At the same time, the community expects to see the best players and a fluid game, which requires players to be familiar with playing together to win, so it places the Real Madrid coach in a difficult position. By the end of the 2014–15 season, Real Madrid's performance started to drop off.[185] The club is more focused on maintaining a balance in the team and replacing star players as they pass their peak age, while relying on a coach to use a system of rotation during the season as well as conditioning during that season. The one thing the club can't completely control is the players' national team commitments.

Archrival Barcelona took a different approach. In midfield, where Real Madrid appeared to suffer the most from fatigue and injuries in the 2014–15 season, the Barcelona coach rotated players more regularly. That coach was heavily criticized for this rotation policy at first, especially as the club had some disappointing losses.[186] Throughout all competitions, the coach went nearly thirty games without naming the same starting lineup. By the end of the season, having endured the early criticism, Barcelona was comparatively full of life, in part because of that rotation.

Tiredness often leads to suboptimal performance, but is difficult to detect, track, and analyze. For example, tiredness may reduce the frequency and intensity of activity off the ball, which can mean missed scoring opportunities (e.g., a player can't catch up to the speed of the ball for a touch when normally he could) or missed defensive assignments (e.g., he doesn't sprint back to help on defense because he is too tired). In addition, insufficient rest and recovery not only impacts players physically, it impacts them psychologically. Tiredness needs to be taken into context when reviewing data and statistics. Krishna Narsu, who consults for the NBA Dallas Mavericks, analyzed how LeBron James and other player's average speeds changed when playing back-to-back days instead of having one day of rest between games. As expected, there was a statistically significant difference when examining

---

[184] Nicholas Rigg, "Rafa Benitez's six Real Madrid action items." *ESPNFC*. http://www.espnfc.us/club/real-madrid/86/blog/post/2478071/rafa-benitez-six-action-items-at-real-madrid.

[185] After winning the Champions League in 2014, many Real Madrid players only had one or two weeks off before the 2014 World Cup and then one or two weeks off before reporting to Real Madrid for the season. At Christmas/New Years, the players had to play FIFA Club World Cup, which limited their holiday. By the end of the 2014-2015 season, the players looked fatigued.

[186] "Enrique Defends Barca Rotation Policy." *FourFourTwo*. http://www.fourfourtwo.com/news/enrique-defends-barca-rotation-policy#:I6p83lrm8_nufA.

regular starters. Interestingly, the players were slower after four days of rest, most likely because of "rust." The differences are small, but when the differences of winning and losing can come down to inches or fractions of seconds in interdependent sports where players need to judge their teammates' speeds, it can impact performance and not be easily detected.[187]

More Speed—It Is a Young Man's Game

The too-tired-and-old effect matters because speed, endurance, and peak age are more important in today's soccer. In the 1970s, an average soccer player ran approximately 2.5 miles per ninety-minute game. Today, an analysis of the maximum running distances of players in La Liga and Champions League games shows that the average soccer player runs approximately 7.1 miles in a game (the minimum is 3.5 miles; maximum is 8.5 miles). The largest distances are covered by central midfielders (approx. 7.5 miles), followed by side midfielders (approx. 7.45 miles), side defenders (approx. 7.1 miles), forwards (approx. 7 miles), and central defenders (approx. 6.6 miles).[188] Studies have shown that with the increased distances covered today, players slow in the second half of play. The rules of soccer, unlike basketball, limit the ability to rest players. In basketball, coaches can rest older players to keep them fresh for key moments. The San Antonio Spurs, for example, won the NBA Championship in 2014 by resting their three biggest stars on the bench 43 percent of the time.[189] In contrast, soccer's limit of just three substitutions per game puts a premium on endurance above all else. The only way for a player to compensate for fatigue is with craftiness and technique—a tremendously difficult feat for even small losses in speed and stamina.

[187] Krishna Narsu, "NBA Players Need Their Rest." *Nylon Calculus*. http://nyloncalculus.com/2015/07/20/nba-players-need-their-rest/.

[188] V. Di Salvo, R. Baron, H, Tschan, FJ Calderon Montero, N. Bachi, F. Pigozzi, "Performance characteristic according to playing position in elite soccer." *International Journal of Sports Medicine* 3: 222–7 (2007). http://www.ncbi.nlm.nih.gov/pubmed/17024626.

[189] "Player age in football: The Clock is ticking." *Economist*. http://www.economist.com/blogs/gametheory/2014/07/player-age-football.

Soccer players run in short bursts, using the time when the ball is on the other side of the field to recover. During the game a player might have thirty-five to fifty "sprints," depending on the player's position. Most of these are of relatively short duration, less than five-seconds. Taking the players' average of forty-five "sprints," they "sprint" about every two minutes. So it's like doing forty-five short sprints with probably a 90- to 180-second recovery jog in between. In comparison, a 100-meter track athlete typically will compete in an average of twenty to thirty races over an entire season. And as previously discussed, sprinters and Olympic-distance triathletes have peak age performances of twenty-five and twenty-seven, respectively. In modern soccer, since the mid-2000s, the average number of sprints a soccer player performs has increased about a third, while the recovery time between the high-intensity sprints has dropped around 20 percent. With soccer demanding more physical exertion than ever, the sport is turning into a young man's game. Responding to these demands, Real Madrid's training has focused on improving the ability to recover between intense sprints, which includes high-intensity interval-type training.

Ronaldo and Messi have extraordinary speed. In a study published by FIFA, both Ronaldo and Messi are in the top-ten fastest soccer players in the world. They reach top speeds of about 20.5 mph in a game. That is equivalent to around eleven seconds in a 100-meter race. Remember, this is in a game, on grass and wearing cleats, shin guards, and soccer uniform. Gareth Bale is slightly faster. The sprint distances have a meaningful impact on the number of goals.[190] Jan Vecer, a former professor in the department of statistics at Columbia University who is working on an upcoming book titled *Soccermetrics: Science of Soccer Statistics*, believes "The sprint distances have a large positive effect on the goals." His hypothesis is that the critical statistic is the acceleration, which captures the change from the fast play to sprints. More importantly, it is not the absolute value of the acceleration, but rather the difference over the opposite team. He believes that both Ronaldo and Messi benefit enormously from being able to accelerate to a level that can overrun the defenders of the opposite team. His hypothesis is that their lower scoring rate in the Champions League (goals per

---

[190] What makes Ronaldo unusual is that he has the length of legs of a sprinter, the body fat of a middle-distance runner, and the powerful thighs of a basketball player. As an example of Ronaldo's athleticism with a two-step run up, he can jump 2 feet, 6 inches off the ground, higher than the average basketball player. He is rumored to have a Vo2 Max of 75 versus an average soccer player of 63. His height is 185.1 cm, chest 109 cm, and thigh circumference 61.7 cm. See http://www. ronaldo7.net for Castrol Edge's documentary/film on Cristiano Ronaldo.

game) is primarily due to the acceleration differential being smaller in comparison to the competition in the Spanish league.

The total distance Ronaldo and Messi run in a season would cover the distance between Madrid and Barcelona. However, there is a difference that gives Messi an advantage on overcoming the too-tired-and-old effect. Ken Early[191] and Benjamin Morris[192] raised an interesting point about Messi, which may shed some light on tactics. According to Morris, over the course of the 2014 World Cup, Messi had the lowest work rate among non-goalkeepers when his team is on defense. More interestingly, Messi had the second lowest among forwards on offense. He expends less energy to exert more influence than anyone else on the field. He spends less time engaged in medium- and high-intensity activity than any other elite forward. And his number of sprints is lower than any other elite forward. When looking at the data, Messi runs about 90 meters per minute; Ronaldo runs about 110 meters per minute. It's possible that Messi's positioning and instructions are to protect him physically from running so that he can sprint whenever he needs to without worrying about the injuries that hindered him early in his career.

Gareth Bale is known for his physical fitness, speed, skill, stamina, agility, and acceleration. When Real Madrid was evaluating Bale, two of the technical things that attracted them to him were age and speed. Bale ran around 12 kilometers (7.5 miles) per game, which is a little above average. But what was remarkable was that more than one kilometer was at a speed near his maximum, which is around twice the distance of the average player. More importantly, he has the ability to perform and use his technique at that speed. Real Madrid signed him when he was twenty-four years old, which is consistent with Galácticos 3.0's shift in signing younger players. His speed not only helps him score goals for himself but creates space and opportunities for his teammates. In addition, he is able to sprint back from offense to help with defense. His speed increases the pressure on the opposing team's players and attacks and reduces their space to maneuver.

[191] Ken Early, "Walking to Stay One Step Ahead." *Slate*. http://www.slate.com/articles/sports/sports_nut/2014/07/lionel_messi_2014_world_cup_the_world_s_best_player_has_figured_out_how.2.html.

[192] Benjamin Morris, "Was Lionel Messi Tired?" *FiveThirtyEight*. http://fivethirtyeight.com/features/was-lionel-messi-tired/.

Spain and the 2014 World Cup

Before the 2014 World Cup started, most experts predicted that the defending champion, Spain, would reach at least the tournament's semifinals. Instead, the defending champions were the first team to get knocked out. Age proved a key factor that negatively impacted their performance: the players' average age was among the oldest in the tournament. Following his squad's early exit, coach Vicente del Bosque dismissed concerns that his players were too old: "This is a mature team with players in their prime."[193]

In a July 2014 article titled, "Player age in football: The clock is ticking," the *Economist* analyzed the average team age and final standing for defending FIFA World Cup champions, and discovered that within this group, age has a remarkably strong impact.

**Table 10.6 Average Age of Team and Final Standing
for Defending Fifa World Cup Champions**

Year	Defending Team	Average Age of Team	Final Standing*
2014	Spain	27.5–28.0	20–25
2010	Italy	28.0–28.5	20–25
2006	Brazil	28.0–28.5	2–5
2002	France	28.0–28.5	25–30
1994	Germany	28.5–29.0	2–5

*Adjusted for continental advantage

After adjusting for the effect of geography, teams that played on their own continent performed six places better than those that had to travel to another continent (a one-year increase in average age for a team correlated with a four-place drop in performance). So if a defending champion simply brought back the same players and coach from four years before, and the team's average age increased by four years, the team would be expected to finish in seventeenth place. The average age of Spain's players was twenty-eight, two years older than when they won in 2010. Also, seven of Spain's twenty-three players were

193 "'Mature' Spain expected to deliver against Dutch." *USA Today*. http://www.usatoday.com/story/sports/soccer/2014/06/12/mature-spain-expected-to-deliver-against-dutch/10382583/.

on the Real Madrid and Atlético Madrid teams that made it to the Champions League final (an additional seven were on the Barcelona team that lost in the semifinals to Atlético), and had the longest seasons. Spain had great leadership in coaching and has a system that many players are familiar with, but being too old and tired has an observable effect.

Understandably, a coach can be reluctant to leave stars with a record of success on the bench or off the team altogether. In addition to prompting criticism or second-guessing from fans and media, promoting an unproven young player over a proven star can easily create tensions among players. The evidence, however, suggests that coaches and general managers should consider a team's age as one of many factors. Older attacking players may not track back as much or as quickly to help on defense or may be just a little bit slower, making the overall defense look worse.

The too-tired-and-old effect may also be more evident later in a season. However, analyzing the average age of a team may not tell the entire story. This effect is more illuminated when digging even deeper and segmenting the roles of the players and their ages in the "Analyzing Stars, Workhorses, and Juniors" sidebar.

Analyzing Stars, Workhorses, and Juniors

Professors Kimio Kase, Sandalio Gómez, and Ignacio Urrutia of IESE Business School in Spain completed an academic study of the business and sports strategy of Real Madrid for the years 2000–06.[194] In their academic paper, they divided Real Madrid players into "stars," "workhorses," and "juniors." In their analysis, stars are recognized as world-class players; "workhorses are top-level players from other national or international clubs; and juniors are players who have come up through the academy or the reserves to earn a place on the first team." Importantly, some players acquired "star" status after performing well at Real Madrid. In extending their analysis to 2014–15, I considered a player's

---

[194] "Real Madrid CF-FC Barcelona: Analysis of Business and Sports Strategy During the Period 2000-2006." IESE Business School Working Paper No. 06/12.

success with both the national team as well as the club in determining whether to categorize them as "stars."[195] Thus, the analysis recognizes that some "work-horses," and even "juniors," became "stars," and re-categorized them as such when appropriate.

The professors' analysis, also published in the book *Value Creation and Sport Management* (Cambridge, UK: Cambridge University Press, 2012), only covers Real Madrid's strategy until 2006. Thus, to better understand changes in Real Madrid's strategy, I have extended and updated the analysis with data from Opta Sports Data and divided the data into three different periods: Florentino's first term as Real Madrid's president (2000–06), the period after he vacated his presidency (2006–09), and since he returned as president in 2009 (2009–14). Appendix D: "Support for Stars, Workhorses, and Juniors Analysis" provides selected information related to the analysis.

The 2000–06 Period

In Florentino's first term as president, he systematically brought "stars" to Real Madrid. In just four years (2000–04), the team signed four high-profile inter-national stars (Figo, Zidane, Ronaldo, and Beckham). Florentino's strategy resembled that of Bernabéu, who consecutively signed stars in the period I refer to as Galácticos 1.0. Florentino grew Real Madrid's stars from 11 percent in 2000 to 25 percent in 2006. Adding stars dramatically decreased the work-horses on the team, from 61 percent to 39 percent. Juniors comprised a sig-nificant portion of the squad (about 37 percent) but insignificantly impacted Real Madrid's on-field performance. Real Madrid's juniors did not receive enough playing time and, in turn, they only contributed an average of 5 per-cent of the goals. The academics wrote:

> *The number of workhorse players continued to decline, and more junior players joined the squad. This is when the problems started, as not*

---

[195] Lionel Messi's and Iker Casillas's careers particularly deserve examination. They both joined the first team directly from the academy but were only considered juniors for two seasons (2004–06 and 2000–02 respectively) and then immediately became "stars." Since the beginning of his career, Messi attracted a lot of media attention and was only nineteen when he scored seventeen goals for the first team. Casillas also became an iconic player for Real Madrid beginning in an early stage of his career, and at only twenty years of age, he had already won a Champions League trophy with Real Madrid as well as a starting spot on Spain's 2002 World Cup squad.

all the stars could be on the pitch at the same time... There were too
many stars, the players' average age had risen, and there were too few
workhorse players. Meanwhile, the juniors were not getting enough
playing time.

In analyzing Real Madrid from 2000 to 2006, I found that stars became older (from 26.0 when Florentino took over to 28.4 in 2005 and 28.1 in 2006), and the goals contributed by the stars decreased significantly. In addition, the workhorses' average age increased from 26.5 in 2000 to 28.7 in 2005. This sheds some more doubt on the explanation that it was primarily or solely Makélélé's absence that caused Real Madrid to struggle. Real Madrid's on-field team performance data is similar to the data and analysis of the average age of team and final standing for defending FIFA World Cup champions mentioned previously and in Table 10.6. My hypothesis is that the drop in team performance has more to do with the players' age and the too-tired-and-old effect, as well as leadership. In 2006, Roberto Carlos was thirty-three years old, and Zidane and Figo were thirty-four.

The academics write in their paper:

.... the risks of Real Madrid's unbalanced squad, with a group of aging
superstars who played in every game, while others spent most of their
time on the bench. The stars were generally older than the other players,
significantly increasing the team's average age... as their age increased,
their playing time and the number of goals they scored decreased.
Also, they played in more internationals and probably had to push
themselves harder than the others, the risk of injury and exhaustion was
significantly higher.

The 2006–09 Period

Florentino was not president of Real Madrid during this period.

There was an increase in the number of workhorses (from an average of 42 percent in 2000–06 to 49 percent in 2006–09) and decrease in the number of juniors (from an average of 37 percent in 2000–06 to 26 percent in 2006–09). In addition, as mentioned previously, the stars were not at the desired level and did not play a style demanded by the community. Workhorses (average age went down from 27.0 to 25.6) were younger than 2000–06. Real Madrid won three titles in three years (two consecutive Spanish league championships and one Copa del Rey), but the club's results in the Champions League disappointed the community.

The 2009–15 Period

When Florentino again became president in 2009, he intuitively recognized what I call a too-tired-and too-old effect, and set out to rebalance the team. Stars represent 22 percent of the team, similar to 21 percent during 2000-2006. However, the average age of the stars is 26.6 in 2009–15 compared to 27.8 in 2000–06. In addition, the average age of workhorses is 26.1 in 2009–15 compared to 27.0 in 2000–06.

The table below gives the average age of members by team, as well as European league averages, at the start of the 2015–16 season. Real Madrid's average age is 26.2, below the La Liga average of 26.6.

Table 10.7: Average Age of Team Members as of October 1, 2015 by CIES Football Observatory

Team/League	Average Age as of Oct. 1, 2015
Juventus	27.8
Manchester City	27.7
Bayern Munich	27.1
Paris Saint-Germain	27.1
Italian Serie A	27.1
Barcelona	26.9
English Premier League	26.9
Spanish La Liga	26.6
Real Madrid	26.2
Chelsea	26.1
German Bundesliga	26.1
French Ligue 1	26.1
Manchester United	25.8
Liverpool	25.0

From an age perspective of its stars and balance between stars, workhorses, and juniors, Real Madrid is about as well positioned as it has been since 2000. Interestingly, when I applied the same analysis to Barcelona since 2011, the mix and positioning were very similar to Real Madrid's.

Dividing Real Madrid players into "stars," "workhorses," and "juniors," and analyzing the data illuminates that when analyzing the performance on the field, it is important to examine not only overall team age but to go even deeper into the composition of the team and the ages of the players playing different roles. For example, an increase in age in stars and workhorses can help explain drop-offs late in the season and the impact of the too-tired-and-old effect. Real Madrid can have the talent, the money, and the data analytics, as well as the values, but we have seen again and again, Father Time is still undefeated.

Chapter 11

EL CLÁSICO—
REAL MADRID VS. BARCELONA

A NY ANALYSIS of Real Madrid would be incomplete without understanding its rivalry with Barcelona. As mentioned, *El Clásico* is the nickname given to any soccer game between Real Madrid and Barcelona. The rivalry is regarded as one of the greatest in the world of the sport. North America has its fair share of sports rivalries, but, in my opinion, none of them reach the intensity of the rivalry between Real Madrid and Barcelona. This is because both clubs have very distinctive identities, brands, and values with passionate and loyal community members. It's difficult to explain how big the game is unless you are a diehard soccer fan. During an El Clásico game, English announcer Ray Hudson entertainingly claimed that not only were Martians watching the game, so were over one billion humans. Most news outlets estimate that over 400 million people around the world watch a regular season El Clásico game. However, Benjamin Morris of *FiveThirtyEight* estimates the viewing audience of the games is most likely closer to the numbers for the Super Bowl.[196] Regardless, the idea that a game that Real Madrid and Barcelona play against each other at least twice a year due to the regular season schedule gets even close to the viewership of the Super Bowl indicates the incredible global interest in El Clásico.

---

[196] Benjamin Morris, "Is Messi vs. Ronaldo Bigger than the Super Bowl?" *FiveThirtyEight.* http://fivethirtyeight.com/features/is-messi-vs-ronaldo-bigger-than-the-super-bowl/.

It is a two-and-a-half-hour high-speed rail trip between Spain's two largest cities. Barcelona, the city, is the second most populated in Spain with 1.6 million people, behind Madrid's 3.2 million. Madrid, the nation's capital, is located in the center of Spain. The capital of the Cataluña region, Barcelona is geographically located in the northeast of Spain, bordered by the Mediterranean Sea to the east and by France to the north.

Barcelona, the soccer club, has always been seen as Cataluña's club, an institution that symbolizes everything Catalan. Barcelona's motto is *Mes que un club* ("More than a club"), which refers to its symbolism beyond soccer or sport in Catalan culture. A soccer club is always taken as a symbol and representation of the local community, but for the people of Barcelona and Cataluña, Barcelona is truly much more than a club, and this political-cultural link and representation is even emphasized in its written identity and values statement. Barcelona's emblem even incorporates symbols of Cataluña. In many ways, Barcelona is a representation of Cataluña, distinct from the rest of Spain. In contrast, Real Madrid consciously positions itself as an international, multicultural, and universal club.[197]

The irony is that the rivalry between the clubs is the one thing that almost everyone in Spain, and the international soccer community, talks about and has an opinion on—the topic unifies the country, and soccer enthusiasts. The respective communities in many ways need the fierce rivalry to help define and strengthen their identities and to make each other better both on and off the field. In recent years, the rivalry has been expanded into heated debates as to who is the best soccer player in the world: Cristiano Ronaldo or Lionel Messi. The fact that Ronaldo and Messi play in the same league, meeting head to head in at least two games per season, and star in El Clásico, the premier rivalry in the sport, encourages the passionate discussion, which helps define and promote their respective communities.

---

[197] To keep with its mission "To be an open and multicultural club that is both appreciated and respected throughout the world...," the Real Madrid crest, which usually contains a cross on top of a crown, has been removed in selected countries to be sensitive to community members. The original design is used in Europe.

Both Real Madrid and Barcelona are extraordinary in their own way. In this chapter, I will examine and compare selected aspects of the clubs.

Comparison of Financial Performance

Upon examination, there are a few financial performance differences between the clubs. Real Madrid has higher revenues from commercial and game-day sources. It is interesting that Real Madrid has higher game-day revenues than Barcelona when Barcelona's Camp Nou Stadium holds 99,354 people, while Real Madrid's Santiago Bernabéu Stadium holds 81,044 people.[198] Dividing game-day revenue for Barcelona of €121 million by the stadium capacity of 99,354 gives us €1,217. Dividing Real Madrid's match-day revenue of €130 million by the stadium capacity of 81,044 gives us €1,604. This indicates that Real Madrid is doing more with less capacity via VIP suites, concessions, and billboard advertising per person. For example, Camp Nou has around 2,000 VIP seats, compared to 4,756 at Bernabéu Stadium.

Real Madrid and Barcelona have benefited from the structure of the TV revenue distribution in Spain prior to 2016–17 season when the Spanish League collectively negotiates broadcasting rights, which mandates Spanish soccer teams to individually negotiate broadcasting deals (as opposed to the collective bargaining system followed in England and Germany). This resulted in the two Spanish giants receiving almost 33 percent of the TV money paid to all twenty Spanish teams. The total numbers of La Liga are less than the English Premier League overall. The Premier League's TV broadcasting deal is worth about €2,100 million per year versus €850 million for La Liga in 2014–15. If you look at

---

[198] Due to security reasons, the available seats of the stadium for sale vary between the Spanish league and UEFA Champions League, as well as the classification of the game. The maximum available capacity is 81,044 seats. In the 2013–14 season, the average attendance was 70,739. In many cases and for different reasons, season ticket holders neither attend all games, nor give their tickets to others, so that those absences are not registered in the attendance control figures. In these cases, it is very likely that there are no tickets for sale although there are unoccupied seats of season ticket holders. In every season there also are games of minimal interest, such as early stages of Copa del Rey playing against a second division club, La Liga games against clubs of lesser importance, and UEFA Champions League games of the first round in which at least two clubs are of lesser importance. Many season ticket holders do not attend these games. Therefore, these few low-attendance games affect the average figure of attendance.

the number of subscribers to soccer on pay TV, in England it is around 15 million, in Spain it is closer to 4 million. Also, in Spain there is the "right to information" that applies to sports news, which means that the goals are shown almost immediately on all free-to-air channels.[199]

It has been reported that Real Madrid and Barcelona have a financial competitive advantage over English Premier League teams because they don't share TV broadcasting revenues like the English League. According to the 2016 Deloitte Football Money League Report, in 2014–15, Real Madrid and Barcelona (and also Juventus) made around €200 million ($220 million) in global TV broadcasting revenues, while Chelsea and Manchester City in the English Premier League made around €178 million ($196 million).[200] Considering Real Madrid's and Barcelona's better performances in the Champions League and larger fan bases, 12 percent over Manchester City and Chelsea is not unreasonable. As for league-specific TV revenues, in 2014-15, Real Madrid and Barcelona both made around €130 million ($143 million) in TV broadcasting revenues from La Liga games only, while Chelsea and Manchester City made around €130 million from English Premier League games only. Therefore, although La Liga has lower numbers than the English Premier League, Real Madrid and Barcelona make what the top English Premier League teams make. However, recent changes to the Spanish broadcasting deal may financially impact Real Madrid and Barcelona negatively in the near term.

Typically, Real Madrid plays six to eight exhibition games per season, all outside Spain. The revenue per game depends on a variety of factors, but the totals range from €15 million to €25 million ($17 to $28 million) per year.

The following table provides selected financial information for Real Madrid and Barcelona to make the comparison easier.

---

[199] The TV broadcasters without TV rights can offer strictly ninety seconds of all the games played the same day (but not of every game), and never after that day. This is a consequence of the "right to inform."

[200] In the Deloitte report, all Champions League income is classified as "Broadcasting." The 2016 Deloitte report indicates for each club, in a footnote, the amount received from UEFA for a team's participation in European competitions. Therefore, the progression in the Champions League, even winning the Champions League, is translated into bigger broadcasting revenues, altering the comparison of the actual TV revenues of different teams in Europe.

Table 11.1: FY 2013-2015 Selected Financial Information (€ in millions)

	Barcelona			Real Madrid		
	2013	**2014**	**2015**	**2013**	**2014**	**2015**
Deloitte Revenues Breakdown:						
Commercial	177	186	240	214	231	248
Match Day	118	117	121	119	114	130
Broadcasting	188	182	200	188	204	200
Total Revenues	483	485	561	521	550	578
Reported Revenues	483	485	561	521	550	578
EBITDA before net gains on disposals	126	100	76	132	125	135
EBITDA (per accounting principles)	118	134	105	150	164	203
Profit (Loss) before taxes	43	55	18	48	48	56
Total Cash	72	49	76	156	174	109
Net Debt[201]	179	165	219	91	72	96
Net Debt / EBITDA	1.5	1.2	2.1	0.6	0.4	0.5
Wages to revenues	54%	55%	66%	47%	49%	50%
Money spent for buying players	101	84	160	86	191	189
Money received from selling players	1	59	51	41	102	114
Net	100	25	109	45	89	75

Note: All this data is calculated consistently with Real Madrid criteria.

Comparing EBITDA, Real Madrid has higher EBITDA before net gains on disposals and per accounting principles, reflecting the power of keeping wages, the highest cost of both teams, to a lower percentage. Barcelona's wages to revenues were 66 percent in 2015 versus 50 percent for Real Madrid.

---

[201] Barcelona reports in its financial statements a net debt of €287 million at June 30, 2014 (debt/EBITDA ratio 1.9), and net debt of €328 million at June 30, 2015 (debt/EBITDA ratio 3.2). The net debt is higher than the Real Madrid criteria because it also includes the net balance of trade receivables and payables, and other recurring operating balances, which, according to accounting experts, should not be considered net debt by international accounting standards.

Real Madrid made €56 million ($62 million) in pretax profits in 2015 versus Barcelona's €18 million ($20 million). There is a misperception in the media that Real Madrid and Barcelona receive some tax benefit by being a not-for-profit entity. This is wrong. Real Madrid (and the other three clubs in Spain: Barcelona, Athletic Bilbao, and Osasuna—all of them not-for-profit entities) are taxed at 25 percent versus 30 percent for corporations by Spanish law. However, not-for-profit entities are only able to deduct 7 percent of reinvestments from pretax income for tax purposes versus 12 percent for corporations. The net result is that in the period from 2000 to 2015, Real Madrid has paid €9.74 million *more in taxes* than if it were a corporation.[202] This is the additional cost of staying a member-owned club, which is a key component of Real Madrid's strategy.

In addition, as a nonprofit entity, Real Madrid may not make distributions or pay dividends, which has a few consequences. From the perspective of the club itself, this restriction promotes economic solvency of the institution and strengthens its shareholder equity (equity at June 30, 2015, was €412 million/$453 million), leading to a more robust financial entity. The economic strength gives the club more flexibility to spend money on players (which is taxed) and investments. However, socio members do not receive a direct economic return from the profits of the club. Although Barcelona is often associated with internal player development, they have increased their spending on players (e.g., Neymar and Suárez). Barcelona's current approach seems to be closer to Real Madrid's of mixing stars with homegrown talent. Real Madrid makes money from selling players to fund the purchases of other players. As discussed in chapter ten's "Real Madrid's Player Selection Process," the discussion about player selection at Real Madrid starts with community values and the technical staff.

Both Barcelona and Real Madrid have modest leverage, both have debt-to-cash-flow ratios below most corporations. Comparing the balance sheets, Barcelona is more highly leveraged than Real Madrid in

---

[202] It should be highlighted that this item is very important, since soccer clubs reinvest revenues and capital gains of player transfers in a recurring manner, and in the end, the compound effect is negative for Real Madrid. Therefore if Real Madrid could choose, it would actually be more economical to be taxed as a corporation.

terms of absolute net debt and EBITDA/interest ratio. Most companies borrow money for working capital and to bridge operating costs and capital expenditures to revenues. Barcelona has been borrowing money to pay the large transfer fees for star players. Barcelona's net spending from buying players minus the amounts collected from selling players is higher than Real Madrid's, increasing Barcelona's debt. Also, Barcelona has been paying a higher percentage of revenues in salaries than Real Madrid, so it has been making less profit than Real Madrid and has less cash flow to pay down debt.

Barcelona's average salary per player is €8.36 million ($7.6 million) over the last five years versus €8.14 million ($7.4 million) for Real Madrid. However, since Barcelona has lower revenues than Real Madrid, its salaries-to-turnover ratio is higher than Real Madrid's, meaning it spends a higher percentage of revenues to pay for the players, reducing profitability. If salaries are indicative of an efficient market, Barcelona and Real Madrid have a comparable level of players on their teams. The table below shows the average salaries for the last five years, total five-year earnings, and salary growth rate for the last five years for the top-spending teams in sports.[203]

Table 11.2: Player Salary Comparison across Sports

Rank	Team	League	Avg salary 2010 survey $m	Avg salary 2011 survey $m	Avg salary 2012 survey $m	Avg salary 2013 survey $m	Avg salary 2014 survey $m	Avg player 5-year earnings $m	% difference annual pay 2014 v. 2010
1	Barcelona	La Liga	6.67	7.91	8.68	7.27	7.45	7.6	12
2	Real Madrid	La Liga	6.94	7.80	7.31	7.31	7.59	7.4	9
3	NY Yankees	MLB	7.66	6.76	6.19	7.15	8.03	7.1	5
4	Manchester City	EPL	2.22	5.86	7.40	8.06	8.11	6.3	265
5	Chelsea	EPL	5.88	6.02	6.80	6.24	6.05	6.2	3

---

[203] "Revealed: Man City, Yankees, Dodgers, RM, Barca best paid in global sport." *Sporting Intelligence.* http://www.sportingintelligence.com/2014/04/15/revealed-man-city-yankees-dodgers-rm-barca-best-paid-in-global-sport-150401/.

Rank	Team	League	Avg salary 2010 survey $m	Avg salary 2011 survey $m	Avg salary 2012 survey $m	Avg salary 2013 survey $m	Avg salary 2014 survey $m	Avg player 5-year earnings $m	% difference annual pay 2014 v. 2010
6	Bayern Munich	Bundes-liga	5.12	5.78	5.91	6.15	6.96	6.0	36
7	LA Lakers	NBA	5.59	6.54	6.28	6.29	5.18	6.0	-7
8	Manchester United	EPL	4.76	5.11	5.52	6.03	6.57	5.6	38
9	Philadelphia Phillies	MLB	4.06	5.77	5.82	6.13	5.79	5.5	43
10	Milan	Serie A	3.32	5.65	6.10	6.59	4.87	5.3	47
11	Boston Celtics	NBA	5.35	5.24	5.32	5.42	5.09	5.3	-5
12	Boston Red Sox	MLB	4.58	5.99	5.09	5.02	5.72	5.3	25
13	LA Dodgers	ML	4.33	3.47	3.17	7.47	7.78	5.2	79
14	Arsenal	EPL	4.29	4.76	5.28	5.64	5.93	5.2	38
15	Internazio-nale	Serie A	3.12	6.00	5.70	6.20	4.64	5.1	49
16	Chicago Bulls	NBA	4.02	4.02	5.32	5.29	6.06	4.9	51
17	Liverpool	EPL	4.15	4.94	5.23	5.16	5.17	4.9	25
18	Detroit Tigers	MLB	4.43	3.91	4.56	5.71	5.82	4.9	31
19	NY Knicks	NBA	5.35	3.87	4.17	5.17	5.87	4.9	10
20	Dallas Mavericks	NBA	5.83	4.88	4.93	4.19	4.49	4.9	-23

It has been reported that players in Spain pay less in taxes than other European countries. In 2005, a Spanish tax law designed to attract talented foreign business executives and researchers was passed, later typically referred to as the "Beckham Law." The law allowed the foreigners who qualified and lived temporarily in Spain to pay income tax on all annual earnings at the minimum rate of 24 percent. At the time, the top English tax rate was 50 percent and the press pointed to avoiding taxes as one of the reasons Beckham left Manchester United. In 2014, the Beckham Law was repealed. However, an international tax expert explained to me that because of various tax loopholes, the typical soccer player playing elsewhere in Europe during the time of the Beckham Law most likely paid similar or marginally higher taxes than a player in Spain, depending on advice, structures, and jurisdictions. In January 2011, the *Sunday Times* reported that it uncovered fifty-five English Premier League players who were taxed at just 22 percent because they get a large proportion of their total earnings from their image rights companies.[204] Therefore, Spanish teams did not have any real competitive tax rate advantage in signing players. Today, the top national income tax rates in Spain, England, France, and Germany are around 45 percent.

Comparison of Player Development—the Academies

Many experts point out, as a key difference in the strategies of the two clubs, the fact that Barcelona spends more on, and develops more talent from, its famous La Masia academy.[205] Barcelona does have two more academy graduates on its 2015–16 team than Real Madrid, eleven for Barcelona and nine for Real Madrid. It also has more academy graduates as regular starters than Real Madrid, although Barcelona's mix is changing. However, the data reveals that Real Madrid's academy may be producing as high, if not higher, quality players. Presently sixty-two players from Real Madrid's academy are playing for teams in the top five European leagues' first divisions: forty-three in La Liga (including nine at Real Madrid), five in the English Premier League, three in the German Bundesliga, seven in the Italian Serie A, and four in the French Ligue 1. In total, 130 players from the Real Madrid academy are currently playing in first- and second-division teams throughout Europe.[206] A study by CEIS revealed that all Real Madrid academy graduates

---

[204] Robert Watts and Maurice Chittenden, "How our top footballers avoid tax." *The Sunday Times.* http://www.thesundaytimes.co.uk/sto/news/uk_news/National/article511544.ece.

[205] Barcelona opened La Masia in the late 1970s on the advice of departing player Johan Cruyff. Cruyff told the incoming Barcelona president that to compete with Real Madrid, Barcelona would need an academy like Real Madrid's and the one that had proved so successful at his previous club, Ajax (illustrating the challenge of copycats to the strategy).

[206] RM Corporate Social Responsibility Report 2014/15, Item "Players from Real Madrid's Youth Academy."

throughout Europe were playing 54 percent of the time versus 43 percent for Barcelona.[207]

The difference in perception may be in the coaching decisions and selection of the players. Barcelona coaches who started as such at the academy (Luis Enrique, Pep Guardiola) prefer to play with academy players, while Real Madrid coaches (Ancelotti, Mourinho, etc., who don't come from the academy as coaches) don't seem to give those players the chance to play in the first team. Real Madrid normally transfers promising players to another team "on loan" to get game experience with a call option to bring them back. When del Bosque was the coach, the playing time of junior players in games ranged from 7 to 15 percent per season—del Bosque had spent time at the Real Madrid academy. Since 2009, the playing time of junior players has ranged from 3 to 5 percent, with one exception—the 2013–14 season when the club won the Champions League under Ancelotti.[208]

Playing Style

As discussed, Real Madrid's community expects the team to play beautiful, exciting, and attacking soccer with elegance, style, and class. At the first Real Madrid game that I went to with my family, the team was winning 3–0 at home. They started to play defensively, making sideways to backward passes to take up time to hold the winning score. The crowd went crazy and starting whistling and yelling at their own players to push forward and attack. They wanted to be entertained and see artistry for a full ninety minutes.[209] Real Madrid's attacking style takes talent and creativity. It isn't as much of a system as it is art. It is beautiful to watch when it works, but when one player or element is out of sync for whatever reason, including injury—or a player who is new or playing out of a

---

[207] Raffaele Poli, Loïc Ravenel, and Roger Besson, "Youth training in European football: a comparative analysis." *Football Observatory.* http://www.football-observatory.com/IMG/sites/mr/mr09/en/.

[208] See "Analyzing Stars, Workhorses, and Juniors" sidebar and Appendix D.

[209] This explains why Real Madrid scores so many goals in a game, and gives up many, as they are vulnerable during attack. Critics who believe that Real Madrid runs up the score, especially at home, don't understand that the community doesn't want to disrespect the other team, they just want to see the art and be entertained until the final whistle blows.

comfortable position—it can disrupt the artistry of teammates knowing each others' tendencies and timing. To get the timing and anticipation right, players may have to invest more minutes on the field, which can put them more at risk of injury or fatigue. Real Madrid doesn't have a consistent offensive or defensive system or template (an "automatic") that they can count on in times of trouble during a game, which is also why a calm coach and presence of the leadership system (a captain with seniority who is first among equals) are important. It is unclear if a system could be developed or how the community would react to such a system—would fans find it too boring, for example?

In contrast, much of Barcelona's game is preprogrammed with players relegated specific tasks and far less freedom.[210] Since the late 1980s, every team in Barcelona's La Masia is taught a version of Johan Cruyff's playing-style philosophy, a traditional 3-4-3 formation with minimal variations. Such a consistent philosophy throughout the club's academy teams allowed young players to not only learn the system well but also take virtually no time to adapt if promoted to the next age group. After Cruyff, the playing style evolved into what today is often called *tiki-taka*.[211] *Tiki-taka* is a style of play in soccer characterized by short passing and movement, working the ball through various channels, and maintaining possession. Barcelona defends with ball possession. In addition, since many of the players learned how to work together and knew their roles in the system, they were more interchangeable for rotations and replacements for injuries. The training of so many Spanish players in the same system helped Vicente del Bosque lead Spain to its first FIFA World Cup in 2010 as well as European Championships in 2008 and 2012 because Spain's players were using a familiar system, while competing against country teams with a collection of their best players that don't typically play together and play in many different systems.

---

[210] Simon Kuper, "What's ailing FC Barcelona?" *FT Magazine*. http://www.ft.com/cms/s/2/83f56d92-acc1-11e4-beeb-00144feab7de.html.

[211] *Tiki-taka* was coined in 2006 by TV commentator Andrés Montes.

Yellow and Red Cards

The Investigation History and Statistics Centre of Spanish Football examined eighty-five years of La Liga data starting with 1928. It found Real Madrid led the way with 487 penalties in their favor, followed by Barcelona with 460 (around 5 percent less).[212] Real Madrid ranks in ninth position of the teams who have given penalties away, while Barcelona has given the fourth most away. The differences are relatively small, as expected, because both clubs have had good teams for a long time. Both Real Madrid and Barcelona have had a reputation for featuring a few tough tackling defenders in their history.[213]

I examined the number of yellow and red cards that Barcelona and Real Madrid players have been issued since 2011–12 from Statbunker.com. Red cards were not used in the World Cup until 1970, so I couldn't examine information about Galácticos 1.0. Also, more yellow and red cards are issued today than in the past, so it is difficult to draw historical comparisons. However, one observation stands out when analyzing the data. Real Madrid received approximately 25 percent more yellow cards on average than Barcelona per season since 2011–12.[214] A Real Madrid fan might interpret the data as bias against Real Madrid; if someone is not a Real Madrid fan they may say that the cards were deserved. Recognize that four years is a small sample size and the coaches' style of play is a meaningful factor; but, whatever the reason, it is an aberration.

The biggest discipline statistic and impact to on-the-field results may be red cards. Since 2011–12 Real Madrid has received seventeen red cards (seven direct), while Barcelona and Atlético Madrid have received eleven (four direct) and sixteen (six direct), respectively. The sample size is too small in terms of data and years to draw any meaningful conclusions. However, regardless of the reasons, the absolute number difference affects performance. In 2008, Jan

---

[212] "Real Madrid have had more penalties than any other team in La Liga history." *Sport EN*. http://www.sport-english.com/en/news/liga-bbva/real-madrid-have-had-more-penalties-than-any-other-team-liga-history-4731538.

[213] In La Liga, five yellow cards result in a one-game suspension. A friend asked me to analyze how many minutes played to each yellow card issued for the following players: Sergio Ramos (RM) 219 minutes; Alvaro Arbeloa (RM) 224 minutes; Rafa Márquez (Barca) 265 minutes; Sergio Busquets (Barca) 300 minutes; Gerard Piqué (Barca) 313 minutes; Pepe (RM) 314 minutes; Manolo Sanchis (RM) 321 minutes; Charles Puyol (Barca) 371 minutes; and Fernando Hierro (RM) 420 minutes.

[214] Atlético Madrid has received approximately 62 percent more yellow cards than Barcelona since 2011–12.

Vecer, Frantisek Kopriva, and Tomoyuki Ichiba of the Statistics Department of Columbia University published a paper titled "Estimating the Effect of the Red Card in Soccer" in the *Journal of Quantitative Analysis in Sports*. They showed that a red card generally leads to a smaller number of goals, typically 33 percent less than what is normal for a penalized team that is favored to win. Also, the team that is not favored to win, with the now-additional player, typically scores 25 percent more than normal.[215] In those six games, Real Madrid was at a competitive disadvantage,[216] and as can be seen in the next section, the differences between Real Madrid and Barcelona's on-the-field results have been very small, and as discussed later, the impact of one goal or one game in La Liga can make all the difference.

Comparison of On-the-Field Results Since 2011–12

Since 2011, Real Madrid and Barcelona have been remarkably similar in terms of winning, scoring, and goal differences.[217] Below is information from La Liga seasons. Both teams have won at least one Champions League trophy since 2011–12. Both teams had magical La Liga seasons with thirty-two wins. Barcelona had a magical 2014–15 season with four major trophies in a season. Real Madrid had a magical 2014 calendar year by winning four trophies—La Décima, the Club World Cup, the European Super Cup, and the Copa del Rey—along with a twenty-two-game winning streak. To put this into perspective, throughout the club's history, Real Madrid has won three titles in the same calendar year on three occasions: in 1957, winning the European Cup, La Liga, and the Latin Cup; in 1989, winning La Liga, the Copa del Rey, and the Spanish Super Cup; and

---

[215] Jan Vecer, Frantisek Kopriva, and Tomoyuki Ichiba, "Estimating the Effect of the Red Card in Soccer." *Journal of Quantitative Analysis in Sports*. http://www.stat.columbia.edu/~vecer/redcard.pdf.

[216] The researchers showed that there are times when a red card is worth it, based on the score, probability of the scoring that may have happened without the red card offense, the time in the game, and whether the red card will result in a penalty kick. Also, there is some evidence that away teams that go down to ten men after seventy minutes into the game may actually have an advantage.

[217] Since 2011 Real Madrid has been to six consecutive Champions League semi-finals. Barcelona also appeared in six consecutive semi-finals from 2008 to 2013, and four of the last six since 2011.

in 2002, winning the ninth European Cup, the European Super Cup, and the Intercontinental Cup.

The table below shows that the wins and goals scored for Real Madrid and Barcelona are very similar. Both teams score and win more at home. Barcelona has many more goals scored against it in away games than in home games. Barcelona lets far fewer goals get scored against it, especially at home, compared with Real Madrid. In away games, both teams are statistically very close.

Table 11.3: FY 2011–2015 La Liga Home and Away Wins/Losses
and Goals For/Against

	Home						Away					
Real Madrid	W	D	L	GF	GA	GD	W	D	L	GF	GA	GD
2011–12	16	2	1	70	19	51	16	2	1	51	13	38
2012–13	17	2	0	67	21	46	9	5	5	36	21	15
2013–14	16	1	2	63	17	46	11	5	3	41	21	20
2014–15	16	2	1	65	15	50	14	0	5	53	23	30
Total	65	7	4	265	72	193	50	12	14	181	78	103
Median	16	2	1	66	18	48	13	4	4	46	21	25
Barcelona	W	D	L	GF	GA	GD	W	D	L	GF	GA	GD
2011–12	17	1	1	73	11	62	11	6	2	41	18	23
2012–13	18	1	0	63	15	48	14	3	2	52	25	27
2013–14	16	2	1	64	15	49	11	4	4	36	18	18
2014–15	16	1	2	64	11	53	14	3	2	46	10	36
Total	67	5	4	264	52	212	50	16	10	175	71	104
Median	17	1	1	64	13	51	13	4	3	44	18	25
Difference	-2	2	0	1	20	-19	0	-4	4	6	7	-1

Comparison of Priorities

Although Real Madrid tries to win all competitions—and the club has won more European Cups (11) and the most Spanish league titles (32)—Real Madrid seems to be more focused on winning the Champions League, while Barcelona seems to be more focused on La Liga.[218] I believe

[218] Pep Guardiola said during his days as Barcelona's coach, "La Liga is the most important

Real Madrid's community sees itself as global, and the Champions League, which Bernabéu helped create, is viewed as the tournament to determine the best in the world. My hypothesis is that the Barcelona community sees the Spanish league with political and cultural meaning and pride, and therefore places a slightly greater priority on La Liga.

Concluding Remarks

As previously mentioned, I believe Real Madrid and Barcelona are both different and extraordinary and, in many ways, need each other to define their communities and measure and push themselves. The comparisons are to provide context only. The teams are starting to have more similarities. The players' salaries are similar. Barcelona, typically known for homegrown talent, recently has been signing big stars to pair with its academy graduates. The balance of players and results are getting similar. Both are driving revenues and commercial opportunities to new heights with many of the same strategies. Both are owned by socios. However, each has its own distinctive identity, values, culture, and history.

---

competition of the year… The Champions League has glamour, but the league is better for me, it makes me more excited." http://www.goal.com/en-gb/news/3277/la-liga/2011/04/08/2432168/barcelonas-pep-guardiola-la-liga-more-important-than.

PART FIVE

Start of Galácticos 4.0 (2015–)

Chapter 12

THE FUTURE
OF REAL MADRID

THE CIRCULAR NATURE of Real Madrid's business model means that it is essentially self-funding, with current initiatives and projects expanding the community and providing the revenues to fund new ones. The increased income generated during the Galácticos 3.0 era (from marketing, broadcasting, and the attraction of new fans through friendly and exhibition games around the world) is providing the financing for the investments that will lead to Galácticos 4.0, to which the team is transitioning. Real Madrid today is investing in grooming the next generation of leaders with its values (once again inspired by and similar to lessons drawn from Galácticos 1.0), while continuing to focus on utilizing history, tradition, and rituals to actively engage its community members.

Investing in the Coach

Note: My research was completed and the majority of this book written before Zidane was named coach of Real Madrid's first team. I decided to keep this section where it was and primarily "as is" to illustrate the thinking of Florentino and his executives.

Zinedine Zidane is an icon for Real Madrid fans, not only for the way he played but also for his behavior on and off the field. He was one of Real Madrid's best players and the fans felt a special admiration for him, but in spite of his international fame, he has a reputation for being very

Zidane, one of the best players in history, with Real Madrid's ninth European Cup in Glasgow, May 2002. He scored what FIFA has considered the best goal in the history of European Cup finals, which gave the victory to Real Madrid.

down-to-earth and serving as a great teammate. He scored the unfor-gettable winning goal for Real Madrid's 2002 European Championship. After his retirement in 2006, Zidane and his wife decided to stay in Madrid and raise their family. His primary focuses were to enjoy his fam-ily; perform charity work for France and North Africa, where he is seen as a symbol of hope; and work with sponsors. In June 2009, Florentino recruited him to the club as his advisor, then, in November 2010, Real Madrid coach José Mourinho asked him to work more closely with the club and become an assistant coach. In 2013, Zidane was appointed assistant coach to Carlo Ancelotti. As an assistant to Ancelotti, much of his work with Real Madrid players was one-on-one. Zidane was very popular and had a strong relationship with both the players and other coaches, and Ancelotti was always quick to praise him. In June 2014, Real Madrid announced that Zidane would be the coach of Real Madrid Castilla, the team right under the first team. It was the first real sign that Zidane was being groomed to coach Real Madrid's first club in the future. He has the right qualifications: he was an elite player, he knows

Real Madrid's values, he knows the academy, he won the Champions League trophy as a player and an assistant coach, and he has a calm demeanor.

Zidane has spent time studying his craft. For example, he spent three days in Munich in March 2015 to watch Pep Guardiola, a former star player and coach for Barcelona, who now coaches Bayern Munich. Soon afterward, he received his UEFA Pro License: a coaching license from UEFA that is required by anyone who wishes to manage a soccer team in the top level of a nation's league system and the Champions League.[219]

The Real Madrid players say that he's inspirational and doesn't have any sign of the arrogance that sometimes prevents great players from being able to improve those with less skills or instinct. The staff praises his tactical brain and says his obsessive character makes him unique. There is also something else about Zidane; there's a quiet authority about him, a presence. As a player he did not talk much, but he led by example. When he did talk, others listened. However, Zidane has had to adapt to being a coach. "If you're soft with the boys, it doesn't work," he told *France Football* in a rare interview in June 2015. "I discovered that, for the common good, you have to know how to tell players things they're not ready to hear...I do it rarely, because I think I have a natural authority, which means I don't have to resort to bawling out players. If I yelled the whole time, I wouldn't be myself. You're going to tell me that a coach has to talk much more than I do, but that's not the case." Crucially, Zidane keeps these rare displays of emotion private and confined to the locker room. The public display of humiliation for a misplaced pass or fluffed chance isn't for him. This is a quality that the players very much respect. Zidane is very serious about his work. When he was the coach of the B team, he was at the practice facility every morning at 8:30 A.M. He was there until late in the evening.

It is difficult to talk about Zidane without talking about one of his closest friends, David Bettoni. "Davi" is part of the technical team that serves the first team and assists Zidane. The two have been inseparable since 1988 when they were teammates at a camp in Cannes when they

---

[219] The course contains workshops involving topics including fitness, injury prevention, player agents, and transfer protocols. There are three levels of progression, with each focusing on more in-depth detail.

were sixteen years old. When Zidane moved to Juventus in 1996, he persuaded the team to find a semipro team in the area for Davi. Also with a shaved head, but a good foot shorter than Zidane, Bettoni acts as a "sounding board" with a "smiley, talkative demeanor" that complements Zidane.[220]

One thing that the general public does not know about Zidane is how he handled the end of his career as a player. Recognizing that he was past his playing peak, at the end of the 2006 season he asked for a private meeting with Florentino. Zidane was entitled to millions of euros for just showing up for the following season, whether or not the coach played him. Wanting to do what was right for the club, Zidane simply walked away, giving up a significant amount of money and releasing a slot for a player who could develop. There is no better example of a player living up to the mission and values of the community.

Investing in Executives

Emilio Butragueño, a retired star player for Real Madrid in the 1980s, is on the club's executive team. Currently, he represents Real Madrid in FIFA, UEFA, and the Spanish Football Federation, as well as the Real Madrid Foundation in multiple events around the world. He is also Director General of Real Madrid Graduate School.

His vision of the game and his ability to improvise led scouts from Atlético de Madrid to try to sign him when he was very young, but Butragueño and his father were socios of Real Madrid and he wanted to play for the team he supported. That's why he eventually signed for the Real Madrid youth academy when he was in his early teens and played in the first team until he was thirty-two. After his career at Real Madrid ended with fifteen trophies and two third-place finishes for the Ballon d'Or, he played for three more years in Mexico before going to Los Angeles, California, to study business at UCLA. After graduating in 1998, Emilio worked for the Los Angeles Dodgers, where most people were not familiar with Real Madrid but respected him because he played

---

[220] Andrew Murray, "Zinedine Zidane the Manager; How Zizou positioned himself to lead Real Madrid." *FourFourTwo*. http://www.fourfourtwo.com/features/zinedine-zidane-manager-how-zizou-positioned-himself-lead-real-madrid#.UCKBKuqOEBdFdA.

on the Spanish national soccer team from 1984 to 1992. Like José Ángel Sánchez, Emilio took a different track than expected. Many would have guessed that he would become a coach—probably in the academy where he started.

Emilio brings a unique perspective to the executive group. He can speak authoritatively about the field, the competition, the players and their needs, the facility, the mindset, and the pressure. He can speak about the value and needs of the academy. He knows and understands the club's mission and values, even though they were not codified when he played; they were drilled into him at the academy. He knows how to balance all of this with the concerns of the business side. In many ways, Emilio is a living example of the values and mission he is so passionate about.

Florentino recognizes this. Emilio's first responsibilities with the club were more closely aligned with activities on the field; now Florentino has rotated him to other parts of the organization to expose him to other areas, to the living and breathing values and mission, and to round out his knowledge of the club. Florentino and the executives frequently get requests or suggestions from a variety of stakeholders from both the sporting and the economic sides. Emilio serves a special role in helping prioritize and consider those requests, and he also has a special bond of trust and friendship with Carlos and José Ángel. When they ask each other questions, they do not feel like they are being second-guessed— rather, they are collaborating. Interestingly, while it took "outsiders" to have the vision to align strategy, identity, and culture to get the circle re-started, to do the same for Galácticos 4.0, it may take an established, experienced president and "insiders" who know and stick to the community values.

Emilio is just one example. In 2014, Real Madrid invested over $200,000 in 107 training programs, including programs on integrity, good practice, prevention of fraud in sports competition, and code of conduct by the club and governing bodies.

Investing in the Next Generation of Management:
Real Madrid University

Florentino and his management team spend a lot of time and effort recruiting and training people for Real Madrid and the industry. At the time they took over in 2000, the club did not put serious academic focus on training future sports management executives. However, the transformation to a lucrative global industry that they helped create caused a strong demand for executives, marketing and media experts, and other professionals schooled in the business of sports.

Therefore, the management team decided to do something about it, teaching its experience and model of management, while making money. In 2006, Real Madrid teamed up with Universidad Europea, a Madrid-based private university that is part of the Laureate group, to establish a series of master's degrees aimed at the sports industry. The program has grown rapidly in recent years. Officially known as the Real Madrid Graduate School-Universidad Europea, it had about 400 students graduate from its Madrid campus in 2015 and over 1,000 in international locations. Student numbers have doubled in two years and are projected to double again by 2020. Teachers at the school include sixty-five Real Madrid staff members, from marketing professionals to media experts and physiotherapists. Emilio Butragueño is the Director General.

The school generates revenues for Real Madrid, but more importantly, it is also a training ground for future executives. Real Madrid takes in about 100 students for internships every year, but recent graduates have also spent time at Chelsea, Wembley Stadium, Atlético de Madrid, and the Spanish basketball association. Real Madrid wants to be able to recruit a multicultural employee base not just on the field but also in management, therefore the endeavor is now global. Presently, the Real Madrid Graduate School is available in thirteen countries.

Investing in the Training of and Facilities for the Players

Santiago Bernabéu realized that to have the best team, he also needed to invest in infrastructure and the development of players. Florentino believes the same—that in order to attract and retain the best players,

Aerial view of Ciudad Deportiva Real Madrid, inaugurated in 2005. It is the largest sport facility of any soccer team. The skyscrapers in the Madrid background are where the old sport facility was located.

the training facilities need to be world-class. His view is that if he can sign the best players in the world that meet the community's values, give them the best training facilities and coaches, and surround them with Real Madrid culture, then he has positioned the team for success. At Grupo ACS, he has also invested in world-class facilities and experts for executive and leadership training.

Since its inauguration in 2005, Ciudad Deportiva Real Madrid has become an international benchmark as the largest sports complex ever undertaken by a soccer team, with an area of 1.2 million square meters, ten times that of the former Ciudad Deportiva. Real Madrid has invested over €186 million ($210 million) in the facilities. All these areas provide a unique space for first-team players and coaches to work in the best possible facilities. The site is divided by a large T-shaped central building measuring 9,935 meters, which houses all the space required for Real Madrid first team and Academy training and competition: changing rooms, gyms, technical conference rooms, medical and recovery areas, etc. The main leisure area looks like a comfortable first-class airport lounge. Everyone is reminded of the club's history and achievements with photographs of players and teams, awards, game balls, letters, news-paper clippings, etc. Additional leisure areas include arcade games, Formula 1 race-car simulation games, and other activities. Each player has his own private bedroom, similar in style and size to a modern hotel room. Each room is only accessible by the fingerprints of that specific player, so they don't have to carry a key. The pillows on the bed have Real Madrid crests. The rooms have flat-screen TVs.

On both sides of the building, with individual team access, there are six soccer fields, surrounded by stands with a capacity to seat more than 11,000 spectators. The facility has a hydrotherapy room that houses four swimming pools, a sauna, and Turkish bath. Selected pools have glass walls around them so that trainers and medical staff can watch the play-ers run or bike while their legs are submersed underwater. One room has a small artificial field and hundreds of high-speed cameras on the ceiling for the players and staff to see how the ball spins with a player's differ-ent motions and leg speeds. The large weight room and gym facilities include every possible type of weights and weight training machines you can imagine. In addition, there are running treadmills that remove the force of gravity so that the players don't hurt their knees.

I was allowed to go inside the private locker room. Typically, only authorized coaches, trainers, and the players have access. I was told that only a handful of unauthorized people each year are ever allowed to see it to respect the players' privacy. When I was in the private locker room, I bumped into a star Real Madrid player who was initially visibly startled to see someone other than a coach or player in the room. Each player has an identical private locker, with his name on it, made out of dark wood, with two coat hangers and a little safe inside to keep valuables and a cushion on the wood to sit down. It was nicer than the locker room in the stadium, but it certainly wasn't over the top. There is a special cleat room that holds extra pairs of the players' cleats on shelves, in which the staff clean and modify the cleats as needed. Different cleats are used for different conditions and environments. Above the locker room, over-looking the main practice field, is a floor that is used for the media and family members to watch training. A movie theater allows players and coaches to watch TV and movies. There is a specific classroom to watch videos of tactics and strategy.

On either side of the T-shaped building, two separate buildings, each almost 8,000 square meters, are used for team functions, nutrition, rest and recovery, and technical facilities necessary for the coaches' preparation and development.

Facilities for junior players from the academy are scattered around the campus. They include classrooms for regular school, boarding facilities, and game and video rooms for the students. The complex is like many leading sports academies I have seen, including the IMG Academy in Bradenton, Florida. They want the junior players to be around the first team. Pictures, statues, and busts of legends, as well as old photographs showing the club's history, can be found around the campus, as can photos of graduates from the academy who have been successful at Real Madrid.

Players can drive whatever car they would like to the training facility. All the players are provided with use of an Audi while they play at Real Madrid, and the same courtesy is given to the executives and coaches. Those driving an Audi can park their cars in a convenient lot near the front entrance. If a player prefers to drive another make, he must park in a much less convenient area that is closed off with high hedges and landscaping and walk much further.

The same exact professionals maintain both the field at Bernabéu Stadium and the practice soccer fields. The grass type, as well as the amounts of sun and fertilizer, is exactly the same at both locations. According to the players, the look and feel of the grass is identical in order to provide a home-field advantage.

Members and fans have an opportunity to apply for a visit to the Ciudad Deportiva Real Madrid. In 2014–15, around 6,000 people visited. Also, media, members, and fans are allowed to watch practices at specified dates and times.

Real Madrid Practice Schedule

Practice typically starts at 11:00 A.M. except in the summer, due to the heat, when it begins earlier. The training session usually lasts between seventy-five and ninety minutes. Practice varies, depending on the day, although most of the time is dedicated to exercises with the ball. In some training sessions, players wear a GPS tracker that provides information on the distance they run, as well as their speed, acceleration, and other parameters that are very useful for the coach. In addition, the device measures the variation of heart rate during each exercise. Players usually arrive at the training facility one hour in advance and some go to the gym before training with the team and some spend time with the physiotherapists. The same applies at the end of the training session with some going to the gym and others going to the physiotherapists. After each training session, there is a buffet for those players and coaches who want to stay for lunch. During the season, it is uncommon to have two training sessions on the same day, and, although training sessions last no more than ninety minutes, players may spend almost the entire morning in Ciudad Real Madrid. Typically, the coaches usually arrive around 8:30 A.M. and stay late into the evenings.

On the eve of an important local game, the coach may order the players to spend the night in the residence at Ciudad Deportiva Real Madrid. While together, they have technical chats, play social games, watch movies, and participate in team-building exercises. Contrary to reports, the club does not have a "sleep consultant" or "sleep program" because, as a matter of policy, the club tries to respect players' privacy as much as possible. However, if a player informs the doctor of any difficulty sleeping, the club's doctors address it.

Digital Ecosystem Transformation

The real innovation with Galácticos 4.0 is a digital transformation the likes of which the world has never seen before. In the Galácticos 3.0 era, there was growth in digital TV, enabling Real Madrid to reach fans around the world in their homes—a sort of virtual stadium. The level of sophistication for broadcasting improves each year to give fans the best and closest visual representation of the action as possible. Bernabéu Stadium has fifty HD cameras for local and international broadcasting. The international feed goes back to the Real Madrid TV center to deliver a live game feed inside the stadium to suites and mobile phones (through WiFi), as well as to offer instant replays. But Galácticos 4.0 will deliver audio, video, and other media over the internet directly from

Real Madrid to fans, which will enable the club to outdistance the copy-cat teams because it brings fans close to the club in a way that has not been done before in the sports industry.

Real Madrid is well over 100 years old, but anyone who walks into the stadium, goes on the stadium tour, or connects with the team online would think the club is modern and cutting-edge. Every day, Real Madrid fights to be entrepreneurial. As an early adopter, Real Madrid was already using technology and social media to tap into and expand its global community, communicating and reinforcing values throughout the organization. For example, during the 2014–15 season, Realmadrid.com had more than 317 million page views from more than 50 million unique users in 112 million sessions. Regarding social media, the most used sports hashtag in the world is #HalaMadrid, with 27 billion uses since the beginning of the 2015 season. Because Real Madrid is so global, all content on Realmadrid.com is available in eight different languages: Spanish, English, French, Portuguese, Chinese, Indonesian, Japanese, and Arabic.

Real Madrid is present as well in the most important social media platforms including Facebook, Twitter, Instagram, Line, Google+, YouTube, Renren, Tencent, and Weibo. Adding up all of Real Madrid's followers on these platforms, the club's worldwide reach totals more than 200 million social media followers, and less than 3 percent are in Spain. Real Madrid has community managers monitoring each platform and is capable of interacting in Spanish, English, French, Arabic, Chinese, and Japanese. Real Madrid wants "to be where the user is, using the channels the user uses." The club's goal is to know the 450 million people who are Real Madrid supporters, to understand who they are, to really get to their passion and love for Real Madrid, and to give them what they want. If they want access, content, and emotions, Real Madrid wants to give it to them the way they want it. Real Madrid wants to make the club frequently and actively available and as close to them as possible. Creating engagement, especially two-way communication, is a challenge. Only about 5 percent of the 450 million fans globally are located in Spain. In fact, both the United States and Indonesia have more Real Madrid supporters than all of Spain.

Real Madrid's players are free to use their social media in any way they see fit, although the club does provide advice and consults with them

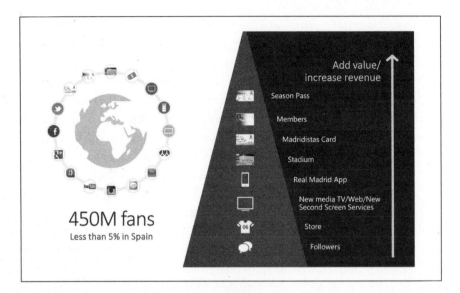

in order to try to avoid any circumstances that might damage their personal, or the club's, image. Real Madrid community managers monitor and advise the players' communications. The club wants the players to generate frequent and respectful communication with the community.

Real Madrid connects and communicates with fans via games and applications for smart phones. As previously mentioned, Director General José Ángel Sánchez's background was at Sega and his knowledge of electronic games has helped Real Madrid design games as a way to connect to fans.[221] For example, Real Madrid has the following game licenses: Real Madrid Imperium, Journey to Real Madrid, Real Madrid Fantasy Manager, Foto Match, Real Madrid Kick, Real Madrid Power Shot, Real Madrid Trivia Fans, and Real Madrid Kids Planet. Real Madrid The Game is an innovative game concept that incorporates a mix of genres (role playing, arcade, simulation). It enables the game player to live a "real life" both personally (shopping, etc.) and professionally (training, press interviews, etc.) as a Real Madrid player. The

---

[221] According to VGChartz, the latest Madden game has sold 4.1 million copies in North America across all platforms, dwarfing FIFA 14's North American sales of 2.12 million. These numbers are, of course, no surprise to American sports fans, as (US) football is by far the most popular sport in the United States. While Madden has sold nearly twice as many copies as FIFA in the US, worldwide, FIFA has outsold Madden 13.9 to 4.6 million. https://www.sccl.org/About/Staff-Posts/June-2014/Madden-vs-FIFA-The-Battle-for-Video-Game-Sports-Do.

game adds original elements such as Santiago Bernabéu Stadium and Ciudad Deportiva Real Madrid.

Real Madrid Fantasy Manager is a soccer team management game. It is the world's leading soccer game—its 2015 version has over one million downloads, and there are over 130,000 monthly active users. A player has three options: to create his/her own team, to play with the whole team of Real Madrid, or to play with another team. Most games licensed by Real Madrid are available on Facebook, iPhone, and Android platforms. In most games, players can invite their friends to play, too. Many of the games incorporate a reward for frequent or daily use.

Real Madrid believes it is the first European professional soccer team in the world to have opened offices in China, headquartered in the Beijing capital. The investment has paid off. Real Madrid topped the 2015 Digital Soccer Index produced by Mailman Group as the most reputable soccer team across the digital landscape. Best described as a hybrid of Twitter and Facebook, Sina Weibo is one of the most popular sites in China with roughly 100 million messages posted each day and is used by well over 30 percent of China's internet users. Real Madrid uses it to communicate directly with fans and grow its fan base in China. The Real Madrid Weibo page allows Chinese fans to view content including game coverage, photos, team history, and background on Bernabéu Stadium. Also, there is an emphasis on the fan experience and the city of Madrid itself since many of the fans in China who view the content may not have opportunities to attend games in Madrid. Real Madrid's Weibo page is a comprehensive source for breaking news, game coverage, and historical moments delivered in real time on the largest social platform in China. Real Madrid even considers the times that information is posted to coincide with high internet and news traffic. The frequent and active engagement, shareable fan content, and strong ties to Chinese media provide Real Madrid the highest level of "buzz," which has allowed the club to develop relationships with community members far outside the largest cities in China. Real Madrid creates personalized content for each country around the world in order to get closer to the community members. It's common in China for fans to support multiple foreign teams because they do not have direct attachment to the different areas like local fans do. Therefore, the Mailman Group ran a study to determine who is "China's second-favorite team." To further back their claim as the most talked-about team online, Real Madrid also finished first in this survey with over 17 percent of the votes. However, the digital ecosystem is not left to itself, it is supplemented and complemented with a physical presence. Real Madrid played two games in China in 2015, generating significant buzz and giving live access to the Real Madrid community in that country.

In addition, Real Madrid tries to work with broadcasters to air games at times in Madrid that are sensitive to the time difference in Asia. The top two games with the highest ratings in China were Real Madrid vs. Barcelona on October 25, 2014, which started at midnight local Beijing time, and Real Madrid vs. Granada on April 5, 2015, which started 6:00 P.M. local Beijing time. Real Madrid must overcome the English Premier League and German Bundesliga, which have achieved 27 percent and 24 percent, respectively, penetration rates for European leagues on Chinese TV channels versus Spanish La Liga at 22 percent. After the 2015 Champions League final, which had the highest TV ratings, both Real Madrid's semifinal and quarterfinal games had the highest ratings (higher than the Barcelona vs. Bayern Munich semifinals). Real Madrid TV is available throughout China and Asia with twenty-four-hour programming to supplement the time in between the live games. The availability has inspired passion, which has led to commercial success in China. Real Madrid was the most searched-for team on Tmall (owned by Alibaba), China's number-one online retail platform. In addition, Real Madrid's digital platform plays an increasingly important role in securing commercial deals in China. The demand for rich, integrated media and sponsorships has created new business opportunities for Real Madrid to promote its community values and brand.

Real Madrid wants to take its digital ecosystem to the next level. Florentino believes that sports media is being consumed in a dramatically different way than in the past. Sports are becoming a multiscreen experience. While Real Madrid fans are watching a game on HDTV, they are also getting rich statistical information through the Real Madrid website, watching a replay, and/or may be tweeting and texting about the game. In fact, the Real Madrid community doesn't even need a TV to watch the team. They can choose the platform they prefer: mobile device, tablet, Xbox, etc.

It is increasingly common for Real Madrid community members to watch the game with a "second screen" up as they communicate with other fans via social media. For example, more than 400,000 community members view Real Madrid's web page on game day. They may want to call up replays themselves; they want to experience the game with more than one screen, but with the inputs that they chose, not the TV producer of the game. One example of drawing the fans into the game: on Realmadrid.com fans can find a heat map of colors showing where each player or players spent their time on the field. This technology is the same that the coaches and technical staff use to evaluate the team.

The Real Madrid App is an application for mobile devices to put its millions of fans in contact under the same interactive platform with complete information on the team. The application comes as a new digital communications channel, covering the all-encompassing social dimension of Real Madrid. For example, there are two GoPro Hero 3s that shoot images from the Real Madrid players' tunnel before the game and Zona Mixta live images after the game. The application, which is still free, was created with an obvious entertainment focus, enabling fans to enjoy a wide range of content and services on their devices. The application's greatest attraction is its audiovisual experience of games: summaries, multi-angle replays, special cameras, and delayed recordings. Fans follow their team in a high-tech way, with all the statistics available and minute-to-minute commentary in Spanish and English. On the anniversary of La Décima, the Real Madrid App offered an exclusive section where fans could again enjoy the game played in Lisbon, see the premiere of a Real Madrid–produced documentary, and listen to the "Décima" song. This comprehensive audiovisual content is complemented by distribution of RealMadrid TV on the Real Madrid App, so that all fans can follow live broadcast club channel television and keep in touch with Real Madrid's latest news. The application is the result of close collaboration with Microsoft over the last year. Microsoft professionals in Spain, the United States, India, Denmark, the UK, the Netherlands, Poland, and China worked together to create the Real Madrid App.

Presentation of the Real Madrid App in November 2014. In suits from left to right: Florentino Pérez, Carlo Ancelloti, and Orlando Ayala.

In the 1950s, the vast majority of revenues for soccer teams came from ticketing. Television rights didn't exist at that time. The club created the current Bernabéu Stadium, with capacity for more than 80,000 people, to increase revenues to afford the best players in the world. Now, sixty years later, Real Madrid believes that with technology and the Microsoft Cloud, the club is building a virtual stadium to host its 450 million fans around the world.

"Opening One Stadium to 450 Million Fans"

On a warm afternoon in November 2014, the Real Madrid president sat front and center for a gathering of mostly media representatives in the presidential box at Bernabéu Stadium. I was seated right behind Florentino in the second row. Marc Reguera, a high-ranking Microsoft executive, was in town to make a presentation on a cutting-edge joint venture poised to launch in the summer of 2015: a platform that will link tens of millions of Real Madrid fans around the world online the way Goodreads connects book readers. The technology itself was a marvel, and for Florentino and the select invited group of media guests who watched as Reguera smiled and bounded around the stage in front of the president's box, showing off features of the planned platform, it was clear that with Microsoft's help, Real Madrid could vault its community experience into the stratosphere. Reguera demonstrated the analytic capabilities that will be open to fans. He pulled up statistics of goals scored by Cristiano Ronaldo dating back to 2003, covering which team he scored for, against which team, and in which stadium. Reguera used this information to create an interactive visual of every city in Europe where Ronaldo has scored, zooming right in on satellite images of the different stadiums. He was able to compare the current Real Madrid team's goal-scoring statistics to prior teams. A fresh-faced, fourteen-year-old blonde girl from Madrid, Esther, came on stage and started to talk about connecting with fellow Real Madrid fans. She touched the large digital screen that showed other fans around the world, and connected with and talked to them, sharing digital information.

By using Realmadrid.com and the Real Madrid App, fans from all around the world can stream all content for which Real Madrid holds the rights. The fans can watch and enjoy, live, the pregame and post-game shows of every single game, players in the tunnel, the press conferences and interviews with players, academy games, basketball games, and different club events. It revolutionizes the experience enjoyed by members and supporters of the club by providing digital services that are accessible anywhere, anytime, and on a host of devices (such as PCs, tablets, smart phones, and wearables).

Microsoft's Chairman of Emerging Markets, Orlando Ayala, described the project as "a long journey that Real Madrid and Microsoft are embarking on together, heading toward the full digital revolution of the club." Florentino focused on the role technology will play in unifying the community: "Today we seal a powerful alliance and the creation of a gigantic digital platform capable of changing the relationship of millions of fans with Real Madrid. Today is the start of the full digital revolution of the club. This new era translates into an unprecedented personalized experience for supporters that will allow millions of fans from all over the planet to enjoy their passion for Real Madrid anywhere, anytime, and on any device."[222]

---

[222] Mike Ozanian, "Real Madrid And Microsoft On Verge Of $30 Million Deal." *Forbes.* http://www.forbes.com/sites/mikeozanian/2014/11/17/real-madrid-and-microsoft-on-verge-of-30-million-deal/#78f946351870.

At the announcement presentation, Florentino focused on the role of technology in unifying the Real Madrid community:

> The Madridistas that constitute this gigantic digital community come from every country, but have one common denominator: their passion for Real Madrid. Those who made Real Madrid the greatest legend in the history of soccer marked out our values. A course whose objective is the conquering of new horizons, goals, and challenges. Santiago Bernabéu and Alfredo Di Stéfano created the greatest factory of dreams in the world and the insatiable necessity to be better every day, and today we seal a digital revolution to channel the emotions of Madridistas.[223]

Satya Nadella, CEO of Microsoft, appeared on a big-screen TV wearing a Real Madrid jersey and talked about the exciting possibilities: "...unprecedented personalized experience for supporters that will allow millions of fans from all over the planet to enjoy their passion for Real Madrid anywhere, anytime, and on any device."

Just as amazing as the view into the future the event afforded was the glimpse of the present and past it offered in the person of Reguera. Reguera's involvement in the Real Madrid project was more than professional responsibility; it was a burning passion. His enjoyable demonstration of this powerful digital tool was full of energy and excitement.

Reguera was still all smiles when I approached him at a reception in the president's box at Bernabéu after his presentation. He was in a group with Antonio Galeno, Real Madrid Communication director; Begoña Sanz, Real Madrid Commercial Director; Enrique Uriel, Real Madrid Technology Director; and Rafael de los Santos, Real Madrid New Media Business. "You have to understand," Reguera told me, his eyes flashing, "Real Madrid is my life. I travel all the time for work and wherever I am the first question is always: Okay, where can I watch the game? When I speak to my parents, children, and friends, we always talk about Real Madrid. I've been working day and night to get ready for this." Reguera

---

[223] Ibid.

even flew his parents to Madrid to attend the event and introduce them to Florentino.

"This man, he loves Real Madrid," Florentino told me, arm on Reguera's shoulder. "You can see it! It's in his heart! His loyalty and passion helps us bring together and connect people from all over the world, so we can serve them."

Chapter 13

CHALLENGES

I N THE BOOK, I've discussed numerous challenges for Real Madrid over the years including:

- the too-much-talent effect;
- the too-tired-and-old effect;
- the potential of manipulation or uneconomic promises to win an election;
- the difficulty of funding potential losses or raising needed capital without a billionaire owner;
- the potential disadvantage of playing a beautiful, attacking game that is more art than system;
- the competitive disadvantage of passing on skilled players whose values don't match community expectations; and
- the delicate role of a coach who's charged with managing players yet upholding the community's values.

Real Madrid executives have addressed the challenges of the too-much-talent effect with the culture and values of the community. The too-tired-and-old effect has been mitigated, in part, by signing younger players, but the club still struggles with players becoming too tired because some factors, like national team commitments, are out of their control. The potential manipulation of an election has been addressed by Real Madrid, which made changes to its organizational structure and by-laws to eliminate some possible loopholes that could have been abused. For example, the qualifications for candidates to the club presidency were changed to double the amount of time that the candidate must have been a club member, to ensure a sense of community values before seeking election.[224] The changes also attempt to prevent the potential of some person or entity financially supporting a "puppet candidate" for president in order to exert influences that may be at odds with the community members. Although some believe a potential candidate's personal guarantee of 15 percent of the operating budget is a Real Madrid rule, it is in fact a Spanish law since 1990 to protect clubs. One of the unintended consequences of the regulation, combined with Real Madrid's incredible financial success, is that only a very wealthy individual, thus a very limited pool of candidates, can meet the personal guarantee to run for president for Real Madrid.

There are some other challenges that the community faces or will face.

Not a Little Club Anymore

Real Madrid in some ways has outgrown being a "club"; it has grown from €118 million in revenues in 2000 to €578 million in 2015 with a 293-page annual report. It is a global corporation. A lot of things have changed in the industry since 2000: inflation in the cost of transfers and salaries of players, media rights commercialization, competition between clubs to increase their fan bases in non-mature markets, competition for sponsorship contracts, data analytics, technology applied to stadiums and social media, and medical science and technology. Real Madrid must continue to grow its revenues significantly in order to have the financial resources to compete and sign the best players. The club needs to stay at the cutting-edge of management science and invest in the tools, just like a multinational corporation. With so much competition and complexity, and an increasing global nature, one has to question whether the president of the club has enough time in the day to also hold down a full-time corporate executive position, like Florentino does as the Chairman and CEO of Grupo ACS. At the same time, unless one has the proven financial sophistication, experience in international

---

[224] On September 30, 2012, the General Assembly of Real Madrid approved a change in the statutes requiring twenty years membership for any candidate to the presidency (formerly ten years), and ten years membership for the rest of board of directors (formerly five years). Additionally, some new solvency requirements of the banks issuing the pledge were approved. Some club members challenged these modifications in court. The court issued a ruling on February 11, 2016 rejecting the challenge and ordering those members to pay all the costs of the legal process.

markets, and management execution expertise that comes from running such a company (Grupo ACS is the largest engineering and construction company in the world with €35 billion in sales and 210,000 employees), it would be difficult to convince the socio members that he or she has the capability to be president.

Copycats Leading to Convergence

In sports, as in business, organizations copy what is successful at other organizations, including Real Madrid. Teams that are backed by owners with significant resources are in an excellent position to imitate, as well as invest, to improve on what Real Madrid has done. For example, in March 2014, the *Financial Times*' Simon Kuper wrote an article titled: "Can Paris Saint-Germain become the world's richest sports club?" The article profiled some of the practices of PSG and many seemed to be very similar to Real Madrid, even signing David Beckham. As mentioned, in 2011–12 PSG was bought by the Qatar Investment Authority (QIA), which reportedly has $170 billion in assets. In addition to QIA owning the team, PSG will earn up to €200 million ($220 million) a year from a four-year deal with Qatar Tourism, which pays the team hundreds of millions of euros in sponsorship fees. That, in turn, allows the team to pay players more and make investments, while still meeting the rules of fair play, although UEFA will only value it at only half that sum in its calculations toward profitability. Similar to Real Madrid, PSG renegotiated previous sponsorship deals to increase their value, and the team has enlarged a VIP section in their stadium. When Manchester United arranged a medical exam for Brazilian winger Lucas Moura in the summer of 2012, a £30 million ($47 million) deal had been agreed to for the Sao Paulo player, until PSG signed the player at the eleventh hour by offering more than Manchester United.

In the article, a PSG executive said, "Our reference points are Real Madrid, Manchester United but also the New York Yankees, the Lakers in LA, Ferrari in Italy." The article explains that PSG has defined (in their new "brand book") exactly what the team should stand for: "PSG is to be as elegant, beautiful and generally excellent as Paris itself. Spectators should be welcomed to the [stadium] as if at an upmarket hotel…the playing style must be chevalier-esque, with panache, Parisian." A PSG executive explained why he believes the team will quickly be one of the biggest franchises in sport: "The world is now instantaneous, digital. It took fifty years to make Real Madrid into a great world club. Now it can be done in five years. If Zlatan [Ibrahimović, one of PSG's star players] scores with a 'pigeon's wing' [a flying back-heel], it goes around the world in 10 seconds." Real Madrid has history and traditions that can't be replicated in five years, but technology can help other teams chase Real Madrid's financial success. A Real Madrid management team that is less adept in these matters than the current one could put the club's position at risk.

Knowledge about the game has spread and successful ideas (on and off the field) have been copied all over the world. For example, Manchester City hired a former vice president and director of soccer from Barcelona in 2012. The *Guardian*'s Sid Lowe wrote an article in February 2014 titled "How Manchester City Embraced the Barcelona Blueprint." In 2016, the former Barcelona executive now at Manchester City hired former star player and former Barcelona coach Pep Guardiola. Slowly but surely, intentionally and through trial and error—and mostly by eliminating errors and weaknesses—teams have become more similar to one another over time. Like result-based sectors in an economy, teams are analyzing and implementing successful structures and playing strategies in the industry—helped by the proliferation of data analytics and an open talent pool—and are growing more similar as a result. Soccer, in essence, is becoming a segment of economy.

Fortunately, Real Madrid has a distinct cultural competitive advantage and an installed community. Real Madrid's history, trophies, heritage, traditions, rituals, best players that share its style of play, club mission, and values continue to attract and retain a loyal and passionate community, which then leads to commercial success to fund more best players. What is unclear is whether that is sustainable without expert management and leadership. External to Real Madrid, there is big money coming into the sport that is disruptive, increasing the purchasing costs of players and their salaries, as well as the stakes. Without a billionaire owner, Real Madrid, and other member-owned clubs, can't afford to make mistakes. Without Real Madrid's successful sustainable economic-sport model, it is difficult to have long-term on-the-field success.

In essence, the sport of soccer is in many ways a saturated market with teams that have access to increasing amounts of financial resources. Soccer games are broadcast almost every day of the week for leagues and tournaments. This is the reason why Real Madrid must innovate and differentiate with its culture. With the popularity of soccer, Real Madrid must manage to attract and retain community members.

The Role of Luck, Defense, and Possession

In 2013, David Sally and Chris Anderson, who are professors at Cornell and Dartmouth, respectively, published a book titled *The Numbers Game: Everything You Know About Soccer Is Wrong* (London: Penguin Books, 2013). The authors attempt to dismiss common soccer beliefs through analysis. One of the most interesting statements they wrote is that soccer results are 50 percent luck. They claim that winning in soccer is 50 percent skill/strategy and 50 percent chance. One of the key analyses they use to support this argument is analyzing the winning percentage of teams that are favored to win:

Table 13.1: Winning Percentage of Team Favored by Bettors by *The Numbers Game*

Sport	Winning Percentage of Favorite
Soccer	50%
Baseball	60%
Basketball	66%

In addition, the study concluded that 50 percent of all goals developed out of some sort of lucky incident such as ball redirections, lucky bounces, and blocks from a goalie, defender, or post that return the ball right to a goal scorer. Jan Vecer, a former professor in the department of statistics at Columbia University who is working on an upcoming book titled *Soccermetrics: Science of Soccer Statistics*, explains, "By the nature of the game, most of the goals happen in situations that cannot be easily replicated even when the players are in exactly the same position. If the situation cannot be easily replicated in terms of scoring, it adds randomness and there is no statistical explanation to it other than luck." Randomness favors the underdog, which is why soccer is so compelling to watch for so many people. There will be players that underperform and others that overperform, plus injuries, distractions, near misses, and other elements that can't be anticipated.

Soccer has a low scoring rate, which means that the entire result can be influenced by a single goal. Vecer explains, "In this sense, soccer is one of the most unfair sports in terms that the probability of the weaker team winning (or not losing) to the better team is quite large."

Sally and Anderson make another argument that relates to the importance of defense. They argue that conceding fewer goals is more important than scoring goals. This conclusion would make it seem that Real Madrid's attacking style of play could be a competitive disadvantage, if that style of play results in more goals being scored against them. The authors conducted a set of rigorous, sophisticated regression analyses based on data between the 2001–02 and 2010–11 English Premier League seasons and concluded that a team scoring ten more goals in a season would have 2.3 more wins on average and that conceding ten fewer goals would have resulted in 2.14 wins (a 7 percent difference). However, since there are draws, they also analyzed the impact of not losing. Scoring an additional ten goals reduced a team's expected number of defeats by 1.76 games on average. Conceding ten fewer goals to a team's opponents reduced defeats by 2.35 games on average. So when it came to avoiding defeat and getting something from a game, the goals that teams didn't give up were each 33 percent more valuable than the goals they scored. Their argument is that defense is significantly more important for avoiding losses while almost as important in helping a team win. The challenge is that this flies in the face of the style of play that the Real Madrid community values and expects to see.

Lastly, there is a philosophical tension within soccer, between those who prefer to see the ball possessed like the game played by Barcelona, and Real Madrid, which prefers to attack. In the last few years, Barcelona possesses the ball on average 60–65 percent of a game, while Real Madrid averages 55–60 percent (typically, a 5–8 percent difference). Possession is in fashion. The theory is the team that has more possession wins more games. Sally and Anderson analyzed 1,140 games over three Premier League seasons. They found that teams that had the greater share of possession generated between 7.7 percent or 11.7

percent more wins. The cause and effect have been debated, however, the data indicates the *tiki-taka* style perfected by Barcelona has a statistical advantage.[225] But it is not a game that Real Madrid community members necessarily want to watch or identify with. The Real Madrid community wants to see the artistic geniuses like Di Stéfano, Zidane, and Ronaldo do something special on the way to winning. The style of play is what makes Real Madrid so mesmerizing to watch and why so many people want to witness their games. However, when the pressure is on, Barcelona team members have what players refer to as an "automatic," a system (learned from young ages at their youth academy) for them to rely upon, while Real Madrid has a less consistent and reliable system (which depends more on familiarity among players). Barcelona didn't have the history of Galácticos 1.0 style to live up to. Real Madrid needs a coach with the credentials and qualities previously discussed to manage and motivate the best players in the world with the community's values of playing a beautiful attacking style in a way to overcome the statistical disadvantage they'd have competing against a team either determined to possess the ball or focused on defense to reduce the goals scored. Phil Jackson and the triangle offense for the Chicago Bulls and Los Angeles Lakers demonstrated that a having a system can lead to selfless, attacking ball movement. The system allowed players who were not regular starters to fit in seamlessly, knowing what their role was and what their teammates were doing and going to do. Lastly, this coach needs to be able to explain randomness and luck to the community and media, when often it is not really explainable or acceptable.

---

[225] This approach, based on speed, unity, and a comprehensive understanding of the field geometry, helped Spain to win the UEFA European Football Championship 2008 (Euro 2008), the 2010 FIFA World Cup, and Euro 2012. Network analysis of interactions among the players (Cotta et al., 2011; Peña & Touchette, 2012) highlighted the importance of passes, yet the ability to do it well doesn't always lead to success—as was demonstrated by the Brazilian team during the 2013 FIFA Confederations Cup (they won despite possessing the ball only 47 percent of the time vs. 53 percent for Spain) and by Netherlands and Chile, which knocked Spain out in the group stage. http://aurametrix.blogspot.com/2014/06/on-luck-skill-and-hard-work-in-soccer.html.

Consistency

Although change in some ways makes a team interesting and engaging, changing coaches can create some difficulties because the players have been selected for a particular coach and his system/formation. Many focus on the number of recent coaching changes during Florentino's presidency, but Real Madrid has a long tradition of replacing coaches. Since 1955, only two Real Madrid coaches have coached more than three seasons, Muñoz (sixteen) and del Bosque (four), both of whom were respected players for the team.

Table 13.2: Real Madrid Managers Who Coached At Least Three Consecutive Years Since 1950 by FootAndBall.net[226]

Coach	Time Period	Seasons	Major Trophies*
Miguel Muñoz	1960–1974	16	14
Vincente del Bosque	1999–2003	4	4
José Villalonga	1954–1957	3	4
Miljan Miljanić	1974–1977	3	3
Vujadin Boškov	1979–1982	3	3
José Mourinho	2010–2013	3	3

* Excluding Super Cups, Latin Cups, and Intercontinental Cups

Three coaches were replaced right after winning a Champions League trophy (the president at the time is in parentheses): Villalonga (Bernabéu), Carniglia (Bernabéu), and Jupp Heynckes (Sanz). Two coaches had to leave the club one year after winning the European Cup: Del Bosque (Pérez) because his contract was not renewed and he chose not to take another role; and Ancelotti (Pérez) because he was fired. In fairness to Pérez, as frequent as Real Madrid's coaching changes have been this century (thirteen), they are on par with many other top teams in Europe:

---

[226] "3 Years: A Comprehensive Look at Mourinho's Real Madrid." *FootAndBall.net*. http://www.footandball.net/3-years-a-comprehensive-look-at-mourinhos-real-madrid/.

Table 13.3: Coaching Changes Since 2000

Team	Changes
Real Madrid	13
Atlético Madrid	16
Chelsea	15
Juventus	11
Barcelona	10
Bayern Munich	10
Manchester United	4*

*Alex Ferguson coached from 1986 to 2013. Since May 2013 there have been three coaches.

Multiple studies found that there is no evidence that changing a coach helps a team win more games.[227] When the coach changes, then the new coach inherits players suited and trained for another system/formation. It can take time for the players to adjust to a new coach's system/formation and then for the coach to sign the right players. During the transition, the team can lack balance. As discussed previously, the difficulty is that the coach has to be able to adapt to changes going on with players, even if the players aren't new, as well as competitive pressures. A soccer team is a complex, dynamic, living organization that has to be nurtured on a daily basis. It takes a special coach to be flexible enough to adapt to an ever-changing group. During the transition, the coach is left with the difficult decisions of putting the players in positions to succeed, rather than implementing a system. With rotations being required and injuries impacting the familiarity of players on the field, it seems that Real Madrid will need to have a system from the first team through the academy. This would take time. The question is as much whether the Real Madrid community, not necessarily the president, will be patient enough and passionately support a more structured system and transition to players who fit into that system. Sometimes, those transitions can be very challenging and take longer than expected.

---

[227] Dave Berri, "Is Changing the Coach Really the Answer?" *Freakonomics*. http://freakonomics. com/2012/12/21/is-changing-the-coach-really-the-answer/.

When researching the value of familiarity to an organization, I discovered a paper by two Harvard Business School professors, Robert Huckman and Gary Pisano. They analyzed cardiac surgeons' performance on coronary artery bypass graft operations where surgeons "open a patient's chest and attach a vein from the leg or section of the chest artery to bypass blockage in an artery to the heart" for a paper published in *Management Science* in 2006. The professors discovered that over time, the performance of the operation got progressively better at the specific hospital where they practiced. The surgeons became more familiar with particular nurses and anesthesiologists, learning about their strengths and weaknesses, habits, and styles. They needed time to develop relationships with specific members to maximize their performance. Also, when the surgeons went to a new hospital, their performance dropped until they could develop relationships with their new team members. The research showed that it is critical to build a familiarity and network of deep relationships with other team members. The intensity, scrutiny, and competitive pressures are not directly comparable, but the research indicates if an organization changes coaches and players too often, it risks suboptimal performance.[228] The stability of Real Madrid's ownership structure, not having different owners buy and sell the club, also may benefit the sustainability of the culture, which may help offset the negative impact.

In the end, on the field, all Real Madrid executives can do is try to exploit the laws of probability over the long term. The probabilities are that if a team has the best players (but not too many and not too old or too tired), then their chances are better than an average team. They try to find players who can perform in Champions League with greater competition or pressure situations to increase their chances, but the data set is limited and data analytics in soccer is complex. Real Madrid focuses on elements to intensify and sustain the culture such as equality and the incorporation of academy players to improve their chances. However, in the end, they can't control the outcome on the field as a casino manager can't control the outcomes of randomness and luck in the casino.

---

[228] Robert S. Huckman, and Gary P. Pisano, "The Firm Specificity of Individual Performance: Evidence from Cardiac Surgery." *Management Science* 52, no. 4 (April 2006): 473–488.

It Is Tougher Now Than During Galácticos 1.0

The difference between an average professional player in the top five leagues in Europe and the best players (the "stars") is smaller than it was during Galácticos 1.0. Data has shown that the gap between the elite and the good and the average is much smaller than most would think.[229] Absolute skill in soccer has never been higher, but relative skill has never been narrower. Players today are grinding to a physiological limit and performance is getting clustered. In his book *The Success Equation: Untangling Skill and Luck in Business, Sports, and Business* (Brighton: Harvard Business Review Press, 2012), Michael Mauboussin, an adjunct professor at Columbia Business School, illustrates this point by showing the difference between first place and twentieth place in the Olympic Men's Marathon in 1932 being around 39 minutes, while in 2012 that difference had declined to around 7 minutes.[230] Similar to soccer, this is due to a greater pool of athletes playing and the amounts of identification, coaching, training methods, and training facilities available to them.

Soccer stars can't dominate as they once did, and, paradoxically, more is being left to luck. In many ways, with a few exceptions, the big teams are paying a significant amount of money for players who are slightly better than other players, because the difference between winning and losing is so small.

Just to put into context how difficult it is to win the Champions League trophy today, since AC Milan repeated as champions in 1988–89 and 1989–90, *no team* has repeated. Before 1990, Real Madrid won five times in a row from 1955 to 1960, Ajax won three times in a row from 1970 to 1973, then six other teams repeated as champions. It is interesting to note that the Bosman ruling allowing more freedom for soccer players in Europe was enacted in 1995. In the NBA, going only back to

---

[229] Harrison Crow, "How Luck Intigrates [sic] with Shots and Our Expected Goal Model." *American Soccer Analysis*. http://www.americansocceranalysis.com/home/2014/11/25/comparing-defenses-and-how-luck-intigrates-with-expected-goals.

[230] In the IRONMAN World Championships, the difference between first place and third place had gone from twenty-three minutes in 1989 to seven minutes in 2011. In 2015, the difference between first and third was four minutes.

1990, there have been six teams that have repeated as NBA champions. The Chicago Bulls (with Michael Jordan and Scottie Pippen) won
three in a row in 1991–93 and in 1996–98, the Los Angeles Lakers (with
Kobe Bryant and Shaquille O'Neal) also three-peated in 2000–02, then
a repeat has been accomplished three other times. This also highlights
the different impacts interdependence and luck have in basketball, a
sport that has lots of shots and scoring (and a NBA finals with a best of
seven games series), versus soccer, which has few opportunities to score
goals (and a one game Champions League final). In case you were wondering, a repeat has happened three times in the NFL and twice in MLB
(including the Yankees' three-peat from 1998 to 2000) since 1988.

Table 13.4: Repeat Champions Since 1990

Champions League	0
NBA	**6**: Bulls (1991–93), Rockets (1994–95), Bulls (1996–98), Lakers (2000–02), Lakers (2009–10), Heat (2012–13)
NFL	**3**: Cowboys (1993–94), Broncos (1998–99), Patriots (2004–05)
MLB	**2**: Blue Jays (1992–93), Yankees (1998–2000)

For those who think that soccer is dominated by a handful of teams,
one can see below that since 1990 the Champions League has had nineteen different teams in the finals, compared to the NBA's twenty-one.[231]

Table 13.5: Different Finalists Since 1990

Champions League	19
NBA	21
NFL	23
MLB	23

---

[231] There is a greater pool of finalists in the Champions League due to the qualification process than
the fixed number of teams in the NBA (thirty), NFL (thirty-two), and MLB (thirty).

Who Gets to Play?

The one question that inevitably comes up when you have a team with so many of the best players in the world: Who plays? Does the biggest, brightest star play? Or is it the player that the community wants to see on the field? What if that best player is not playing at 100 percent because of injury or the too-tired-and-old effect? What about giving the younger players a chance to play and develop? These are difficult questions for a coach to answer. With the too-tired-and-old effect it seems that some sort of rotation is necessary. Real Madrid's fans have been critical of the coaches using rotations, and the stars themselves may not be happy with a rotation or being substituted. This puts the coach in a very difficult position, especially if he realizes what is in the best long-term interests of player performance. In addition, whenever a player believes he should be playing more minutes but doesn't, it affects him not only from a soccer perspective, but also at home and in his personal life. Based on the data analysis, the Real Madrid community will have to embrace rotations of players. A coach must have the credentials to overcome the second-guessing.

In addition, there is the aging-superstar dilemma that has plagued every team throughout the years. As discussed, the too-tired-and-old effect impacts performance on the field. Each starting position is hotly contested at Real Madrid. Sometimes a "less famous" player who is less known to the community is playing better than a "more famous" player loved by the community. This puts the coach in a very difficult position. If the more-famous player is not played then the media attention is overwhelming and the media, coaches, players, etc., essentially are left in the awkward position of choosing sides. Not every aging player is going to be as thoughtful and gracious as Zidane. A lot of times, the aging star can still play and contribute, but maybe not at the level to start at Real Madrid on a regular basis.[232] If an aging player wants to continue starting,

---

[232] After sixteen seasons at Real Madrid, Iker Casillas, the classy Real Madrid captain and academy graduate who is loved by fans, agreed in July 2015 to move to the Portuguese soccer club Porto. Real Madrid called him "the greatest goalkeeper in the history of the club and in the history of Spanish football" and "a symbol of the best in our history." Through November 25, 2015 (admittedly a small data set), the 34-year-old Casillas, a former "Best European Goalkeeper" and "FIFA World Cup Golden Glove" winner, captain of the Spain's 2010 World Cup win, and three-time Champions League champion, had been responsible for the most defensive errors in the Champions League and

management is left with selling or releasing the player. Depending on all parties and the circumstances, this can be handled with class or become a public relations disaster. Real Madrid has no incentive but to try to make the exit as elegant and gracious as possible to protect its brand and image, as this is what the community would like, and the club wants to maintain excellent relationships because it involves former stars in its rituals and traditions after they retire. However, sometimes other factors, miscommunication, and influences get involved and it impacts the transition. Through my interviews with executives and coaches, this challenge seemed to be the one that personally impacted them the most, and it is one of the reasons for executives to maintain more distance from the players—it is difficult for coaches who develop close personal bonds with players to be involved in the personnel decisions.

What Happens After Winning a Championship?

After a team wins a championship, the team can become complacent and satisfied, or, feeling that he or they sacrificed for the betterment of the team, individuals or groups of players can demand more recognition, a larger role, or more money. This can threaten the culture and values as well as the sustainable economic-sport model. It is a challenge any successful organization is likely to confront. In the good times, when things go a player's way and the player wins a lot of trophies and receives all kinds of awards, then the player becomes susceptible to thinking he is the best and no longer needs to improve; often, this is the first step toward failure. As for complacency or lack of motivation, it mostly likely comes down to the leadership of the coach, the captains, the "first among equals," and academy players. As for players feeling justified in seeking additional money or recognition, it seems that this is more complicated. In the end, an organization has its values and its sustainable economic-sport model to consider in making tough decisions.

---

has a Champions League save percentage of 68.4 percent, ranking twenty-first among goalies. In contrast, his replacement, Navas, was ranked number one and had a save percentage of 100 percent.

English Premier League Develops into the NBA of Soccer

In the sink-or-swim world of European soccer, where there's no salary cap and the richest teams can outspend most of their competitors, the English Premier League has gained an edge in becoming the richest league.[233] When I refer to the "NBA of Soccer," I am referring to the idea that all basketball players in Europe want to go to the NBA because it's recognized globally as the highest level of basketball competition and has the highest average salaries.

"We run the risk of having the Premier League become the NBA of football in the next five years, with the rest of European leagues turning into secondary tournaments," according to Spanish league president Javier Tebas.[234] English Premier League soccer is growing ever more popular worldwide. The league broadcasts to 212 territories for a possible reach of 720 million homes, with more and more Americans watching the games. The English Premier League has close to 11 million more subscribers and around $1.4 billion more revenues per season than the Spanish league. Also, there is a fear that a number of very wealthy owners in the English Premier League have the resources to sign the most talent in any league and increase its large lead over the Spanish league in its broadcasting and marketing revenue opportunities. Fourteen of the thirty richest soccer teams in the world (based on 2013–14 revenue) are from the English Premier League. Five of the top thirty are from the Italian Serie A. Four are from Germany. Three are from Spain. Two are from France. The other two are from Turkey and Portugal. None of the other leagues have the upper-middle class of teams that the English Premier League can produce with its television money. This may raise the question of whether Real Madrid (and Barcelona) can be perceived as a global leader playing in the Spanish league and make enough money in broadcasting and marketing if the club is not regularly playing the

---

[233] Although the English Premier League is the richest league, Spanish league teams have won forty-five of the past forty-eight games in competitions against non-La Liga teams. Since 2011, Spain has had fourteen teams in the Champions League, Europa League, and UEFA Super Cup finals.

[234] "La Liga goes abroad to try to keep pace with Premier League." *USAToday.* http://www. usatoday.com/story/sports/soccer/2015/11/01/la-liga-goes-abroad-to-try-to-keep-pace-with-premier-league/75018236/.

teams with the most talent. However, recent large investments by entities controlled by foreign billionaires in Atlético Madrid and Valencia
may start to change the dynamics in the Spanish league.

The concern that the English Premier League's new TV deal "poses a
great threat to all other European leagues" is leading to more speculation
of a European Super League.[235] In 2016, the Bayern Munich CEO said
that he is not ruling out a potential European Super League that consists
of twenty teams from England, France, Germany, Italy, and Spain. The
income of the European Super League's participants would be much greater
than the present income from the UEFA Champions League. In 2009,
Florentino said he would consider an alternative to the Champions League
that "guarantees that the best always play the best."[236] He added that he
hoped a new system could be designed "without abandoning the national
leagues." The manager of Arsenal has previously said that he expected
such a league to be created "because the income of the Champions League
is basically owned by UEFA and they distribute the money to the clubs."[237]
In the future those games could be held in the United States or Asia to
increase global interest and revenues.

Stadium Limitations

Teams are constantly trying to upgrade and enlarge their stadiums for
additional revenue opportunities. In January 2014, Real Madrid presented plans for a remodeled stadium with a 150-room hotel, two external giant screens, expansion of the museum, and shopping complex, as
well as a retractable roof. The capacity would increase from 81,044 to
approximately 90,000. However, the plan has been stalled because of
urban issues. Meanwhile, Barcelona has released plans to take their stadium's capacity from 99,354 to 105,000 and to complete the project by
2021. The additional seats and opportunity for naming rights will give

---

[235] Stephen Uersfeld, "European Super League possible – Bayern Munich CEO Rummenigge."
ESPNFC. http://www.espnfc.us/bayern-munich/story/2785910/european-super-league-possible-
bayern-munich-ceo.

[236] "Real Madrid's Florentino Perez reveals 'European Super League' ambition." *Telegraph*. http://
www.telegraph.co.uk/sport/football/european/5748825/Real-Madrids-Florentino-Perez-reveals-
European-Super-League-ambition.html.

[237] David Hytner, "European super league will be here in 10 years, says Arsène Wenger." *Guardian*.
http://www.theguardian.com/football/2009/aug/17/arsene-wenger-european-super-league.

Barcelona an economic advantage. If Real Madrid can't upgrade its stadium, then the club either risks having lower revenue opportunities than competitors.

One Goal Makes a Difference

...and can change the perception of history.

When I researched performance on the field, I was shocked at how much history and narrative is determined by one goal, which, as discussed above, has a large element of randomness and chance. As discussed earlier, Real Madrid was close to losing in the first round of the defense of the European Cup in the 1956–57 tournament until Di Stéfano scored a goal to tie the game and then win in the play-off. In the 2013–14 final, Real Madrid scored a goal with 150 seconds left to tie the game, then won in extra time.

In 2011–12, as discussed, Real Madrid had the best statistical season in their history, winning the Spanish La Liga over Barcelona. Real Madrid's total of 100 points was one point better than the previous record that was set by Barcelona in the 2009–10 season. Real Madrid won a record thirty-second La Liga title and finished the season with a record of 121 goals scored and goal difference of +89, and a record sixteen away wins and thirty-two overall wins. However, Real Madrid lost in the Champions League semifinals at home in a penalty shootout. At the ninetieth minute of the first Champions League semifinal against Bayern Munich, the German side scored a late goal to win 2–1 at home. It was Real Madrid's first loss in the Champions League that year. The commentators questioned whether Bayern Munich was offside. The goal would prove deadly, as Real Madrid went on to 2–1 at home, resulting in an aggregate 3–3, but then lost 3–1 on penalties.

In 2012–13, Real Madrid lost in the semifinals of the Champions League by one goal on aggregate. They let an opposing player become the first player to score four goals in a Champions League semifinal as Borussia Dortmund defeated Real Madrid 4–1 in the first game. Real Madrid won 2–0 at home. One more goal at home or one less goal given and Real Madrid would have been in the final. Instead, Real Madrid lost 4–3 on aggregate.

In 2013–14, Real Madrid finished three points behind Atlético Madrid in La Liga, which is the difference of winning one game in an entire season. One goal would have made the difference in several games to give Real Madrid the three points.[238] Real Madrid won its semifinals game against Bayern Munich 5–0 on aggregate on April 29, 2014. In May, Real Madrid tied both Valencia (finished eighth in La Liga) and Real Valladolid (finished nineteenth out of twenty in La Liga that season) and had a loss to Celta Vigo (finished ninth). All of the teams had more losses than wins. A change in any of those games would have allowed Real Madrid to win the league, as it had a higher goal difference (+15) than Atlético Madrid. Once again, the late-season disappointing performance raised the question of the impact of the too-tired effect.

In 2014–15, Real Madrid finished second behind Barcelona by two points in La Liga, which is less than the three-point difference of winning one game in an entire season—which could have been just one goal in a game, hitting the back of the net instead of the crossbar in one game—that small of a margin. During the season, Real Madrid had a twenty-two-game winning streak and was on pace to challenge the best season ever. Then the team lost in the semifinals of the Champions League by one home goal in aggregate. In the second game, Ronaldo scored at twenty-three minutes, and Real Madrid was going to go to the finals. Then Juventus scored at fifty-seven minutes, equalizing the game—and sat back, defended, and advanced to the final.

It is shocking when one examines the effect of the slimmest of margins—one goal, which can result from a ball that deflects in versus out from the crossbar, or an offside call that isn't called versus is, or a penalty is called in the penalty box versus just outside or five minutes of stoppage time being added versus three or a player being sent off for a hard foul and reducing his team to 10 men versus just receiving a yellow card. Also, in a sport that requires so much interdependence, the effect of players being too tired, showing the slightest difference in speed or concentration, or incorrectly anticipating speed by a teammate can create an offensive or defensive action that will win or lose a game. Many of these possibilities can't be truly captured in data analytics.

---

[238] Winning one more game could not have been enough because of Real Madrid's head-to-head against Atlético (0–1, 2–2). Head-to-head points are the second rule of classification. Goal difference is third.

Below is a chart summarizing Real Madrid's performance since the 2011–12 season. It highlights that one goal can make a difference and change the perception of history.

Season	Coach	Goals Allowed	Goals Scored	Net	End of Season Standing	Total Points	Comments	Champions League Performance	Aggregate Score	Comments
2011–12	Mourinho	32	121	+89	1	100	9 points ahead of Barca	Semifinals	3–3, 1–3 penalties	Lost on penalties at home. Best statistical year in RM history.
2012–13	Mourinho	42	103	+61	2	85	15 points behind Barca	Semifinals	3–4	Lost by 1 home goal on aggregate, lost 1–4 away when one opposing player scored 4 goals.
2013–14	Ancelotti	38	104	+66	3	87	3 points behind Atletico (1 win). Tied points with Barca but lost on head to head. One of the games was 1–2.	Winner		Tied Atlético with 150 seconds left in stoppage time and won in extra time.
2014–15	Ancelotti	38	118	+80	2	92	2 points behind Barca (1 win)	Semifinals	2–3	Lost by 1 home goal on aggregate. Juve scored with 33 minutes remaining.

CONCLUSION:
LESSONS FROM
THE REAL MADRID WAY

WHAT IS THE GREATEST competitive advantage? Real Madrid's executives believe that, in the end, it is a team's values and culture that have the greatest impact on performance on and off the field. To them, culture means everyone working around a common mission in a selfless way, and everyone knowing the goals and how to achieve them in a collaborative way. What makes Real Madrid such a fascinating case is that its entire strategy both on and off the field is based on a culture and values system from its community members.

The Real Madrid way is a sustainable economic-sport model centered on the community values. It starts with Real Madrid getting the world's best players that match those community's values to play an attacking beautiful style of soccer with class to win championships and capture the imagination and inspire the current and potential global audience. Technology enables the means for experiences and engagement to be scalable around the world. This leads to passion, and the club's traditions and rituals reinforce the identity association. Since Real Madrid's values are inclusive and universal, appealing to a global audience of all ages, the community grows globally, which leads to international sponsors spending big money for association with and access to Real Madrid, as well as television broadcasters paying lots of money to distribute the games to the large, passionate worldwide audience. The passion leads to an increase in stadium receipts, the value of broadcasting rights, and marketing and sponsorship opportunities, which then leads to higher revenues. See Appendix A: "Comparison of Galácticos 1.0, 2.0, 3.0, and 4.0" to see a comparison of key characteristics between the different eras.

Culture and values don't guarantee trophies, just like data analytics don't.[239] Culture and values provide a statistical competitive advantage over the long term both on and off the field. As discussed, on the field, luck and one goal can easily change the narrative. One person can flip a coin five times and get five heads in a row, and a history and narrative can then be created, but we know that over time, statistically heads versus tails is 50 percent. Real Madrid's executives look for any competitive statistical advantage. As discussed, executives can't control many factors on the field, and money and talent don't guarantee trophies either. Executives can control their active engagement with the community and try to live up to their values and expectations.

Since Florentino and his executives implemented their sustainable economic-sport model, revenues have soared as fans more closely identified with the club and its players, as demonstrated below in Table C.1. Coming full circle, the high revenues allow the club to sign the world's best players that share their community's values. The culture and values inspire the best players to work together as a team, play a certain style, and conduct themselves in a way the community expects. This is Real Madrid's statistical competitive advantage, and one that many others are desperately trying to copy in many ways.

---

[239] Maureen Mullen, "Sox: Too Much Math: Boston Owner Blames Heavy Analytics for Decline." *Valley News*. http://www.vnews.com/sports/21226802-95/sox-too-much-math-boston-owner-blames-heavy-analytics-for-decline.

Table C.1: Fiscal Year End 2000 and 2015 Real Madrid Financial Information

	June 2000	June 2015
Revenues	€118m	€578m
EBITDA (before net gains on disposals)	€10m	€135m
EBITDA (as per accounting principles)	(€30m)	€203m
Wages to revenues	66%	50%
Profit (Loss) before taxes	(€23m)	€56m
Net debt	€126m	€96m
Net Debt / EBITDA	4.2	0.5x[240]
Result	Auditor's opinion: unsustainable model	Season Investments: €240m (Players: €189m; Repurchase of Rights: €30m; Sports Facilities [CRM]: €7m; Stadium €14m) Total 2000–2015 Investments: €2,259m (Players: €1,785m; Repurchase of Rights: €48m; Sports Facilities [CRM]: €186m; Stadium €240m)

The club is financially as strong as it has ever been. Taking all of the club's assets and subtracting all of the club's debts results in an equity total of €412 million ($453 million) as of June 30, 2015. Since Real Madrid does not make distributions of dividends, the annual variation of equity corresponds to the yearly after-tax profit. Due to profit earned, Real Madrid has increased its equity on a year-over-year basis of 11 percent since 2000 and has a 14 percent pretax return on equity (€56 million/average equity of €391 million), which, considering its low leverage, is an excellent return on capital. Net debt of €96 million ($105 million) is 23 percent of the value of equity and 0.5 times EBITDA, representing a solid financial situation.

For the skeptics who don't think culture and values impact organizations, I provided performance data from McKinsey & Company that illustrates it

---

[240] The calculation of ratio Net Debt/EBITDA is done with EBITDA as per the official accounting principles of soccer.

is a key competitive advantage. The surveys from McKinsey & Company show that executives of the best companies in the world believe in culture. However, for some reason in sports management, it is not actively discussed. I have looked in the indexes of most sports management books and the words "culture," "values," and "mission statement" often do not appear. For those who don't think values and culture are applicable to sports, I provided statements from the leaders of winning sports organizations that believe they are important. When Florentino and Ballmer, two extremely successful business executives worth billions of dollars, took over sports organizations, one of the first things they did was develop a mission statement, and both used surveys of their communities to help them do so. They know that you have to start with organizational culture. Everything flows from this critical element because the values and culture facilitate the maximization of team performance both on and off the field. The extraordinary element about Real Madrid is that the community itself dictates the culture. I believe that organizations interested in performance and finding a competitive edge both on and off the field and in business need to give culture, mission, and values more serious consideration. They need to be paranoid that their competitors are. With the increased accessibility of data analytics, the teams and organizations with more resources will be able to afford better players and analytics staff. Organizations with fewer resources can still compete on culture and values because these are not something a team can go out and "buy." Cultures and values can make a community more loyal and passionate, which can lead to more commercial revenue-generating possibilities. I don't necessarily believe that an organization has to literally go as far as Real Madrid does in being owned by a community, but I do believe that when the organization is focused on aligning the community's values and expectations with its strategy, it can be powerful in generating extraordinary loyalty and passion. When this passion and loyalty are carefully, actively, and frequently supported, they can lead to extraordinary commercial performance. This loyalty and passion can be sustained for a long time, even without winning. Real Madrid's community has shown multiple times that values are more important than winning, and this may shock many sports management teams. It is not just Real Madrid's community. I demonstrated that in the NFL and NBA, winning or large markets don't necessarily lead to more team jersey sales, which is an important indicator of identity and connection. It is what you stand for and how you prove it that matters most. Keep in mind, the vast majority of the time a sports team won't win a championship, so a strategy is flawed if it relies on winning as a part of the reason why the community will support the team. Also, it takes time to establish a culture and identity; it doesn't happen overnight.

In sports and businesses with employees, there is a tension between the interests of the team and the interests of the individual. The game or the way compensation or recognition works in most organizations continually tempts the people who play it to do things that are not necessarily in the best interests of the group. Soccer, like business, is highly interdependent. In business you have no guaranteed at bats, like in baseball. In business, most of the time you need a teammate to help you get the best opportunity to score a deal or perform. In soccer, Ronaldo needs his teammate to get him the ball at the right place at the right time. In soccer, and business, you need teamwork and coordination to maximize performance. A mission, purpose, values, and culture are the elements that maximize performance, especially in organizations that are highly dependent on talent. When the culture is known and accepted throughout the organization, decisions become easier, less time is wasted, and power and decision making can be more distributed.

One of the biggest ideas that Real Madrid opened my eyes to is that a sports community could care more about *how* their sports team wins and *who* it wins with instead of "just winning." It is tempting to try to take a shortcut and sign a player whom the data analysis (and/or talent evaluator) says would be best in order to win. Entrepreneurs like Zappos' CEO Tony Hsieh and venture capitalist Brad Feld have made the case that when they look to hire, cultural fit trumps competence. Having the culture and values to turn down that player, even if it costs your community or your organization a championship or business deal in the short term, is remarkably brave but ultimately smart. It is a tough pill to swallow when that player or employee goes to a competitor and helps them win. Having studied Real Madrid and related organizations, I believe that in the long run, values, how you do things, and who represents you will differentiate the community, make it more loyal and passionate, and can lead to greater commercial success to fund what the community desires.

Culture can also help retain players. The culture, community support, history, environment, world-class facilities, and the exposure are some of the reasons players are attracted to Real Madrid and on the margin may give Real Madrid an advantage of attracting or keeping a player. The San Antonio Spurs are an excellent example of culture attracting and retaining talent. Keeping a player and not needing to pay a new player a transfer fee—or, for a corporate organization, the equivalent would be avoiding a headhunter's fee—will save money in the long run; also that employee or player will have more familiarity, which can maximize performance. Similarly, developing and investing in homegrown talent may require an upfront expense, but in the long run the talent knows the organization and can help assimilate new employees and optimize performance.

Real Madrid management has instilled trust through radical transparency. Real Madrid creates trust with actions such as standard contracts and treating players fairly and equally. This goes beyond 293-page annual reports, or having the same locker, this is something that is instilled throughout the organization. There is an air of transparency when dealing with Real Madrid; the people that I encountered were straightforward and professional. When I observed their interactions, they treated each other with respect. They were eager to bring experts into discussions to elaborate and give me access to whatever I wanted. My understanding is that most sports teams do not act in this manner. Many corporations don't either. When an organization doesn't act with full transparency, it is difficult for the community to completely trust the organization, which can have a negative impact on the passion and loyalty.

Over time, sports teams, like businesses, keep getting more and more competitive and efficient. Processes and trade secrets become more widely dispersed. Most teams will become similar. In baseball, most teams have adopted data analytics, which was being used to level the playing field, so the big competitive advantage has been eliminated. Culture is a unique, authentic differentiator. I don't think it is just the words in mission and values statements (although it is a start) but how they are emphasized and reinforced. For Real Madrid that includes considerations such as how captains are selected and employees are treated. I believe those organizations that can differentiate with history, traditions, and legacies combined with a community of values can differentiate their performance both on and off the field. This opportunity exists for small market teams or organizations that seem out-resourced or outmanned.

In my analysis, I learned that the single-reason narrative, such as the loss of one player, is not likely. There are many complicated and inter-related factors. From Real Madrid, I learned that culture can help priori-tize data analysis and provide context. For example, Real Madrid selects data and uses data analysis to choose the best players that match its goals and its values. Real Madrid also utilizes context in analyzing the data. Context matters a lot.

I also learned that there is a correlation between what happens off the field and on the field.[241] Not just in sports, but in most organizations certain people seem to focus on the numbers/business aspect and others on the revenue generation/creative/content aspect. The two are inter-related. The revenue generation/creative/content people don't want to hear about how the numbers work but they have to—it impacts the resources and therefore the strategy that can be followed. The two sides need to have a sustainable model, an economic-sport model, even if the purpose is not to make a profit; losses can't be funded forever and dona-tions can't be counted on forever. Ultimately, in today's world, a sustain-able model is the best way for a long-term success.

Culture is hard to define, let alone analyze, measure, and compare, and it is difficult for the media to report on culture. There is bound to be resistance, just like when data analytics was introduced and people had to learn a new way of thinking and a new language. The fact that quantifying culture is difficult and an obstacle is what actually makes it a competitive advantage that is not easily dispersed and copied. Every winning culture has its own unique personality and soul that can't be invented or imposed.

---

[241] Francisco Cutiño in his unpublished thesis paper identified the issue: "So here a potential conflict arises in most of the clubs. Business managers care about winning matches, but what they have to give account of is about increasing revenues. On the other hand, football managers care about having a club financially wealthy, but they only have to give account of the matches they win. So most of the times, in most clubs, team management and club management do not seem to be rowing in the same direction. There is a problem of accountability. Business managers do not get bonuses for the team winning matches...Football players do not get bonuses for the club making profits. In this situation, it is difficult that employees in different areas look beyond the immediate results of their own jobs."

As Fournier and Lee state in their 2009 *Harvard Business Review* article, aligning strategy, culture, and identity "requires an organization-wide commitment and a willingness to work across functional boundaries. It takes the boldness to reexamine...organizational design. It takes the fortitude...to cede control" to the community's values and beliefs. Centering the culture on community values increases loyalty and passion, validates brand identities, and yields sponsors and promoters to grow the business. Real Madrid demonstrates that the alignment of strategy, culture, and identity can create a powerful sustainable model if it is approached with the right mind-set and commitment.

Talent-oriented businesses need specialized leadership, and that leadership needs to be flexible and adapt because people, goals, expectations, and conditions change. For Real Madrid, a calm coach with credibility matters. It seems that leaders managing highly talented people deep in the organization need to be respected for their applicable accomplishment by those that they manage. Getting Real Madrid's sustainable economic-sport model working required outsider thinking and a deep commitment from the top, but the coach—the fulcrum, managing and leading the talent day-to-day—needs to be an insider. Real Madrid is making the necessary investments for the next generation. There seems to be a commitment or openness to search for new ideas and adjacent domains. They constantly want to refresh their systems and processes. That energy and drive comes from the top. The executives are eager to listen to best practices in other industries and understand how those could apply to Real Madrid. For a club so steeped in tradition, I found it impressively open to technology, change, and unconventional ideas. The executives took a business that was constrained by the physical space of a stadium of 81,044 people and used technology to connect to 450 million community members. The environment of trust, respect, collaboration, and debate fosters openness and speed to adapt. Utilizing executives with certain roles (e.g., visionary, execution, etc.) helps. However, one thing is consistent: the center revolves around the values of the community and the sense of purpose from its mission seems to drive the commitment. The commitment and constant reinforcement from the top, as well as putting in place processes, procedures, and environment, is critical.

Lastly, leadership requires an ability to tweak and adjust strategy, but without losing sight of being centered on the community's values, attitudes, and beliefs (culture). Florentino is the first to admit that he and the club haven't made every right decision, but he is humble enough to reflect on missteps to learn valuable lessons about how to stay true to the mission and values, which is incredibly difficult considering the intense pressures and scrutiny. It takes courage to withstand the criticism and second-guessing when sticking to values. Similar to how a coach who has won as both a player and coach has leeway, Florentino and his executives get leeway. Although leeway can be very advantageous in making courageous decisions, it has to be earned. The leeway is smaller in the Real Madrid community when there is an election every four years, compared with a sports team or organization that is privately owned, or a public company where the board of directors has a good rapport with the CEO, or a sports team in a league without relegation.

Florentino and his executive team created the modern, global sports team, one that cherishes the community's values and expectations, that aims for success off the field as much as victory on it, and in the process secures the long-term future of the club. Interestingly, the inspiration came from its past. By studying Real Madrid, I learned why they have been able to win on and off the field. Money, certainly. Talented players, of course. Data analytics, without a doubt. In the end, however, the Real Madrid way is the creation of value through its community's values.

Real Madrid provides a compelling alternative model with lasting competitive advantages for leading any organization, not just a sports team. Big data and statistical analysis is taking over business strategy. However, Real Madrid shows that an organizational culture and identity that engages a community can demolish competitors.

Aligning strategy, culture, and identity requires commitment from the entire team. It takes courage to rethink organizational design. It takes time and patience to establish a culture and identity. It takes confidence to depend on the community for directing the mission and values. Doing so authenticates brand meanings, and produces the loyalty and passion of both community members and employees to grow the business. This alignment is powerful if it is approached with openness, accountability, and transparency, and can deliver superior and sustainable returns and performance.

Appendix A:

COMPARISON OF GALÁCTICOS 1.0, 2.0, 3.0, AND 4.0

The following table compares the various elements Real Madrid has found to help create an environment of success.

Table A.1: Galácticos 1.0, 2.0, 3.0, and 4.0

	Galácticos 1.0	Galácticos 2.0	Galácticos 3.0	Galácticos 4.0[242]
Selected year	1959	2002	2014	2016
Title (RM's total at time)	European Champions League (4th)	European Champions League (9th)	European Champions League (10th)	European Champions League (11th)
President	Bernabéu	Pérez	Pérez	Pérez
Years of prior pres. experience	16	3	11	13
Coach	Miguel Muñoz	Vicente del Bosque	Carlo Ancelotti	Zinedine Zidane
Coach credentials as a player	• RM midfielder • Scored 1st RM goal in ECL • 1956, 57, and 58 ECL	• RM midfielder • 5 Spanish league titles • 1 ECL Final	• Milan midfielder • Scored against RM in ECL semifinal • On Milan team that was last to repeat as ECL champions	• RM attacking midfielder • Scored winning RM goal in 2002 ECL • 3x FIFA World Best Player

	Galácticos 1.0	Galácticos 2.0	Galácticos 3.0	Galácticos 4.0
Coach credentials as a coach	Coach of RM #2 team	Coach of RM #2 team	2003 and 2007 ECL (Milan)	• 2014 RM Assistant Coach • 2014-15 RM Castilla Coach
Personality	Calm	Calm	Calm	Calm
Selected galácticos (*italics if ever placed in top 3 of Ballon d'Or*)	• *Alfredo Di Stéfano*[243] (Argentina) • *Ferenc Puskás*[244] (Hungary) • *Raymond Kopa*[245] (France) • *José Santamaría* (Uruguay) • Francisco Gento[246] (Spain) • Louis Del Sol • Didi[247] (Brazil)	• *Luis Figo*[248] (Portugal) • *Zinedine Zidane*[249] (France) Academy/on team before Florentino Pérez: • *Raúl*[250] (Spain) • *Roberto Carlos*[251] (Brazil) • Iker Casillas (Spain) Added for 2003: • *Ronaldo*[252] (Brazil) • *David Beckham*[253] (U.K.)	• *Cristiano Ronaldo*[254] (Portugal) • Karim Benzema[255] (France) • Gareth Bale[256] (U.K.) Academy/on team before Florentino Pérez: • Iker Casillas[257] (Spain) Added for 2015: • James Rodriguez[258] (Colombia)	• *Cristiano Ronaldo*[259] (Portugal) • Karim Benzema[260] (France) • Gareth Bale[261] (U.K.) Added for 2016: • Casemiro (RM exercised buyback clause option) • Lucas Vázquez (Academy graduate brought back from loan)
# of players ever placed in top 3 of Ballon d'Or	3	4 6, after season	1	1
"First Among Equals"	Di Stéfano	Raúl/Zidane	Cristiano Ronaldo	Cristiano Ronaldo
Age of "FAE"	33	25/30	29	31
Total revenues	N/A	€152m	€550m	€608m
Lead revenue source	Stadium	Marketing	Marketing	Marketing
% of revenues from stadium	90+%[262]	26%	24%	25%
% of Players from academy	12%	27%	39%	33%

	Galácticos 1.0	Galácticos 2.0	Galácticos 3.0	Galácticos 4.0
% "Stars"		16%	28%	22%
Stars average age		28.6	26.7	26.6
% "Workhorses"		50%	48%	50%
% "Juniors"		34%	24%	27%
Captain (position)	Juanito Alonso (goalkeeper)	Fernando Hierro[263] (central defender)	Iker Casillas (goalkeeper)	Sergio Ramos (defender)
Appearances	292	601	710	337
Vice-Captain (position)		Raúl	Sergio Ramos[264]	Marcelo

[242] Some of the information is from 2015 due to timing constraints.

[243] 1957 and 1959 Ballon d'Or. Second place 1956 Ballon d'Or. Pelé described him as "the most complete footballer in the history of the game." Along with Francisco Gento and José María Zárraga, he was one of only three players to play a part in all five Real Madrid Champions League consecutive victories (from 1955–56 to 1959–60).

[244] Voted best player of the 1954 FIFA World Cup. Second place 1960 Ballon d'Or.

[245] 1958 Ballon d'Or. Second place 1959 Ballon d'Or.

[246] Only soccer player to win six Champion Leagues in his career as a player. He played in eight finals (6–2 record). Gento's teammate, Di Stéfano, had a 5–2 record.

[247] First player to score a goal at Maracaña Stadium in Rio de Janeiro. Credited with being the first person to call soccer "the Beautiful Game."

[248] 2000 Ballon d'Or. 2001 FIFA World Player of the Year.

[249] 1998 Ballon d'Or. 1998, 2000, and 2003 FIFA World Player of the Year. Third place 1997 and 2002 FIFA World Player of the Year. Voted best player of the 2006 World Cup tournament. Scored famous winning goal in 2002 UEFA Champions League final.

[250] Graduate of RM Academy. Second place 2001 Ballon d'Or. Third place 2001 FIFA World Player of the Year. Replaced Emilio Butragueño in a symbolic "passing of the crown" in 1994.

[251] Second place 2002 Ballon d'Or. Second place 1997 FIFA World Player of the Year.

[252] 1997 and 2002 Ballon d'Or. Second place 1996 Ballon d'Or. Third place 1998 Ballon d'Or. One of four players to have won the FIFA World Player of the Year award three times or more, along with Zidane, Messi, and Cristiano Ronaldo.

[253] Second place 1999 Ballon d'Or. Won 1999 UEFA Champions League with Manchester United.

[254] Ballon d'Or. Second place 2009, 2011, and 2012 Ballon d'Or. 2008, 2013, and 2014

[255] 2011, 2012, and 2013 French Player of the Year.

[256] 2011 and 2013 PFA Players' Player of the Year.

[257] Graduate of the RM Academy. 2008, 2009, 2010, 2011, and 2012 IFFHS World's Best Goalkeeper.

[258] 2014 FIFA World Cup Golden Boot.

[259] 2008, 2013, and 2014 Ballon d'Or. Second place 2009, 2011, and 2012 Ballon d'Or.

[260] 2011, 2012, and 2013 French Player of the Year.

[261] 2011 and 2013 PFA Players' Player of the Year.

[262] Estimate.

[263] Won three UEFA Champions League trophies. Assistant coach of Real Madrid.

[264] Scored game-tying goal in 2014 UEFA Champions League final in stoppage time.

Appendix B:

SEASON AVERAGES VS. POSTSEASON IN BASEBALL

I WILL ADD A LITTLE DATA analytics on baseball because many data analytics supporters love baseball statistics and believe it is the most "pure data" between a batter and pitcher. The analysis will help illuminate why Real Madrid focuses on a player's performance against top level competition (e.g., Champions League, World Cup, etc.). As a qualifier, Real Madrid recognizes that the data against top-level competition is limited. But as mentioned, they are looking for any statistical advantages they can to win the Champions League, which is against the best competition because of such small differences and the impact of luck. How a player performs over a long season in the Spanish League or in MLB may not be the same in the Champions League or MLB Playoffs for a variety of factors, including the level of competition, being at the end of the season, weather, etc. So a player's performance may be able to help you get to the playoffs, but the player's performance against better players (or better pitching) may not be able to help you win it.

For example, there is a startling difference between the statistics of baseball players Derek Jeter and Alex Rodriguez. Derek Jeter's batting average and on-base percentage in the regular season (0.310 and 0.377, respectively) and postseason (0.308 and 0.374, respectively) almost mirror each other. However, if you look at Alex Rodriguez, his postseason batting average and on-base percentages are less than his regular season averages (0.297 versus 0.259 and 0.382 versus 0.365, respectively). If you built a team assuming Rodriguez would perform the same in the postseason as he did in the regular season, then you would have made a wrong assumption. His batting average is 13 percent worse in the postseason.

	AVG	OBP
Jeter		
Reg Season	0.310	0.377
Postseason	0.308	0.374
A-Rod		
Reg Season	0.297	0.382
Postseason	0.259	0.365

If you only looked at Rodriguez's time at the New York Yankees, his postseason batting average is 19 percent worse than his career average.

A-Rod (NYY Only)

	AVG	OBP
Postseason	0.240	0.363

Compare this to Reggie Jackson, nicknamed "Mr. October" for his postseason home runs, which seemed to come right when his teams needed them. His postseason numbers are slightly better than his regular season averages.

	AVG	OBP
Jackson		
Reg Season	0.262	0.356
Postseason	0.278	0.358
Jackson (NYY Only)		
Postseason	0.280	0.363

In New York, his postseason batting average seems the same as his overall postseason career. However, the big difference is that around 30 percent of Jackson's hits in New York were home runs in the postseason, much higher than his season career average of 22 percent. In comparison, Rodriguez's career average percentage of home runs was around

22 percent. In the postseason in New York and overall, Rodriguez's was lower, around 18 percent.

When I spoke with Vince Gennaro, Director of the Master of Science in Sports Management program at Columbia University and author of *Diamond Dollars* (CreateSpace, 2007), he told me that postseason baseball is a different game than regular season baseball, based on one critical factor—teams can deploy pitching very differently in the postseason…and they do so. A batter cannot come to bat more than once every nine times during a game, but a top pitcher can be used more heavily in the play-offs. The net result is that the quality of pitching is about 40 percent higher in the postseason than in the regular season. In the 2009 postseason, when the Yankees last won the World Series, their top five pitchers (starting pitchers Sabathia, Burnett, and Pettitte, combined with Hughes and Rivera in the bullpen) accounted for approximately 81 percent of their postseason innings but only 53 percent of the team's regular season innings. The net effect is that postseason batting performance is expected to go down somewhat as the run-scoring environment is lower. He thinks it may be partly psychological, but it is also dependent on which players hit high-quality pitching disproportionately well. For Jeter, there is very little "spread" in how he performs against the number one starter versus the number five starter. For Rodriguez and other players, there is a difference. Certain players build up statistics against weaker pitching (number three, four, and five starting pitchers) during the season. So context and priorities matter.

When examining the regular season and postseason Earned Run Averages (ERAs) of Cy Young (the top pitcher) winners since 1969, there is no difference at 3.26. However, if you look at the list below of selected players who have pitched at least fifty innings of postseason baseball, you may be surprised.[265]

Player	Reg. Season ERA	Postseason ERA	Difference
Clayton Kershaw	2.43	5.12	+111%
David Price[266]	3.09	4.78	+55%
CC Sabathia	3.69	4.53	+23%
Roger Clemens	3.12	3.75	+20%

[265] Ross Benes, "Postseason Price vs. Regular Price." *Sports on Earth*. http://www.sportsonearth.com/article/153773346/david-price-blue-jays-postseason-era-cy-young.
[266] Only forty-seven innings pitched.

Player	Reg. Season ERA	Postseason ERA	Difference
Pedro Martinez	2.93	3.46	+18%
Randy Johnson	3.29	3.50	+6%
Greg Maddux	3.16	3.27	+3%
Catfish Hunter	3.26	3.26	0%
Tom Seaver	2.86	2.77	-3%
Justin Verlander	3.52	3.39	-4%
Tom Glavine	3.54	3.30	-7%
John Smoltz	3.33	2.67	-20%
Orel Hershiser	3.48	2.59	-26%
Fernando Valenzuela	3.54	1.98	-44%

Examining the top four players with the most innings pitched, Tom Glavine and John Smoltz pitched over 200 innings in the postseason and defied the probabilities and pitched meaningfully better in postseason, Greg Maddux pitched 198 innings and was essentially the same, and Roger Clemens pitched 199 innings and was clearly worse in postseason.

Mariano Rivera, the New York Yankees star closer pitched in 141 innings in the postseason. He never won a Cy Young, which typically goes to a starting pitcher, but he finished four times in the top three. When you examine his numbers, he is remarkably better in the postseason than the regular season, and possibly the greatest postseason pitcher in the modern era. Andy Pettitte (276 innings pitched) is about the same between the postseason and regular season. David Cone (111 innings pitched) was about 10 percent worse in the post season.

Player	Reg. Season ERA	Postseason ERA	Difference
Mariano Rivera	2.21	0.70	-70%
Andy Pettitte	3.85	3.81	-1%
David Cone	3.46	3.80	+10%

I asked Gennaro about the pitching discrepancies, and he admits he does not have a good explanation other than possibly small sample size, or the fatigue and durability of adding October innings to an already taxing workload, or colder weather in the fall impacting grip. I thought that the play-off teams would have a better hitting average and that would account for some of the discrepancies, but it is not as statistically significant as I thought.

Appendix C:

REAL MADRID ORGANIZATION CHART (2015)

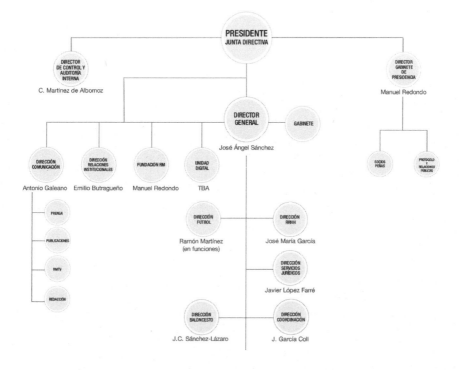

Continued from previous page

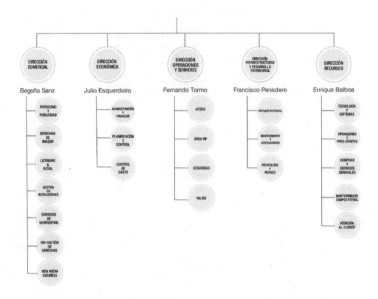

Appendix D:

SUPPORT FOR STARS, WORKHORSES, AND JUNIORS ANALYSIS

Our Classification of Real Madrid's Stars for Analysis from 2000–01 to 2014–15

Season	Name	Position	Age	Total playing time (minutes)	Goals
2000–01	Roberto Carlos	DF	27	4490	10
	Luis Fígo	MF	28	4375	14
	Raúl	FW	23	4315	32
2001–02	Roberto Carlos	DF	28	4525	6
	Fernando Ruiz Hierro	DF	33	4209	5
	Zinedine Zidane	MF	29	4052	12
	Luis Fígo	MF	29	3910	11
	Raúl	FW	24	4854	29
2002–03	Iker Casillas	GK	21	4950	-64
	Roberto Carlos	DF	29	4896	7
	Fernando Ruiz Hierro	DF	34	3320	1
	Luis Fígo	MF	30	4241	12
	Zinedine Zidane	MF	30	4107	12
	Raúl	FW	25	4042	25
	Ronaldo	FW	26	3359	30
2003–04	Iker Casillas	GK	22	4500	-63
	Roberto Carlos	DF	30	4346	8
	Luis Fígo	MF	31	4516	14
	Zinedine Zidane	MF	31	4127	10
	David Beckham	MF	28	4036	7
	Raúl	FW	26	4553	20
	Ronaldo	FW	27	3917	31
2004–05	Iker Casillas	GK	23	4223	-41
	Roberto Carlos	DF	31	4034	4
	David Beckham	MF	29	3107	4

Our Classification of Real Madrid's Stars for Analysis from 2000–01 to 2014–15 (Cont'd)

Season	Name	Position	Age	Total playing time (minutes)	Goals
	Zinedine Zidane	MF	32	3204	6
	Luis Fígo	MF	32	3115	7
	Ronaldo	FW	28	3639	24
	Raúl	FW	27	3487	13
	Michael Owen	FW	25	2427	16
2005–06	Iker Casillas	GK	24	4290	-51
	Roberto Carlos	DF	32	3962	6
	David Beckham	MF	30	3617	5
	Zinedine Zidane	MF	33	2739	9
	Robinho	FW	21	3779	12
	Ronaldo	FW	29	2154	15
	Raúl	FW	28	2230	7
2006–07	Iker Casillas	GK	25	4050	-50
	Roberto Carlos	DF	33	2651	3
	Fabio Cannavaro	DF	33	3358	0
	Ruud Van Nistelrooy	FW	30	4004	33
	Raúl	FW	29	3334	12
	Robinho	FW	22	2509	8
	David Beckham	MF	31	1936	4
	Ronaldo	FW	30	645	4
2007–08	Iker Casillas	GK	26	4140	-51
	Fabio Cannavaro	DF	34	3601	1
	Raúl	FW	30	4035	23
	Robinho	FW	23	2835	15
	Ruud Van Nistelrooy	FW	31	2624	20
	Arjen Robben	MF	23	1588	5
2008–09	Iker Casillas	GK	27	4230	-67
	Sergio Ramos	DF	22	3629	6
	Fabio Cannavaro	DF	35	3076	0
	Arjen Robben	MF	24	2693	8
	Raúl	FW	31	3838	24
	Ruud Van Nistelrooy	FW	32	980	10
	Robinho	FW	24	64	0
2009–10	Iker Casillas	GK	28	4140	-44
	Sergio Ramos	DF	23	3513	4
	Kaká	MF	27	2524	9
	Cristiano Ronaldo	FW	24	2914	33
	Karim Benzema	FW	22	1714	9

Our Classification of Real Madrid's Stars for Analysis from 2000–01 to 2014–15 (Cont'd)

Season	Name	Position	Age	Total playing time (minutes)	Goals
	Raúl	FW	32	1513	7
	Ruud Van Nistelrooy	FW	33	129	1
2010–11	Iker Casillas	GK	29	4802	-40
	Sergio Ramos	DF	24	4049	4
	Mesut Özil	MF	22	3823	10
	Cristiano Ronaldo	FW	25	4605	53
	Karim Benzema	FW	23	2760	26
	Kaká	MF	28	988	7
2011–12	Iker Casillas	GK	30	4800	-49
	Sergio Ramos	DF	25	4497	4
	Mesut Özil	MF	23	3840	7
	Cristiano Ronaldo	FW	26	4898	60
	Karim Benzema	FW	24	3448	32
	Kaká	MF	29	2055	8
2012–13	Iker Casillas	GK	31	2528	-28
	Sergio Ramos	DF	26	3539	5
	Mesut Özil	MF	24	3562	10
	Cristiano Ronaldo	FW	27	4632	55
	Karim Benzema	FW	25	2878	20
	Kaká	MF	30	1323	5
2013–14	Sergio Ramos	DF	27	4350	7
	Karim Benzema	FW	26	4040	24
	Cristiano Ronaldo	FW	28	4026	51
	Ángel Di María	FW	25	3749	11
	Gareth Bale	FW	24	3327	22
	Iker Casillas	GK	32	2115	-12
	Mesut Özil	MF	25	134	0
2014–15	Iker Casillas	GK	33	4230	-46
	Sergio Ramos	DF	28	3533	7
	James Rodríguez	MF	23	3506	17
	Cristiano Ronaldo	FW	29	4644	61
	Gareth Bale	FW	25	4036	17
	Karim Benzema	FW	27	3653	22

		Age Average				Team Composition			Average Playing Time			Average Goals		
Season	Coaches	Team	Stars	Workhorses	Juniors	Stars	Workhorses	Juniors	Stars	Workhorses	Juniors	Stars	Workhorses	Juniors
2000–01	Del Bosque	24.6	26.0	26.5	20.0	11%	61%	29%	86%	44%	12%	47%	50%	0%
2001–02	Del Bosque	24.8	28.6	26.6	20.5	16%	50%	34%	73%	36%	15%	49%	46%	2%
2002–03	Del Bosque	25.0	27.9	26.8	20.8	24%	41%	34%	74%	42%	7%	60%	24%	15%
2003–04	Queiroz	25.0	27.9	27.1	21.8	25%	32%	43%	81%	45%	12%	80%	16%	4%
2004–05	Camacho, García Remón, Luxemburgo	24.8	28.4	28.7	20.7	25%	28%	47%	73%	45%	8%	80%	18%	1%
2005–06	Luxemburgo, López Caro	24.9	28.1	26.5	20.9	25%	39%	36%	70%	38%	19%	59%	26%	12%
Average	N/A	24.8	27.8	27.0	20.8	21%	42%	37%	76%	42%	12%	62%	30%	5%
2006–07	Capello	25.2	29.1	25.3	21.6	28%	41%	31%	62%	42%	11%	70%	26%	1%
2007–08	Schuster	25.4	27.8	25.6	22.0	24%	56%	20%	67%	44%	14%	60%	34%	5%
2008–2009	Schuster, Juande Ramos	25.2	27.9	25.8	22.1	22%	50%	28%	59%	37%	10%	46%	51%	1%
Average	N/A	25.3	28.3	25.6	21.9	24%	49%	26%	63%	41%	12%	59%	37%	2%
2009–10	Pellegrini	25.5	27.0	26.1	20.8	27%	58%	15%	54%	47%	3%	53%	46%	1%
2010–11	Mourinho	23.9	25.2	26.1	20.6	17%	46%	37%	66%	42%	3%	68%	29%	2%
2011–12	Mourinho	24.3	26.2	25.5	21.0	20%	50%	30%	75%	41%	4%	64%	27%	8%
2012–13	Mourinho	24.9	27.2	26.8	20.3	18%	52%	30%	56%	43%	3%	62%	33%	1%
2013–14	Ancelotti	25.1	26.7	26.1	21.2	28%	48%	24%	58%	52%	13%	72%	17%	11%
2014–15	Ancelotti	24.8	27.3	26.1	20.4	23%	50%	24%	64%	41%	5%	77%	17%	4%
Average	N/A	24.8	26.6	26.1	20.7	22%	50%	27%	62%	44%	5%	66%	28%	4%

REAL MADRID'S SEASONS SUMMARY

Sources: OptaPro Sports Data and http://www.bdfutbol.com/

Notes: Goals do not add to 100% because we exluded Own Goals.

Playing time is calculated using the average number of minutes played per season per player category ("stars," "workhorses," and "juniors"), expressed as a percentage of the total number of minutes played in one season.

Average Playing Time for each group ("stars," "workhorses," "juniors") represents the percentage of total minutes each entire group of players could have played during the season. Thus, if all players in a group played all minutes of all games, that group's percentage would be 100 percent.

Includes all other competitions, not only La Liga as the previous academic analysis did.

The analysis of classification of players is very subjective. We tried to consider a player's transfer value, ranking in publications, and starts for national team.

Players could move in and out of classifications by year.

Arguably all, or most, of Real Madrid's players could be classified as "stars." Therefore, we also had to use some weight to relative position and contribution to the team.

Lastly, when classifying players as "stars," we tried to stay consistent with the original approach of Professors Kimio Kase, Sandalio Gómez, and Ignacio Urrutia of IESE Business School in Spain in their academic study.

We did update the professors' analysis on Barcelona as well.

ACKNOWLEDGMENTS

I WOULD LIKE TO THANK the many kind people of Real Madrid who gave me permission to conduct my study, answered my many questions, escorted me around, made introductions, and provided me with information. Everyone was incredibly kind, thoughtful, professional, and patient. Thank you to those I interviewed. I would love to recognize your contributions and time on an individual basis, but I want to respect your privacy. I have had the pleasure of working with some of the largest and most prestigious companies in the world, and I can truly say that Real Madrid's commitment to professionalism, transparency, and excellence was exceptional. The people that I interacted with were incredibly forthcoming, responsive, and detail-oriented.

This book is a result of the love and support of my wife, Alexandra, and two daughters, Tatiana and Isabella. My parents, brother, Dean Mandis, sister, Vivian Mandis Flynn, cousin, Gus Menoudakis, and the Kairis and Keralakis families have always been loving and supportive.

I would like to give a special thank-you to my best friend, Borja Arteaga Fierro, who read multiple drafts of the book and gave me feedback as well as encouragement. He also made vital introductions to many people, including David Stern.

I would like to express the deepest gratitude to Fabio Lopez. He made the first introduction that started a fascinating chain of events that ultimately led to this project.

I had the true pleasure and luck to be given invaluable constructive feedback by three of the greatest leaders, minds, and people in sports management history. I would like to give a special thanks to Billy Beane, Executive Vice President of Baseball Operations and minority owner of the Oakland Athletics, Sir Alex Ferguson, former Manager of Manchester United, and David Stern, former Commissioner of the NBA. They all have been incredibly thoughtful, responsive, patient, and generous with their time. In many ways they served the role of my "doctoral dissertation committee," challenging my analysis and conclusions. As one can imagine, I have had absolutely fascinating discussions, debates, and communications with them. They do not agree with everything that I have written. Billy Beane was kind, and brave, enough to return my "cold call." Sir Michael Moritz, Chairman of Sequoia Capital and co-author with Sir Alex Ferguson of *Leadership: Learning from Life and My Years at Manchester United*, was also kind, and brave, enough to return my "cold call" (suggested by John Radziwill), give me his thoughts, and make an introduction to Sir Alex Ferguson.

I would like to thank Vince Gennaro, Director of the Masters of Science in Sports Management of Columbia University; Jim Pallotta, President of A.S. Roma and minority shareholder of the Boston Celtics; the Green Bay Packers organization; the St. Louis Cardinals organization and Ron Watermon; and Paul Wardlaw, head coach of the Women's tennis team at Brown University. They carefully reviewed information and added unique insights and nuances.

As one can probably tell from my descriptions of the games, the commentators (such as Ray Hudson and Phil Schoen) add tremendously to my enjoyment. The comments from the commentators in my descriptions of the games didn't really happen; they are just what I imagined they would have said. I did have the pleasure of reviewing the commentary I made up for Ray Hudson with him. I would like to thank him for his contributions and good humor.

I would like to thank Glenn Yeffeth, publisher of BenBella Books. He immediately saw the vision and potential for this book. Many people in the United States were skeptical about publishing a book about a soccer team, especially one in Spain, which was geared to the "smart thinking" genre interested in both sports and business. Also, I would like to thank Vy Tran, my editor; Roger Domingo of Grupo Planeta; and editor Alexandre Casanovas, who handled the Spanish version of this project.

I would like to thank Tony Kornheiser and Michael Wilbon of ESPN's *Pardon the Interruption* show. Their work, and many in the ESPN family, stimulates my thinking and keeps me entertained. In many ways, comments on data analytics, leadership, aging players, and management by them and their guests (including Charles Barkley) inspired my thinking and curiosity. Also, thank you very much for the "shout-out" on your December 10, 2013, show.

I would like to thank some of the wise mentors that my family and I are lucky to have had in our lives: Kairis, Keralakis, Menoudakis, Mavromichalis, Clive Worms, Coumantaros, Jaharis, Livanos, Neff, Radzwill, Taubman, Theodoracopulos, and Tisch.

There are many large loving families to thank in Madrid: Alcaide Justel, Amusátegui, Arteaga, Báez, Barreiros, Beca, Blázquez, Bonte, Cano, Colino, Cotoner, de las Bárcenas Fitz-James Stuart, Denizot, de la Peña, del Pino, del Rey, Domecq, Elzaburu, Entrecanales, Fazzini, Fernandez, Fierro March, Franco, Garcia, García de la Rasilla, Gelardin, Gómez-Acebo y de Borbón, González, González Cortés, Herrera, Ibáñez, Kronholm, Lopez, Lopez de la Osa Escribano, Maesso, Moyá, Murgui, Narvarte, Osío de Talayero, Peña, Piaggio, Porcar, Posner, Primo de Rivera, Puregger, Restaurante El Landó, Ritz Hotel, Roca de Togores, Sajonia-Coburgo, Serra, Soler-Roig, Spínola, Sweatman, Vallés, Villalba, and Zaforteza.

I would like to thank my primary research analysts Andres Galicia and Scott Spencer, students at Columbia University Masters of Science in Sports Management program, and my primary Spanish translator in Madrid, Ainara Azcona.

Many thanks to the professionals and professors who helped with the book: McKinsey & Company's Asheet Mehta, Alexander Edlich, Aditya Sanghvi, Michael Bazigos, Bill Schaninger, and Dan Singer; Columbia University Masters of Science in Sports Management's Francesco Avella Jr., Akash Bhat, Timur Chernykh, Laurajean Holmgren, William J Koessler Jr., Jason Kosasih, Christina LaBrie, Andres Loaiza, Nathan Stender, and Bradley Tuyay; Columbia University Business School's Paul Ingram, Stephan Meier, Adam Galinsky, Eric Anicich, Ronnie Sacco, and Elizabeth Gordon; Columbia University's sociology department's David Stark; United States Soccer Federation and Columbia University's Sunil Gulati; Vega Factor's Neel Doshi and Lindsay McGregor; Notre Dame's Richard Sheehan; Central Washington University's César García; Florida State University's Nader

Rahnama; Northwestern University Kellogg School of Management's Alexander Chernev; Frankfurt School of Finance and Management and the Charles University in Prague's Jan Vecer; Opta Sports Data's Oliver Miller-Farrell; PJT Partners' Don Cornwell; Kalamata Capital's Brandon Laks; ManagingMadrid.com's Gabe Lezra, Kiyan Sobhani, and Josh Zeitlin; messi-vs-cristiano.com's Míchel Acosta, Emily Loose; Steve Kettmann; Kirby Kim; Susan Rabiner; and Harvard Business Review Press' Tim Sullivan.

I would like to thank those who have researched and written about topics related to this book, because without their diligent work, it would have been impossible to write this book. Many are cited in the book and some are not, but I wanted to specifically acknowledge a few writers: Phil Ball, John Beech, Jimmy Burns, Simon Chadwick, Francisco Cutiño, Anita Elberse, Richard Fitzpatrick, Susan Fournier, David Goldblatt, Graham Hunter, Simon Kuper, Tim Kuypers, Lara Lee, Michael Lewis, Sid Lowe, Jorge Mendes, Alfredo Relaño, John Samuels, Ferran Soriano, Stefan Szymanski, and David Winner, as well as writers from a few critical sources: AS, BBC, Bleacher Report, Daily Mail, ESPN, FiveThirtyEight, Harvard Business School Cases, Marca, Mirror, Mundo Deportivo, New York Times, Sport, and the Telegraph.

I want to thank Craig Alexander (3x IRONMAN World Champion) for providing suggestions and support, as well as Mark Allen (6x IRONMAN World Champion), Marcantonio Antamoro, Jeffrey Appel, Red Ayme, Mike Beys, Cliff and George Brokaw, Alberto Cribiore, Bo Curry, Dave and Kara Deschenes, Joe Farina, Javier Fente, Mark Flynn, David Ford Jr., John Freund, Rohan Goetzke, Marty Halbfinger, Cris Howard, Memo Içöz, Murphy Jensen (French Open Doubles Champion), Craig Kennedy, Aaron and Meredith Kessler (IRONMAN Champion), Harry LeFrak, Todd Martin (2x Grand Slam Finalist), Walter McCormack, Ryan McElvenny, Robert McKeown, Andrew Messick, Prakash Melwani, Mike Miele, Krishna Narsu, David Pauletti, Geoffrey Pope (2008 NY Giants Super Bowl Champion), Doug Polley, Jason Rosenfeld, US Representative Kyrsten Sinema, Jay Tee, Nicholas Titley, George Walker, Jared Weitz, and Joann Willard.

A shout-out to a few young Madridistas: Borja, Beltrán and Bruno Arteaga Barreiros, Miguel Báez Herrera, Marcos Fernández Barreiros, Lucas and Diego Kronholm Fierro, Diky Izmirlian, Iñigo Lopez de la Osa Franco, Alvaro José Talayero, Gunnar S Overstrom, IV, and Charles Villalba.

Lastly, I want to thank those who take care of me when I am writing: Chef Daniel Boulud, Jason Ferretti, Edouard Bourgeois, Cherif Mbodji, Wander Barbosa, and the Café Boulud staff; Sergio Vacca and the Harry Cipriani staff; Carlos and the SushiAnn staff; Vito and the Mediterraneo staff; Chef José Andrés and the Barmini staff; PDT NYC/Crif Dogs bartenders and staff; the Four Seasons Georgetown; Miguel Gonzalez, Marsida Guzia, and the Mr. Chow staff; Gianni and the Fodera staff; Dr. DSB; Dr. AR and Beth; Dr. BGC, Dr. PGP; Dr. RGP; Dr. AJR; the 1165 PA staff; and the ladies at 12AB.

ABOUT THE AUTHOR

STEVEN G. MANDIS is an adjunct professor at Columbia Business School. He also teaches at Columbia's Masters of Sports Management Program. His previous award-winning book, *What Happened to Goldman Sachs: An Insider's Story of Organizational Drift and its Unintended Consequences*, is a rigorous analysis of if, why, and how the culture of Goldman Sachs changed. Mandis worked at Goldman Sachs in the investment banking, private equity, and proprietary trading areas. After leaving Goldman, he cofounded a multibillion-dollar global alternative asset management firm that was a trading and investment banking client of Goldman's. During the financial crisis, Mandis was a senior adviser to McKinsey & Company before becoming chief of staff to the president and COO of Citigroup and serving on executive, management, and risk committees at the firm. Mandis is Chairman and Senior Partner of Kalamata Capital, a provider of online small business financing. Mandis holds an AB from the University of Chicago and an MA, MPhil, and PhD from Columbia University. Mandis was a two sport varsity athlete in college and currently competes in triathlons, including having competed in the IRONMAN World Championships in Kailua-Kona, Hawaii; IRONMAN 70.3 World Championships in Zell Am See-Kaprun, Austria; and Escape from Alcatraz in San Francisco, California. He was awarded the Ellis Island Medal of Honor, given to children of immigrants who exemplify a life dedicated to community service.

INDEX